Dear Eddie

Dear Eddie

DANNY RUSSELL

god, turtles and
letters about mum

PIER

9

In memory of Kerrie (Fahey) Russell
who taught me life really is beautiful

16 May 2006

Kerrie is dead and I want to escape. I want to abandon her breathless body and run from the hospital, flee with the same scared urgency I felt when my wife first told me that cancer had entered our lives. Her body is the reason I want to get out of there – it is a shadow of the vibrant woman I married; auburn hair and freckles are all that I recognise. I can't even shut the lids of her eyes. It is another of the many misconceptions I have had about death and losing someone you love.

By the end, the only thing I understand about cancer is its devilish ways. That is why I want to run: to be someplace where I can feel like none of this has happened, where I don't feel like I've lost twice over – the so-called fight and my wife. Only a voice of reason keeps me at the hospital. Father John tells me not to rush.

'You'll never get this time again,' he says.

So I make myself walk into the dying room and lie beside my wife, wrapping my arms around her lifeless body and holding her tight. And I discover it isn't me who wants to get out, it's the tears. They come in a flood, rising from a great well of sadness. Each drop a testament for every smile, laugh and good time we have shared.

How much time passes? I don't know. Sit and stare at a river, lie on the ground and look at the clouds, push a child on a swing. There's no time.

All I know is that when the last tear falls I'm ready to say goodbye.

26 November 2002

I rang Kerrie to tell her I was going for an after-work drink with my best friend for his thirty-third birthday. She told me to come home because she had cancer.

'How do you know?' I asked, my desk phone starting to tremble in my hand.

'There was an urgent message to call the doctor. The scan has shown a lump in my abdomen. They've found a tumour. It's come back.'

'Shit.'

'Don't worry. We'll talk about it when you get home. I'll meet you at the train station with Eddie. I'll be all right. I've beaten it before.'

It's a date I'll never forget: 26 November 2002. Almost a month after Eddie's first birthday and the reason he stopped breastfeeding.

Kerrie hadn't told me she feared the cancer was back, and even though the swelling in her abdomen must have been causing her mental anguish, she had continued on occupying our time as if we were the only three people that mattered.

Kerrie filtered worrying news like a prospector sifted for gold, leaving nothing more than nuggets of gleaming ore. I knew she'd had a scan, but I'd thought it was a precautionary measure. So this phone call came as a massive shock. And I wondered how I'd missed it. Had I been so buried in my new newspaper job that I'd forgotten to read my wife?

A person's battle with cancer could end happily ever after. I'd read Tour de France legend Lance Armstrong's autobiography. But even he would admit there was never a happy beginning. I cried my first tears of dread. Soon after the phone call I walked into a Flinders Lane bar to tell Brian that I couldn't stay, but the tears came first. I looked at him and was unable to hold them back.

'Kerrie's cancer is back,' I spluttered.

For ten years she had been clear, beating the first tumour three years before I even knew she existed. But this was different. Now we were married and we had a one-year-old son. This time, she had a reason to fear death.

As much as Brian assured me that things could and more than likely would work out, I wasn't so sure. Not many people beat cancer once, and no one I knew had beaten it twice. I bade him farewell and took the lonely train ride to Strathmore Station, numb to the rockin' and rollin' of the carriages, and impervious to the shouting school kids hitching their afternoon ride home.

Ironically, the only comfort came from seeing Kerrie. She wore bravery with the same ease that our son wore his pyjamas. Usually babies fed off their parents' vibes, but Kerrie held together so well that Eddie was a bundle of joy sitting in his Winnie-the-Pooh baby seat. I kissed him and then slumped into the front of the car, waiting for the news. Unbelievably, she asked me about work.

It was a glimmer of hope. If she wasn't falling apart, then maybe things weren't going to be so bad after all.

'So what does this mean?' I asked.

'It will probably mean an operation,' she said. 'Don't worry, it worked the first time and I'm determined to beat it quickly again. I'm just really pissed off that it's come back.'

I bit back the tears, gazing out the front window, trying desperately not to break. Trying to remain strong for Kerrie. Every word that I had ever read about beating cancer, every word that I had ever heard spoken about winning the fight centred around staying positive. The mind could do amazing things, they all said. So I figured the last thing I should do was sap her strength or weaken her fight by bursting into tears.

Looking back, I'm not sure I did the right thing. Fighting cancer isn't a war and people who die aren't losers. It's an uninvited houseguest – sometimes it stays, sometimes it goes. To this date, nobody knows why.

Kerrie saw my red eyes as we drove into 48 Gallipoli Parade, Pascoe Vale South and her facade dropped.

'I'm so sorry, babe,' she said.

'Sorry? For what? For getting cancer? Honey, don't be sorry. It's not your fault. You've done nothing wrong.'

As far as I was concerned no one deserved cancer. No one deserved pain, torture or a life-threatening illness. But somehow I don't think Kerrie believed me.

27 November 2002

Kerrie wanted to protect her parents. It was the one point at which she visibly weakened, tears forming each time I suggested she should call Adelaide and tell them. People say one of the worst things in life is outliving your child, but Kerrie experienced this agony from the other side. She didn't want to put them through the pain of the first operation again.

Kerrie was just twenty-two in 1992 when a kind woman offered her a bus seat, thinking she was pregnant because of her swollen belly. The woman's assumption shocked Kerrie, who until then thought she'd been putting on weight.

'I thought I was getting fat. I was chubby as a child so it wasn't impossible to believe and I guess you don't notice yourself changing shape when it happens gradually. But I hadn't been eating that much and when the woman offered me a seat, I realised something was wrong,' Kerrie said.

'After the initial scan they said I had a tumour the size of a tennis ball above my right hip. The next estimation had it at the size of a football, and when they operated it turned out to be the size of a watermelon.'

It was an amazing story, made even more amazing by the flippant way in which Kerrie told it: she had a 3.9-kilogram liposarcoma arising from her pelvis, underwent surgery to have the growth removed, lost her right kidney in the process and flew full tilt back into life.

Six weeks after the operation, much to her mother Elsa's dismay, Kerrie packed her bags and drove to Melbourne, starting work as a sub-editor with the *Herald Sun*. And in her new world she wore the battle wound – a purplish scar running from the base of her sternum to the top of her pubic bone – proudly, showing if off to her workmates at the pub after a couple of her trademark bourbon and Cokes.

'Do you want to see my scar?' she would say, devoid of any self-consciousness while boldly lifting her shirt.

That's how she dealt with the first bout of cancer, thumbing her nose at the illness, adopting a mocking tone. For this I was glad. It was her joie de vivre and refusal to get bogged down by petty matters that made me fall in love with her and forget that she even had a whopping big scar running down her belly. Because of her approach, I never worried much about the possibility of the cancer returning.

28 November 2002

While I bumbled through work for two days, I couldn't bring myself to talk about Kerrie's cancer. I had to get my own head around it first.

Kerrie told me that before her first operation in April 1992, doctors warned her that she might not wake up. At twenty-two, she faced the prospect of death. But back then, she said, she had no fear because she felt she had nothing to lose.

'The night before the operation I stood on a balcony at Flinders Medical Centre and told my family not to worry. I had never felt more alive,' Kerrie said.

She was also warned about the probability of further surgery. 'My surgeon said he would be very surprised if the tumour didn't recur within ten years.'

She made it to ten years and eight months and had considered herself safely over the line. After the first five years of CT scans looking for a recurrence of the cancer, she said she'd been advised to stop because the radiation would be doing her more harm than good. She had the last one in 1997, about a year after we fell in love while working together at the

Sunday Herald Sun. It was only on the night before these scan results were due, she confessed, that she would smoke more, drink more and act a touch flighty. I didn't know the name of her cancer then, only that it was not aggressive. I didn't worry because she did not seem to worry.

But now I was experiencing fear. Dread bounced in my gut like coal on a conveyor belt as we drove to meet Kerrie's professor at the Alfred Hospital and settle on a plan to evict this intruder. As she walked to the hospital, I took Eddie to adjoining Fawkner Park and he took off for the other side. I followed in a cloud of vagueness, wondering how the hell our insular world had been shaken so violently and where it would all lead: Eddie running as fast as his unsteady legs would take him towards new worlds and Kerrie walking on her unsteady legs towards darkness. I kept changing the subject, distracting myself from thoughts of losing my wife. I had to stay positive, remember.

Then, as later, I relied on Kerrie to relay the news. Specialists didn't need to be distracted by a pessimistic husband and a curious thirteen-month-old boy with a penchant for pulling out cupboards and finding it near impossible to sit still.

This first visit – like so many others with doctors, oncologists, radiologists, surgeons and specialists – ended with more questions than answers. We were playing the game of hope, being drip-fed information that didn't provide a best-case scenario, but never delivered a card announcing the end of the world. Not yet, anyway. Kerrie was referred to a professor at Peter MacCallum Cancer Centre, who, although he specialised in breast cancer, was 'an excellent surgeon'. First, she would need to undergo a raft of tests.

We drove home feeling empty, talking about anything but the cancer. Kerrie still hadn't telephoned her parents and I hadn't told anybody at work.

10 December 2002

Within two weeks, Kerrie had seen The Professor at Peter Mac and sought a second opinion. They all pointed to an operation – the only effective way to treat liposarcomas. Kerrie's cancer was rare and non-aggressive but did not respond well to chemotherapy. Radiation was more effective as a follow-up treatment.

She was given the choice: have the surgery on Monday, 16 December, two days before her thirty-third birthday, or wait until after Christmas. She didn't deliberate.

'I just want to get it out and get better,' she said.

'What about Christmas?' I asked.

'I don't want to be distracted over Christmas by the thought of an operation. How could that be enjoyable for anyone? No, I want the tumour removed as soon as possible.'

Heartening news came when The Professor said he would treat Kerrie as a public patient. I hadn't given a thought to costs, but having her family freed of crippling medical bills gave Kerrie peace of mind.

The Professor's reputation was further good news. People with connections in the medical profession told us that Kerrie could not ask to be in better hands. Our situation was starting to look up.

11 December 2002

Grandma Elsa marched through our door within days of Kerrie's telephone call. I only had two weeks' holiday coming up over Christmas and someone had to run the house.

I opened the door and there she was: 155 centimetres, grey curly hair, thick-rimmed glasses and the power of her personality looming large. She could have passed for royalty – holding herself with class, and expecting to get her own way. She had driven the entire nine-hour trip from Adelaide to Pascoe Vale with Grandpa Des in the passenger seat. From the moment she walked inside she took over, ordering Kerrie to sit down and rest.

The following morning Des began his daily routine of wheeling Eddie in the stroller to the nearby service station for a Kit Kat and grabbing the paper for himself. Meanwhile, Elsa became Eddie's surrogate mother and matriarch of the house. While her intentions were always kind-hearted and well meaning, she boxed Des and me around the ears to get things done. Des didn't say much, but it was obvious he was churning away inside about his daughter's health because he was always sneaking off for a drink.

As for me, I felt under siege. Reluctant to carp to Kerrie, I lightened the load over a coffee with my best mate. But it was hard not to feel a sense of betrayal, like biting the hand that was feeding us.

15 December 2002

The day before her operation Kerrie put on a new dress – bought for a bargain while shopping with her thrifty mother – smoothed her mouth with red lipstick, lined her eyes with blue-tinted mascara and we drove to St Kilda for a friend's post-wedding celebration. It would have been hard to believe her life was in peril if not for her sombre mood. Cancer came with us. As a result, the champagne did not taste right, she didn't dance and she didn't engage in her usual witty small talk. The only time she truly escaped was looking at video footage of her friend's original wedding ceremony on a Greek island. Her gaze was lost in fantasy and her smile was back.

She only told one person that day about the tumour: her friend Helen, who could hardly believe it was true. But the more questions Helen asked, the further Kerrie pushed the topic away, until she'd changed the subject entirely.

If the wedding was a minor distraction, there was no avoiding the truth that night. Kerrie had to begin preparing for the following day's operation by drinking 'four litres of gunk' to clean out her bowels. She mixed the first sachet of Colonlytely powder with a litre of water and got halfway through the first glassful when she started to gag.

'This stuff is awful. I can't drink it,' she complained.

'You have to, honey. They wouldn't give it to you otherwise,' I said. 'Try holding your nose while you drink it, that can mask the taste.'

She pegged her nose between two fingers and took another swig. Immediately she gagged. At this rate, there was no way she was going to swallow the required amount.

'It tastes like ... well, I'm not saying what it tastes like, but it tastes disgusting,' she whispered, out of her parents' earshot.

'Oh, I wouldn't know anything about that,' I said. 'C'mon, it can't be that bad, just skol it quickly and get it over and done with.'

She refused. 'I didn't have to drink this stuff for the first operation. They can give me bowel prep beforehand. That's what they did last time. And besides, there is no way you need to drink the whole lot. They're just being over-cautious.'

'What will you tell them tomorrow?'

'I'll tell them I couldn't drink it all. They won't care.'

I really should have been supportive, but I was worried she was jeopardising the operation. I tried to cajole her but it was no good, she'd made up her mind – there was no way that she was going to get through two litres, let alone four. And in spite of my concern, I admired her defiance.

16 December 2002

Orderlies scurried in and out of the waiting room like giant worker ants, while Kerrie waited on a trolley for her final briefing and I tried to shake the image of Eddie and his grandparents waving goodbye from the porch.

A surgeon arrived and in the process of warning Kerrie of the imminent dangers, she scared the hell out of me. She said it was possible the tumour was attached to Kerrie's liver. She said it was possible they might need to resect Kerrie's bowel. She said it was possible Kerrie might need a stoma.

'We won't know for sure until we get in and have a look,' she said. 'You do understand what I'm saying?'

Understand? I had no idea what she was saying. It was not until later that I learned she was talking about the possibility of Kerrie needing a colostomy bag. But my wife, who knew about medical terms such as 'resect' and 'stoma', nodded peacefully. She appeared anxiety-free, maybe because the coming hours were out of her control.

'Just do what you have to do,' she smiled.

'Are there any questions?' the surgeon asked.

'No, darl,' Kerrie said.

But when the surgeon turned her blue eyes towards me for some form of confirmation, a dumb nod was all I had to offer. Because what did I matter? I mean, I had innumerable questions – How will I know when the operation is finished? How will I know if everything is all right? How will they know where to find me if something goes wrong? – but they were inconsequential to scalpels and incisions and saving my wife's life.

An orderly and a nurse wheeled Kerrie towards theatre, allowing me to kiss her goodbye, hold her hand for a short time and wish her luck, before closing a sliding door between us.

'I love you, honey,' Kerrie said, lifting her head, her auburn hair covered by a surgical cap, and the rings on her finger hidden by tape. She seemed calm. As she said, she had done it all before.

The theatre nurse who was stealing my wife said the operation could take a number of hours and afterwards Kerrie would be taken to the Critical Care Unit. Then the communication lines were down and I was left with a knot of fear.

I should have had an inkling of how it would be. For the past two days, Des had been drinking more and Elsa had been bordering on a nervous wreck. They said Kerrie's first cancer shattered her self-assuredness. I was beginning to understand why. We had no control.

There was no sign telling distressed husbands where to wait. There were no staff members handing out leaflets on what to do while your wife's life was in the balance. There was nothing. Nothing but my jangled nerves.

In the end I took them to the pub. I didn't know where else to go. I met Brian and Chel and ordered a counter meal. Their company momentarily settled my anxiety. Momentarily, because before long my mind kept drifting back to Peter Mac: is Kerrie okay? Should I be drinking a beer? Is Kerrie okay? What should I do? Is Kerrie okay? I've gotta go back.

The critical care nursing staff had not seen Kerrie or heard any updates, but said I was welcome to wait in their lounge and help myself to a coffee. I just wished they'd told me I'd be there for six hours.

I began by reading the paper and then writing things down. I stared out the window, hardly registering the view. And still no word of Kerrie.

I had another coffee. I re-read the paper. Surely I'd get word soon?

Wailing broke my fretful silence. A family was crying because someone had died. As nurses did their best to placate them, I wished for a calm voice to unwind my fear. I couldn't drink another coffee or read another word; people were dying in this monstrous labyrinth of strangers and Kerrie was still missing.

I needed information. A word. Something. Anything.

The crying faded, and as time shuffled past I settled again.

I phoned home to pass on the lack of news, to speak to a familiar voice and tell them I was bravely standing by while nothing was happening. Elsa wasn't impressed.

Reluctantly, I made another coffee and began drawing biro moustaches on pictures in the paper.

Tick. Tick. Tick. Nothing. Nothing. Nothing.

I don't know what I'd expected, maybe that I would walk into a room 30 minutes after the operation and see Kerrie sitting up in bed, sore but smiling. That's how it happened on *ER*.

What I didn't expect was an excruciating six-hour wait to be punctured by the sight of Kerrie so bloated she looked like a puffer fish, barely able to open her swollen eyes and almost too groggy to talk. There were two unsightly fluid bags hanging off her bed – one for a catheter, the other a drain from her wound. She looked like she'd plunged over Niagara Falls in a barrel, without the padding.

'Hi, honey,' she whispered.

I nodded my head and touched her arm, barely able to contain the shock.

'Hi, babe, do you feel okay?'

'Pretty sore.'

After the initial jolt, my dread faded. Now that I could see Kerrie and touch her, I felt all right. I asked the nurse, who was hovering around checking drug charts and vital signs, about the operation, but other than thinking it was a success, there was little she could tell me.

I had missed the surgeons, she said.

Hang on a minute. Did she say I'd missed the surgeons?

She did?

I almost lost control. How? How in the hell did I miss the surgeons? I'd been sitting down the corridor in a waiting room all bloody day.

Elsa received this news with equal disquiet. She was desperate to be told that everything had unfolded perfectly.

'After the last operation the surgeon said the tumour had peeled away like a melon. That's all I want to hear this time.'

17 December 2002

Kerrie was more alert the day after the operation, but still swollen and I winced at the amount of bloody fluid draining from her wound.

'How do you feel?' I asked.

'Okay, but I didn't have a very good night. I had chest pains and I kept bothering the nurses all night, didn't I, darl?' she whispered to a loitering nurse.

'And so you should have,' the nurse smiled back.

Kerrie talked softly, saving her energy for recuperation, and occasionally thumbing a little button dangling by her side for a shot of morphine.

'Do you remember me coming in last night?' I asked.

'Yes, but it's all pretty vague.'

'Any word from The Professor about the operation?'

'He said it was a success, but he'll be around later this afternoon so you can talk to him then.'

I stayed bedside most of the day, reading the newspaper from the back, stopping for a coffee and then reading from the front. I started a book, poring over pages until my eyelids started to droop and the words began to slur, telling Kerrie I needed to go for a walk and a feed before I fell asleep. Time passed no faster than yesterday, but it mattered little because Kerrie was in my sights – when she was dozing and when she occasionally appeared out of sleep asking about pain control or to be shifted in bed.

I rushed food breaks, hurrying back to the critical care ward so The Professor didn't elude me again. His summary was worth hearing. They'd removed the tumour en bloc. There had been complications such as the painstaking dissection of the tumour from Kerrie's liver and a need to divide and later rejoin the large and small intestines, but in layman's terms they'd got it all.

The next steps, before eating could start, were rumbles and wind. So as we rejoiced in the surgeons' skills and the success of their operation, we anxiously waited for Kerrie to fart.

18 December 2002

Dear Eddie,

Your mum has big feet. Not many husbands can buy their wife a pair of shoes after trying them on first. But that's what I've done. She turns thirty-three today, stuck in hospital, unable to eat until she passes wind and all I can think to buy her is dress sandals. Well, she can't have champagne. Perhaps I should have bought her baked beans.

Kerrie is too zonked to properly show her appreciation, but I reckon she'll be rapt because she's always complaining about the struggle to find appropriate footwear for her ungainly feet.

'Look at them, they're like my father's,' she says.
They look fine to me, better than Grandpa's, but she won't entertain high heels. She always feels avenged when women walk home from the races on blistered feet. 'Serves them right,' she says, slightly tongue-in-cheek.

Mum's still in intensive care, becoming brighter by the hour, and I'm back at work, glad for the distraction. I finish soon after midday and make the hospital by 1 pm. We go through the newspaper together and do the quiz, Kerrie getting most of the answers right.

I always ask the questions within earshot of the staff so they can marvel at her general knowledge.

'Will you want me to bring Eddie in for a visit when you are shifted to a ward?' I ask.

'No,' she says.

'Why?'

'Because I want to concentrate on getting better.'

Kerrie doesn't say so, but I think she is scared of letting you see her so vulnerable, even though you've not long turned one. She thinks you are better off at home, not in a hospital ward seeing your vivacious mother with a drip in her arm. Such things can be irresistible to the curious clutches of an infant.

Tears appear when Kerrie talks about keeping you away, but your antics are news of the day, with me relaying your mischievous ways: taunting an enchanted Grandma Elsa by throwing pumpkin on the floor; coming back from the shop with Grandpa Des each morning with your face smothered in chocolate.

Then, despite myself, I complain to Kerrie about Elsa controlling my life.

'I know that we couldn't get by without her help and I know she is a very kind-hearted person, I just find it hard being told what to do all the time, being treated like a teenager again,' I say.

'I know, honey, but it won't be for much longer.'

I shouldn't say these things to Kerrie because the pain of responsibility shows on her face. It is selfish to unload my problems on top of her enormous strain, but she is my confidante. And as soon as I spew out these little dramas, I immediately feel better.

'Look, it really is fine, Kerrie,' I apologise. 'I'm being trivial. Elsa is a great help, I just needed a little whinge.'

'That's great, honey.'

So know that she misses you and that she'll be home soon.

Love Dad

19 December 2002

The Professor swept into the room followed by an entourage of assistants, interns and who-knows-what.

'How are you feeling today?' he asked.

'I'm starting to feel a lot better,' Kerrie replied.

He felt her tummy, listened for activity and asked if there had been any wind.

'Not yet.'

'Okay, well, there's some grumbling there so it might not be far off.'

I think he genuinely liked Kerrie. She was sharp. She would often make nerdy specialists smirk by quickly comprehending their medical jargon and twisting it into a gag, making light of her situation. And I think Kerrie genuinely liked The Professor. He acted real, and I guess you learn to appreciate people when you think they hold the key to life and death. You probably like them more when they say you can have a cup of tea and a dried biscuit or a piece of toast.

'He said I could have a little treat. Isn't that exciting?' she said.

With Kerrie optimistic and improving, the weight was lifting from my shoulders.

Unfortunately, Grandma Elsa spoiled my mood by starting Eddie's sleep lessons.

'He's got to learn to be put down and go off to sleep by himself. Kerrie can't stand around nursing him in her arms, she'll be too tired,' she insisted.

I agreed. It had always been too tiring for Kerrie, but what I differed on was the timing. I had to get up at 4 am for work the following morning and sleeping was impossible with the truculent screeching and screaming of my son as stubborn Elsa sat by his cot, humming inanely, trying to lure him into dreamland.

I turned and tossed and rolled and sighed and became so agitated I started wrestling the bed sheets. Give it up, Elsa. Give it one more day. Start again tomorrow when I'm on FUCKING HOLIDAYS, and it doesn't matter if I don't have a decent night's sleep.

But Elsa wouldn't tune in to my thoughts or feel the bad energy emanating from my room or listen to my groans of frustration as I pinned down the bed sheets. She'd made up her mind; Eddie was going to cry himself to sleep, tonight.

20 December 2002

I visited Kerrie as she was having lunch – a bowl of flavourless broth – and we laughed about my grandma-induced sleep deprivation from the night before. She was in good spirits after positive news from the lab about the margin around her tumour. It was clear of cancerous cells. She insisted that I go to my work Christmas party and have a drink. She didn't need to twist my arm.

I kissed her goodbye and turned up at the Mountain View Hotel in Richmond. I'd only told three work colleagues about Kerrie's operation, including my editor, and they were all discreet enough to respect my privacy, so I hooked in to a few drinks without having to delve too deeply into my emotional state or answer any probing questions.

It was a relief to let go for the afternoon with almost everyone oblivious to my wife's cancer. Soon I was almost oblivious myself.

We drank more and more and sang and danced and started drinking shooters and before I knew it there were three of us left and I could barely stand up. My drinking partners walked me outside, flagged a taxi and pointed the driver towards Pascoe Vale South.

The problem was, I woke up on a train. In Broadmeadows, five stations past my stop, being prodded by a couple of pitiless inspectors.

'Where are you going to?' they asked.

'Strathmore station,' I mumbled.

'Well, you're at Broadmeadows. How are you going to get to Strathmore?'

'I'll catch a train back,' I snapped, still half-asleep.

'You can't, this is the last train.'

So there I was, stuck at the end of the line at 1.30 am Saturday, trying to work up the courage to venture out among the notorious youth gangs that supposedly roamed the Broadmeadows streets at night.

As I stumbled through the station, fumbling with my wallet, I was relieved to be able to dig out enough cash for a taxi home. That's if one was game enough to stop.

I stepped out onto the street preparing to shield my face from a barrage of bottles and empty spray cans. But the gangs did not materialise. The road was busy and the line for taxis stretched ten deep. I soon realised my biggest problem would be convincing a cab driver to open his door for me, the only disreputable-looking character in sight.

23 December 2002

Kerrie's gift two days before Christmas was to have a tube whacked down her nose. She'd taken a turn for the worse, vomiting overnight, and the tube was needed to aspirate her stomach, relieving pressure on the bowel.

'What's happening?' I asked.

'They think my bowel has kinked because of all the adhesions from the operation,' she said, struggling to talk with the intrusive pipe rubbing the back of her throat.

'What does that mean?'

'The bowel moves around and they think it might have caught on scar tissue, causing it to kink.'

I imagined a fizzing hose winding itself in a knot.

'How can it be fixed?' I asked.

'By waiting. They expect the bowel to unravel itself. But in the meantime I have to keep this tube in and I'm not allowed to eat.'

25 December 2002

Kerrie was allowed out of hospital for a couple of hours even though she hadn't grazed properly in nine days. We did our best to give the house a Christmas feel before I picked her up from Peter Mac. I was excited and nervous at the same time.

Elsa had warned me to warn Kerrie that she could not over-extend herself and strain her delicate stomach. Under no circumstances was she to lift Eddie. We didn't want her guts all over the carpet. This was one area in which I was happy to acquiesce, almost grateful to be bossed around by Elsa.

'Your mum said you couldn't pick up Eddie.'

'I know.'

'Your mum said you have to be extremely careful.'

'Okay, I will.'

'Are you listening, Kerrie?'

'I am.'

The first thing Kerrie did when she walked through the door on Christmas Day 2002 was pick Eddie up and give him a delicious hug.

The doctors had told her not to strain herself, the nurses had cautioned her about unnecessary pressure on her stomach and I had warned her repeatedly on the drive home from Peter Mac not to pick Eddie up or else she'd have to answer to her mother. But despite her weakened state, despite the scar from the operation and despite the nasogastric tube dangling from her nose, she simply thought giving her son a hug was worth the risk.

Elsa didn't say a word, standing in the hallway, mouth agape. The admonishing was left up to me.

'Your mother was very naughty, picking you up, wasn't she?' I said to Eddie.

'I didn't,' Kerrie said. 'He jumped into my arms when I was bending down. I just used my legs to pick him up, that's all.'

And who was I to argue?

It was a tough Christmas Day. Kerrie couldn't have a slice of ham, a glass of wine or a serve of Christmas pudding. So while she was there none of us ate. And despite our best intentions, we overdid the fussing. Irritated, and with her energy levels flagging, Kerrie asked to go back. So I put her in the car and drove her to hospital.

* * *

31 December 2002

At the turn of the millennium Kerrie and I had stood under the Sydney Harbour Bridge swigging from a bottle of champagne and staring up as hundreds of fireworks exploded across the sky. The possibilities were endless. Each turbo-charged cracker cascading its sparks over the harbour was like a new opportunity imprinting itself on the night sky.

We handed the bottle back and forth as the sky pop, pop, popped in a shower of sparkles.

We were engaged, childless, and contemplating life in this big city. As we played pass the bottle, like two naughty teenagers in the shadows of a high school disco, we were amazed that, despite the throng, the world seemed to belong to us, like we were the only two people under the bridge.

'I'm so glad to be standing here and sharing this with you,' Kerrie said, as I swigged and the sky popped.

'There's no one else I'd rather be with,' I replied, as she popped and the sky swigged (all right, by this stage we'd probably had enough champagne).

'Happy New Year!'

'You too, babe.'

Turn your eyes away now for cringe-worthy, couple-in-love pash.

Two years later, we were married, parents and scared of cancer. The only fireworks we wanted to hear, or indeed prayed to hear, was an explosion of Kerrie's making. One fart – and it didn't have to be an ear-splitter – would set our sky alight and once again open up a new world of possibilities. But someone forgot to order the pyrotechnics.

Each day since Christmas I had returned from the city hospital to our Pascoe Vale South house and dreaded opening the door, fearing Grandma Elsa in the kitchen waiting with her demanding eyes. She visited Kerrie during the mornings, but that wouldn't stop her from wanting a positive change by nightfall, hoping upon hope that her daughter was getting better. I felt like a doctor, needing to give her some positive news, to tell her that with a couple of Panadol and a good night's rest Kerrie would be okay, but there was nothing to give.

'They are still hoping that the bowel will rectify itself,' was all I could offer, and all I had offered for about ten days.

Grandma Elsa's questioning eyes would disappear in a blink, and re-open with disappointment. Sometimes they welled with tears, and once she allowed herself to cry, but most often she retreated into her surrogate mum persona and cleaned the house. Or fed her grandson. Or started bossing Grandpa Des around.

Because Kerrie's bowels didn't want to count in the New Year with a pop, pop, pop, or allow her to swallow a swig of champagne, I think she was going slightly mad.

She didn't start hallucinating – amazing, considering her undernourished state – she fantasised. First it was talk of dining out.

'If I ever get out of here, we are going to the Flower Drum as a special treat. I need a goal. I need something to make two weeks without food worthwhile.'

Kerrie wasn't bothered by the financial aspect, that the only way we'd afford a table at leading Melbourne restaurant the Flower Drum was for our son to win a lucrative baby competition, me to start winning on the horses, or for her to sell a kidney. Unfortunately, she wouldn't let me enter Eddie in competitions – 'we are not going to exploit our son' – I was having as much luck finding a winner at the track as she was of farting, and she only had one kidney (the other having been removed with her first tumour ten years ago).

The second hint of my wife's madness came during KFC ads – a plunge into fast-food mediocrity from the reputed lofty heights of the Flower Drum. Usually people watched TV and then talked during the commercials. Not Kerrie. Starving in hospital, she insisted that visitors kept quiet during KFC's 'cricket box' ads so that she could drool and dream about being marooned on some undiscovered island paradise with a fistful of greasy drumsticks and a mouthful of mashed potato.

'Doesn't it look delicious?' she would say. And then: 'I can't believe I'm salivating over KFC!'

'Neither can I, honey. You're not even hung-over.'

Fantasy, it seemed, was her best defence against this uncontrollable hunger. Even the doctors were bewildered by her ongoing problem. They were talking about a second operation.

'Just think, this time two years ago we were unmarried, childless, planning a life in Sydney and pissed,' I said.

'I know. How things have changed. Life was so decadent back then. I just want to get out of here so that we can go back to enjoying our little life,' she said.

'Me too.'

'What are you doing tonight?'

'Brian and Chel have asked me to meet up with them. Some of their friends have a motel room in the city to watch the fireworks. But I don't think I'll go. I don't really feel like celebrating.'

'You should go, Danny. Go out and enjoy yourself. It would make me feel better. Let your hair down.'

'I haven't got any hair.'

'You know what I mean.'

So I did. I went to that hotel room and I had a couple of drinks with Brian's friends and I watched the fireworks at midnight and as much as I tried to be distracted by the conversation I couldn't help but think of the blazing word that lit up the Sydney Harbour Bridge at the turn of the millennium with all its fizzling promise of happiness: 'Eternity'.

4 July 2006

Dear Kerrie,

Eddie has grown even in the two months since you have been gone. I wish you could see him. He might not have the best manners of all the four-year-olds in Cobram, he might not always listen or do what he is told, but his vocabulary and imagination set our son apart.

He is halfway through tonight's dinner, a plate of noodles, when a song on TV captures his attention. A couple are murdering 'You're the One That I Want' from the *Grease* soundtrack on *Singing with the Stars*. He obviously doesn't share my distaste of the version because he soon asks if he can dance.

'No way, not until you have finished your dinner,' I say.

I don't want him getting into the habit of waltzing around the dinner table halfway through a meal, spreading sticky noodles across Granny Kath's tiled floor.

Well, he has the ability to improvise. He cheekily looks across at my mother with his fork in hand and says: 'Granny, my toes are dancing.'

He then turns to me: 'Look, Dad, my toes are dancing.'

I lift the tablecloth to unveil wriggling toes and I have barely lowered it back to table level when he defiantly asks again to dance.

'No way, finish your dinner.'

I feel mean for quashing his meal-time frivolity, but it's not as if I'm slamming my fist and yelling every time he drops a dollop of sauce-smeared mashed potato on the table. I'd lose my voice.

He is developing a unique language. During the middle of the night he comes into my room complaining of a sore ear. Grumpily I bark at him to stop crying. But the pain is bad and when I ashamedly shake from slumber, I give him some Baby Panadol to dull the ache.

First thing in the morning I book in with Dr Chrissie and a more buoyant Eddie waltzes into the surgery, announcing to the receptionist, 'I have bruises in my ears.' She looks stunned and I giggle nervously.

While we are waiting for Dr Chrissie, Eddie spots a mobile dangling from a doorway, using the spectre of three nefarious 'flu germs to encourage people to have 'flu injections.

'Look at the frogs, Dad. What are the frogs saying?'

Stupidly, I tell him the green cardboard figures are germs.

'But they're not around Cobram, right?'

This has become his safety blanket – he can cope with bad things as long as they don't live in Cobram. He is fascinated by piranhas, sharks and all those nasty flesh-eating creatures but does not fear them because they don't live in the Murray River or surrounding bush.

I tell him the evil 'flu bugs don't live in Cobram, because I don't have the heart to tell him otherwise.

'Why don't they live in Cobram, Dad?'

'Because the Murray River is too strong for them and they get swept away.'

'Why?'

'Because they're not very strong swimmers.'

'Why?'

'Let's just leave it at that, okay?'

Thankfully, Dr Chrissie breaks the impasse and we are ushered into her room. You'll be pleased to know she's as busy as ever, rushing around as if the electricity is about to be cut.

Eddie doesn't wait to be seated before declaring, 'I've got bruises in my ears. Can you get them out?'

She takes a look and says he has a slight infection, but won't need antibiotics unless it becomes worse.

'So am I healthy?' Eddie asks.

'Well, sort of,' Dr Chrissie says.

'I'm healthy then?' he says, not totally convinced.

'Well, you've got a little infection in your ears.'

'Can you get the bruises out?'

'Well, we won't need to do anything for the moment.'

'Why?'

'Ask your father,' she laughs.

So I tell Eddie he is healthy, and needn't be scared of 'flu bugs or nasty-looking frogs or piranhas and if he starts feeling worse, we'll get some medicine. He must be happy with that, because there's no more 'why?s', only 'how come?s'.

Miss you,

love Danny

6 July 2006

Dear Kerrie,

We are spending two weeks with your father in Adelaide and he's deriving great pleasure from Eddie's self-nominated role as the 'swear man'. You wouldn't believe how many times Grandpa Des and I utter the words 'bloody' or 'shit' during the course of normal conversation.

This is a common exchange.

Des: 'Oh shit, I left the bloody paper in the bedroom.'

Eddie: 'Uhh! Grandpa, you sweared.'

Des: 'No I didn't, did I, love?'

Eddie: 'Yes you did, you said bloody and shit.'

Des: 'Ooh, I'm sorry, I won't do it again. You keep reminding Grandpa, won't you, love?'

Me: 'It's swore, Eddie. Not sweared.'

And this conversation is replayed about ten times a day because these words are so ingrained in our everyday speech, Des and I don't know we are saying them.

I much prefer when Eddie is the 'Kissy Monster', roaming the house and planting big smooches on our whiskery cheeks. 'Here comes the Kissy Monster,' he shouts. He's very affectionate, which no doubt stems from you because I've never been an overly 'kissy' person.

It is strange being in your family house, Eddie sleeping in your childhood bed and you no longer being around. I sit in your seat with your dad on the porch each night, while Eddie buzzes away at our feet. I talk about how special you were or how special Elsa was and Des nods in agreement.

'God bless her,' he says about you. 'God bless her,' he says about Elsa.

We talk about his years working at Adelaide airport or his time at the gas fields of Moomba, and we talk about football and we talk about horse-racing and we talk about the weather but we never talk about the fact we might be falling apart.

Miss you,
love Danny

23 July 2006

Dear Kerrie,

We are back in Cobram and one second Eddie is running down a wooden ramp, the next he slips, bounces on his bum and catapults off into the Murray River. The water is only 60 cm deep because we haven't made it as far as the houseboats, but he's completely submerged and I have to lean over and yank him out, stifling the laughter as he starts sobbing, water dripping from his beanie, his jumper, his tracksuit pants and his new sneakers.

'Are you all right, Ed?' I ask, trying hard not to laugh at his misfortune. 'Don't worry, I'll take you home and get you all dried up.'

It is a cold, overcast day and the river is chilly. A puddle is forming at his feet so I walk him home. I strip him off at my parents' front door and take him inside to stand on the heated tiles while towelling him dry. He has stopped crying and I have stopped laughing. The image of Eddie falling in the river loses its humorous edge. What if he'd fallen in the deep, flowing water? I mightn't have got him out.

That night at the dinner table, he theatrically explains to Granny, Pa and Grandpa Des, who we have brought back from Adelaide for ten days, about his frightful experience.

'Yeah, yeah, I fell in the river. But Daddy grabbed me. Daddy saved me; he's my hero,' he says.

This puts Des's nose out of joint.

'What about me?' he says. 'I killed a spider for you.'

'Yeah, Grandpa killed a big black spider in the lounge room. He's my hero, too.'

Equilibrium is restored to the house and I go off in search of the Vicswim brochures.

Miss you,
love Danny

28 July 2006

Dear Kerrie,

As I try to make sense of losing you, I'm sorting through your old letters and emails. I can't believe how often I took your sentiments for granted. Reading our correspondence from the time I left you in Melbourne to live in the UK is like watching an old movie of our romance. I'm falling in love again.

Remember when I was living on Portobello Road in a London pub and you were coming to visit for Christmas in 1997? You couldn't contain the excitement:

Well, it can now be measured in a matter of weekends – only four more before the Tuesday I fly out. Yippee. And the time is absolutely galloping away, probably because all I do is work and sleep. Had a 14-hour day yesterday – 10 am 'til midnight. But, as with everything in life, there is an upside – I've only been to the River (bar) twice in about three weeks. I've completely lost my thirst for alcohol and gained one for nice, strong cups of tea. Tonight I'm breaking the drought with a lovely Coonawarra cab sav, simply because it seemed the right thing to do while writing to you. Like toasting you, or something …

I've lived these past seven months with you like a ghost at my shoulder, a presence only I can feel. I've felt indescribable grief, self-pity and loneliness, but also euphoria (when I get a letter or phone call) and peace that come from solitude. A state of grace, if you like. I think I've grown up a bit in your absence, probably you have, too.

On to things fluffier: My thighs are growing as wide as my nails are growing long. Saddlebags and claws. I hope you still find me desirable. I want to spend a week in bed (or the broom closet, or on top of the bar) because we have a lot of catching up to do. I love you, dannyboy. I play 'Imaginary Friend' by the Lemonheads every morning on the way to work in your honour. Every time I see the moon I send up a prayer to her to look after you. You are everywhere around me and inside me, no matter how much I try to put you aside for fear of losing you and having nothing left. Your voice and face are so close I can touch them. I can feel the hairs on your chest still. And somehow – somehow – I know with all my heart that you will, in my mind, be part of the best years of my life.

Sometimes I want to burst – with happiness about life. Are you ever just going about some mundane task and then it hits you – I'm alive? All my bits work. I love people who love me back.

Can it get any sweeter than that? Yes, it can. You can be at Heathrow on December 10 at 6 am. I want to hold your face and stroke your ears then nestle into your neck and inhale you. I want to kiss your hands and put my fingers to your mouth so I can feel your breath on them. I want to look into your eyes, your beautiful green eyes, and see the passage of these months in them.

I want to hear you laugh at any old absurdity. More than anything, I just want to be in your orbit, with that invisible thread holding us together as we go spinning about life. Separate but together. Smiling across a room at each other over the din of strangers and going, 'hey, this is an adventure!'

Is this over the top? I hope so. Cos when I get over there, I want to dazzle you. There's so much living to do. Let's dance through the streets. Let's make fun of every poor miserable bugger who frowns at us, people who simply don't know they're alive. Let's show them what it's all about. I wanna get high on existence, the thrill of uncertainty. And I want you to come with me. Honey, no matter how broke we are, we can own the world.
Kerrie XXXX

2 January 2003

Among The Professor's New Year's resolutions was to make Kerrie's bowel work again. And to make sure he didn't renege on this little decree he operated the following day. This time in nearby St Vincent's Hospital.

Far from being scared, Kerrie was glad for action. I, too, would be better prepared. Rather than wait anxiously in a hospital lounge, tangling my insides like a jumbled mess of fishing line, I would go to the movies. I would catch a tram to Bourke Street, buy a big box of popcorn, a large Coke, grab a ticket to *Lord of the Rings: The Two Towers* and lose myself for a couple of hours. There was no way I'd be caught up among grieving relatives this time. I told Kerrie of my plans before the doors closed between us and she was taken to surgery.

'Good for you, honey. You go enjoy yourself,' she said.

Except, I didn't enjoy myself. The popcorn didn't have enough salt and tasted like cardboard. Butterflies in my stomach wouldn't make room for the Coke, and as loud as the on-screen hordes of 'nassty Orcses' were as they battered the crumbling defences of Helm's Deep, my mind wouldn't allow me into the fantasy.

We'd cast out cancer, a foe more real than any invading Orcs, but could the surgeons invoke their wizardry to repair the damage? Could they make my wife better? Were the good guys going to prevail in our story?

As soon as the credits rolled, I was on my way back to St Vincent's. And once again I was greeted with blank faces and a lack of news. My wife was locked away in the hospital's caverns, and I couldn't breach the defences. The nurses had no idea when Kerrie would be returned to the ward.

'Why don't you go home and I'll ring you when we get any news?' a desk nurse suggested after spotting me in a corner walking around in circles like a dog chasing its tail.

Yes, why didn't I go home? Why didn't I go back to Pascoe Vale South so that we could all worry together? Perhaps seeing Grandpa Des, Grandma Elsa and Eddie could help fill the hollow pit in my gut.

'Are you sure that's okay?' I asked.

'That's fine.'

So I stopped chasing and went home. But I didn't wait for the desk nurse to ring. I rang her. Every ten minutes. And when I waited longer than ten minutes, Grandma Elsa asked me why the delay.

8 pm

Ring, ring, ring.

Me: 'Hello I'm just inquiring about Kerrie Russell. I'm her husband and I want to know if she's back on the ward yet.'

Nurse: 'No, not yet.'

Me: 'She's not back yet, Elsa.'

Elsa: 'Any idea when?'

Me: 'Any idea when she might be back on the ward?'

Nurse: 'She's out of theatre and in Recovery, but we'll let you know as soon as she comes to the ward.'

Me: 'They'll let us know, Elsa.'

Elsa: 'Do they know whether the operation was a success?'

Me: 'Do you know how Kerrie's operation went?'

Nurse: 'No, but we'll let you know.'

Me: 'Thanks.'

8.12 pm

Elsa: 'How come you haven't called yet?'

Me: 'Shit, is that the time?'

Ring, ring, ring.

'Hello I'm just inquiring about Kerrie Russell. I'm her husband and I want to know if she's back on the ward yet.'

'No, not yet.'

'She's not back yet, Elsa.'

'Any idea when?'

'Any idea when she might be back on the ward?'

'No, but we'll let you know.'

'Thanks.'

Finally, before our ten minutes was up, one of Kerrie's surgeons called me. She said the operation had been long, tedious and tiresome (no shit!) but, ultimately, a success. Basically, the surgeon said, they'd had to unravel the bowel and unpick numerous adhesions over the course of three and a half hours. They did not, the surgeon was delighted to say, perforate the bowel.

'What do we do now?' I asked.

'We wait for the bowel to start working again,' the surgeon said.

Hooray.

She's okay.

The operation was a success.

Before Grandma Elsa and I drove to the hospital to give Kerrie a goodnight kiss the three of us danced around the lounge room, chasing each other's tails.

January 2003

The unspoken side effect of having a wife in hospital for a month was no sex. There's no physical counterbalance to the stress, fear and hopelessness. I tried not to talk about this abstinence in front of Kerrie, although I might have mentioned it once or twice. Well, I couldn't very well raise the subject with her mother. And it wasn't a topic that I expected my friends to understand.

Me: 'This drought is starting to affect my moods. Or it's failing to affect my moods. There's no upside to my life.'

Pick a friend, any friend: 'Sex! You're worried about sex! For God's sake, you dissolute twat, your wife's in hospital after not one, but two life-saving operations. Get your mind out of your Calvin Klein underwear for a second and think about the person who is really suffering.'

They were right. Or they would have been right if I wore Calvin Kleins and had the nerve to start the I'm-not-getting-my-rocks-off conversation. And yet I couldn't stop my hormones buzzing. 'The month without' was making me see strange things. Women. I was seeing women. Everywhere. Tall women. Short women. Young women. Skinny women. Plump women. Sexy women. Gorgeous women.

In the past, I would sit on a train and read the paper or stare out the window at houses flashing by, barely bothering to acknowledge the cardboard cut-outs filling the surrounding seats. Now I was seeing it all: wavy, blond-tresses; jet-black hair finer than fibre-optics cables; eye make-up; lipstick hues; tight butt-hugging jeans, loose butt-hiding skirts; jiggling breasts, wobbling breasts; and, eyes. Brown eyes, blue eyes, bored eyes, sorrowful eyes, nervous eyes and, my favourite, eyes that sparkled and smiled. Then there were smells. Subtle perfumes that gently tickled the tip of your nose, the scent of shampoos and conditioners that fairy-danced around women's heads, and the inescapable nasty potions that were so overbearing they would hang around the carriage for minutes after their wearer had alighted from the train.

Once the looking and the noticing and the smelling started, I couldn't stop. I reminded myself of what my friends might think. I told myself it was immoral, considering my wife's predicament. I tried to make myself read the paper.

Most times the hormones settled once I arrived at the hospital, like a belligerent swarm of bees returning to the hive. Sometimes they stayed sedated until I massaged Kerrie's shoulders. And it was at these times that the hive would stir. I couldn't help but mention how tough I was doing it in 'this month without'.

For the most part Kerrie was sympathetic, saying she would do her best to come home. Sometimes she even sounded guilty, but mostly, I think, she ignored my fizzing libido and concentrated on getting better. It was either that or douse me with a bucket of cold water.

While I was getting hot under the collar, the outdoor temperatures, too, were searing. Asphalt-bubbling heat. Even after visiting hours when I had left Kerrie for the night, and walked the fifteen minutes from Strathmore station up the hill to our Pascoe Vale South home, my sweat-soaked shirt adhered to my back.

Grandma Elsa always chastised me for not calling.

'Why didn't you ring? We would have driven down and picked you up. Eddie loves the train. You're mad walking in this heat. Tomorrow, ring up and we'll come down and get you,' she demanded.

'I don't mind the walk,' I said.

'Don't be silly. It's too hot. Ring tomorrow and we'll pick you up.'

'All right.'

But I didn't ring. Elsa didn't understand. I needed the walk. I needed to tire myself out each night by marching up our hill until my calves were screaming. I had to feel grossed out by that soggy shirt on my back. It took my mind off sex.

6 January 2003

As Kerrie improved, the Flower Drum dream faded. Doctors were cautiously optimistic because her bowel had started grumbling, but my problem was that I couldn't back a winner. I was trying. But luck wasn't on my side.

It was my first day back at the newspaper after the Christmas break, starting an intense eight-hour shift as production editor at 4.30 am, pulling the pages together by midday so that the edition could be on the streets before the commuters started streaming home. I barely had time to fret. Once the paper was rolling on the press, I would take the lift nine storeys down to the foyer, walk through Southgate across the Yarra River footbridge to Flinders Street Station, catch a train to Parliament Station, walk to St Vincent's Hospital and then catch a lift to Kerrie's bedside. All this via the TAB.

Every evening, before I saw Kerrie, I felt the urge to gamble. I needed to challenge fate or God or whoever it was that re-routed our lives to change our luck.

'I dare you to let me win, God.'

'I dare you, fate, to let my horses win.'

'I dare both of you to let me actually feel like I can do something that makes us better off.'

I didn't scream these words, I muttered them like a homeless man as I filled out betting slips, trying all sorts of combinations to strike it rich: lucky numbers, lucky names, closing my eyes and trusting the fall of a pen. I even tried testing my intellect by studying the form guide – carefully noting previous starts, previous opposition, track conditions, barrier draws, trainers and jockeys.

But none of these systems worked. When I placed a bet based on form, my lucky numbers came up. When I reverted back to the numbers, a lucky name would bob. I backed No. 7, and Heaven Can Wait saluted. I backed Courageous Girl, and the horse with the best form and carrying No. 7 finished five lengths ahead. Gambling made me feel worse. And, strangely, somehow I think that helped. It gave me something else to blame, an outlet for the hurt and sense of injustice bubbling away inside.

Occasionally, I told Kerrie about my hard-luck stories. Every so often, I would tell her the name of a horse that had seemed like a perfect omen and yet had 'lost by a nose to a horse that I was going to back which paid fifteen dollars'. She nodded her head and smiled. She would half-heartedly say 'bad luck' or 'better luck next time'. Because for Kerrie, luck was swallowing a cup of tea or a couple of spoonfuls of tasteless broth and having it reach the other end. She didn't need to tempt God, she simply asked Him to give her strength.

13 January 2003

Dear Eddie,

Your mum is regaining power and has been transferred back to Peter Mac to see out the last of her incarceration. The second operation has been a success. She is eating. She is farting. She is even 'doing poo'. The cancer is out and her bowels are working. In three days' time she will be sent home so that we can start our lives again. Your mum was right. She's always right.

'I've beaten it before, I can do it again.'

Love Dad

16 January 2003

What do you eat after a hunger strike? What sort of goodies do political activists stuff down their throats when they decide to end their foodless protests?

Steak?

Vegetables?

Steak and three vegetables?

If they are incarcerated, are they stuck with the prison's menu? Do they get a choice, or are they that mind-bogglingly hungry that they eat the first thing in sight? 'Attention Prisoner 101! Prisoner 101, please remove the warden's foot from your mouth.'

Kerrie settled on McDonald's. Five minutes out of hospital and she steered me into the Golden Bloody Arches.

She ordered a McChicken.

She ordered fries with that.

She ordered McNuggets.

She ordered fries with that, too.

Did she want a drink?

Of course, she wanted a bloody drink. She'd been stuck in hospital for a month, literally starving.

We had to get past the menu board, I thought, before she filled the boot. 'Yes, that's all,' I said as I hit the accelerator and fishtailed up the drive-through until we reached the 'please pay here' window (all right, burning rubber might have been a slight exaggeration, but we took off pretty darn quickly).

Although McDonald's hadn't been a premeditated gastronomic decision, merely a fast-food restaurant in the right spot at the right time, she enjoyed that meal like it was Babette's feast. She took pleasure in every bite. She took pleasure in licking the salt from her fingers. She slurped at the Coke, and she burped. Not little, 'excuse me' burps, but big-bellied belches.

She ate until the corners of every bag, box and container were wiped clean. Then she sat back and smiled, a full-as-a-fisherman's-cat smile that made me laugh.

'Kerrie, are you meant to be eating this shit?' I asked.

'Probably not, but I don't care. It's only today. I'll start eating properly tomorrow.'

January 2003

Dear Professor,
A small scribbled note is small recompense for a life-saving operation, but it's all I can offer at the moment (unless you want to join my husband and I at the Flower Drum in a couple of months).

Thank you so much for all you have done for my poor old body, and for your optimism and 'hang in theres' when I was miserable waiting for things to start working.

My spirits always lifted when I saw you bustle through the door. I felt safe and reassured after your visits. The knee pats were an extra-kind touch.

I guess I'll see you for follow-ups, but until then I wish you all the best, and hope your well-earned holiday was fabulous.
Thanks again
Kerrie Russell

I agreed with her on all except one thing, the 'life-saving operation'. Surgeons were extremely gifted people, no doubt, but I couldn't invest my faith in 'life-saving'. These brilliant minds with their deft and steady hands could prolong our time on earth, but that was all. Everyone died. I needed to convince myself of this so that my appreciation of surgeons' unique abilities didn't become one of unconditional reverence. I knew they could help Kerrie, but they couldn't work miracles. That's why I occasionally prayed to her God.

January 2003

Looking back, Kerrie made the most of her second shot at life. Following her operation in 1992, she changed. She shed her innate shyness, saying goodbye to the timid girl who hid in cupboards when visitors called, and became an open, insouciant woman. She sought adventure in her backyard and abroad. She went overseas ... three times. She worked at a backpackers' hostel in Ireland. She made new and exotic friends. She smoked cigarettes. She drank Guinness. She drank whisky. She drank bourbon.

Amazingly, she lived without fear. She even altered her approach to work. She would turn up late if she felt like sleeping in; she would go for an hour-long coffee break if a colleague needed to chat; she never watched the clock; she just enjoyed doing the work when it needed to be done. Whether a job took ten minutes or five hours, she simply made sure she did it well.

Kerrie would while away Sundays in her pyjamas. She would spend hours reading the papers. Sometimes she would go to a movie, sometimes she would go see a band, and sometimes she would sit at the bar until late after work and grab Chinese takeaway on the way home. It didn't matter what she did, as long as it was random and as long as it was fun.

If there was something missing, it was love. And that's where I came in.

Four years after her first operation, Kerrie began to think cancer was on permanent vacation and she wanted a companion. She even asked God.

I distinctly remember one evening after work in Melbourne almost six years ago. I was in one of those public transport-induced reveries thinking about my life and, wonderful though it was, knowing something very important was missing.

As I stepped off the tram, I said a spontaneous (and apparently quite powerful prayer): 'Please God, send me someone to knock

*about with. Nothing serious – just a nice, funny, smart man to have
dinner with and go to the movies with. Someone I can really talk to
who won't be scared of me or run off as soon as I hold his hand in
public. Someone who knows I'm a sensational woman with a very
independent and balanced view of life who would never manipulate
or try to change him. That would make life perfect, God. I know I'm
selfish to ask for something when I have so very much already, and
I don't expect you to do anything about it because you're busy with
so many more urgent and tragic matters. But it never hurts to ask.
Thanks.'*

About three weeks later, he sent me Danny. I'm glad I asked.

That was Kerrie's second shot at life. She changed, she travelled, she
married and she became a mum. Now, almost eleven years later in 2003,
she had a third shot, decisions to be made under a menacing cloud: 'This
time I have something to lose.'

Kerrie settled on three things: she wanted to cook, she wanted to keep
moving and she wanted to find ways to lock out cancer. As soon as she
was strong enough, as soon as she was capable of running the house so
that Grandma Elsa could return to Adelaide, these were the things she
would pursue. This was Kerrie's life, take three.

Early February 2003

There's a joke about a man who goes for a drive with his mother-in-
law. While out on the open road, he is pulled over by a policeman. The
policeman asks the driver whether he is aware that his mother-in-law fell
out a couple of kilometres back.

'Oh, thank God for that,' says the driver. 'For a while there I thought
I was going deaf.'

Grandma Elsa was still bossing Grandpa Des and me around, although
with Kerrie home we were taken off the boil and reduced to simmer.
Grandma Elsa might have even mellowed. She fussed over Kerrie like she
was a newborn, making sure she had a bottomless cup of tea, a kitchen

landscape dotted with food, and a newspaper. At the start of each morning she would bark at Grandpa Des to wheel Eddie to a nearby service station for the *Herald Sun*, *The Age* and a Kit Kat for her grandson.

Kerrie reintroduced laughter. No longer did I feel like a recalcitrant teenager when ordered around by Grandma Elsa. Instead I gave her cheek. And she responded. This playful banter melted whatever barrier I had placed between us and we became closer than friends; we became family. As for Grandpa Des and me, we continued talking about horses, or the weather, or who would get the next beer from the fridge. We were already family.

Grandma Elsa said the reward for her three-month tour of duty was to see Kerrie home safely and to watch her grandson grow. She said three months might not seem like a lot in a lifetime, but each day with Eddie had brought new tricks, new adventures and new problems to solve. What she didn't tell us about was the strain that being a worried grandmother and a surrogate mum had placed on her heart. We weren't to find this out until a week before she died.

Prior to marriage and fatherhood, chief among the many things that stretched my paper-thin tolerance levels were self-absorbed parents who waffled on with under-stimulating anecdotes about their kids. I couldn't stand that these blinkered adults would consider a semi-nocturnal person such as myself with a background in late nights and mayhem even remotely interested in their snotty-nosed, overproducing poo factories that they liked to quaintly refer to as 'our Bobby' or 'our Katy' or 'the only child that exists in the world right now'. As far as I was concerned, they could take their 'goo goos' and 'gaa gaas' and shit stories someplace else because I wanted to sit around bars discussing more pertinent things such as why my favourite Australian rock band You Am I had become a four piece.

Grandma Elsa helped change these perceptions. Not about You Am I, I still couldn't understand why they became a four piece. No, she made those blinkered parents seem normal. Through osmosis and the dark art of 'grandmother knows best' I learned to treat baby talk as a second language. Having had my night-owl licence revoked helped, too.

Hitherto, terms such as 'time for food, bubba' used to make me cringe and want to throw up mushy peas; now it had me mesmerised sitting at the table watching Grandma Elsa steer Spoon Flight 689 towards my son's tongue for landing.

Grandma Elsa was all right. I started watching her more closely. Sometimes she would leave Eddie with Kerrie and zip out to the back step for a special Grandpa Des-rolled cigarette. As she puffed away she would look at the sky and I'm pretty sure she was thanking God.

If moments in our lives are defined by songs or words, Grandma Elsa's catchphrase for that Christmas became 'Uh, uh, argh – not the glasses', uttered in response to her inquisitive grandson trying to snatch the specs from her nose. She would emphasise the 'Uh, uh, argh' with shakes of her head and then let out a witch-like cackle. Every time she said it, Eddie would giggle and then grab for her silver-framed glasses again. We all watched and we all laughed – Grandpa Des, Kerrie and me. Sometimes I would find myself parroting the line on the train to work. 'Uh, uh, argh – not the glasses.'

I was glad I wasn't going deaf.

Mid-February 2003

Luck found me sitting in the Cross Keys pub on a Saturday night. Finally, after two months of feeling-sorry-for-myself fist-shaking at the sky, someone heard my call. Brian and I won $6000 on a quadrella at the Moonee Valley trots.

When Chris Alford steered Mont Denver Gold first past the post to snare the Hunter Cup, I couldn't believe my luck or my heartbeat. I had won. At last. Six fucking grand! Thanks, God. Thanks, fate. Thanks, Brian for picking the horses. I was so ecstatic I upgraded from beer to spirits. Hey, big spender. All that money in my phone account, if … if I had punched in the right numbers.

I felt my racing heart skip. What if I'd punched in the wrong numbers by mistake? It wasn't hard to do with fat fingers on a crowded phone pad. I'd done it before. Shit!

I raced outside to a phone box and dialled my account. No money. Yet. The stewards wouldn't have given the all clear, I told myself. I waited, and waited, and waited. One minute, maybe two, maybe ten. I didn't want to ring, but the pub's TAB screens were flashing 'all clear', the paying sign was up, I dialled my numbers again.

'Your account balance is …'

'Yes? Yes? Yes?'

'Your account balance is …'

'Yeeeessss? Yeeeeesss?'

'Your account balance is … six thousand and fifty-four dollars.'

Yes! We're rich!

Elsa, who had been next door feeding coins to the pokies, was shocked when I raced up and excitedly threw her some cash.

'Here, double your bets,' I yammered, 'I've just had a win. I'll see you back at home.'

Kerrie, who had been unaware of the building excitement, couldn't believe her ears. She congratulated me and I accepted the praise. That's why I gambled, because I was a winner. Forget the horses or the drivers or the fact Brian did the form, I was making our little family's future better. Me.

'This will pay off our credit card,' Kerrie said, snapping the legs off the little dancing man in my head.

'What?'

'This will pay off the credit card,' she repeated with delight.

'But – '

'You're always complaining about our credit card debt and now we'll be clear.'

'Yes, but – '

'After the next win we can go to the Flower Drum.'

Mid-February 2003

Kerrie was growing restless – suburbophobia meant she fingered weekends as a time to keep moving. She needed trees, and mountain ranges and ocean views. She needed to escape. She needed to calm the fear of becoming rooted in our concrete-laden pocket of Melbourne, if only for an afternoon.

Getting away would prove difficult. For one, we had a sixteen-month-old son. For two, I usually had my head buried in a form guide for the best part of a Saturday trying to win us a night at the Flower Drum, and for three, even though we had paid off the credit card, we were broke. Unlike Kerrie's life, take two, there would be no flights of fancy to Ireland.

Our first excursion was a bunny hop, driving to a nearby suburb and its duck-filled park with a sprawling wooden playground – a perfect setting for Eddie and his desire to run. He shunned walking soon after he learned to stagger (at about ten months old), and every so often his body would overtake his nappy-hindered legs, causing him to topple on the grass. Overbalancing in this park, however, was perilous – a minefield of duck shit. I ambled after Eddie, carefully picking my way through the squishy mess, while Kerrie sat on a bench, still regaining her strength from the operation, but looking incredibly relieved and relaxed.

It was like she was watching us on a home movie, the way she sat back and smiled, and I hammed it up for the imaginary camera, swinging Eddie in the air, chasing after him and, the part of the home movie Kerrie didn't appreciate, a mock attempt to toss him in the lake.

After being admonished for foolish parenting, and tired of chasing Eddie around, I grabbed some bread to feed our little web-footed friends. Eddie failed to grasp the purpose of the exercise, instead shoving bread in his mouth.

'No, no, you don't eat it, Eddie. The bread's stale.'

This only encouraged him to eat more, so I commandeered the bread.

I found it a cruel exercise, feeding the ducks. There was always a small bird with a gammy leg struggling at the back, looking underfed and desperate, while its fitter, stronger cousins monopolised the bounty. As hard as you tried, throwing a crumb within pecking distance, these weaker ducks never pounced on time. And while I was worrying about ducks, our son's little legs had started working again and he was halfway across the park, heading for the playground.

'Yes, Kerrie, I know. Don't worry about the ducks.'

After catching Eddie and chasing him up the ramps and down the slides, around the poles and through the tunnels, we sat on a park bench dipping into our picnic bag and it occurred to me that our serendipitous afternoon wouldn't have been possible six months ago – not when my eyes were closed.

I took a photo to freeze the moment, a picture of Eddie with his mum. And I wondered, the way she held her arm around his waist, looking totally enamoured, if she would ever let him go.

3 March 2003

I lost Kerrie in April 1997 when I left Melbourne to discover America and Europe and found her again in Ireland two years later. Initially, she kept her distance, literally – she set up home in the southern coastal town of Tramore, a six-hour bus trip from my workplace at a newspaper in Belfast. Re-injecting spark into our relationship took some planning, mainly stealing time from our jobs so we could meet halfway in Dublin. After a couple of months, countless hours on the bus, dreamy-eyed meetings at the depot and lost nights boozing in the Temple Bar, we decided to get married so that we never had to be apart again. I'd realised I'd travelled halfway around the world searching for the very thing I'd left behind.

The next step was to ring Adelaide to get the all clear from Kerrie's father. Except he couldn't remember who I was. We'd met, but the place, date and face had slipped his mind. I'd just assumed Kerrie had told her parents we were an item again. I'd actually assumed she'd told them we were an item in the first place. Wrong on both counts, even though I'd been sending them postcards of my travels.

'Why didn't you tell them? You invited me to your father's birthday dinner in Melbourne, for fuck's sake. Who did they think I was? Another friend?'

'Yep. I didn't think you saw any future in our relationship, so I didn't bother telling them. What was the point?'

'But I sent them postcards.'

'I'm sure they loved them.'

So there I was, stuck in a Belfast phone box, mentioning that I was calling from Northern Ireland and that Kerrie and I were getting engaged, while her father was bamboozled and kept interrupting me to ask about the weather.

'It's overcast,' I said, 'it always is in Ireland, but is it okay if I marry Kerrie?'

'Who is this again?' Des asked.

'It's Danny. Danny Russell.'

'Danny? Danny who?'

'Danny Russell.'

'Oh. Well, guess what, Danny Russell?'

'What? … What? … Whhhaaaaattttt?'

'No, you can't.'

'What?!' This was absurd. It was a perfunctory call, playing along with tradition. We were getting married whether he liked it or not. I didn't need his permission. I didn't even need him to remember who I was.

Thankfully, Des read the mood.

'I'm just joking,' he said. 'Sure you can marry my daughter.'

Kerrie grabbed the phone and chided her father for being blasé about such a momentous occasion, but before she could finish he had interrupted her, too.

'It's overcast, Dad. It always is in Ireland.'

My mother was different. When I told her the news, she started crying. She couldn't understand why I had left Kerrie in the first place. So with Granny's tears, Grandpa Des's semi-blessing and a weather report, on 24 July 1999 we announced our engagement.

July 1999: Just in case the rumour mill has been hangared for maintenance, thought I'd let you know, in time-honoured cadet-journalist-intro fashion, that IT'S OFFICIAL. I'm getting married. Married. Aaaarrgghh. Yep, Danny and I have decided we've done just about every

*foolish, heat-of-the-moment, ill-advised thing a nearly-thirty-year-old
person can do except tie the knot, so we're gonna do that, too. And you
know what? It feels fantastic. And not nearly as weird as it did the first
week after he popped the question (for a few days Danny and I just kept
looking at each other and laughing).*

*I guess it's strangely appropriate that we've done this now, living our
lives as we do amid the chaos of a houseful of fringe-dwelling 22-year-olds
in varying degrees of flux. How can I give you a picture of our lives here?
Erm, try combing a less sinister version of 'Trainspotting' with 'Withnail
and I' and 'This Life' and you'll get a fair idea of our days. When they're
not a haze of Belfast clubbers crashing at our place, they're filled with
cups of tea and Match of the Day and silly stories about the human
flotsam that marches through our home on a regular basis. Needless to
say, it's another lifetime entirely from the one I led in Oz, and I'm very
pleased to have tasted it.*

*Maybe the relentless pursuit of fun and experience has led us to this
place of comfort now. We've had enough of it. It's time to count our
blessings and settle on an Ikea couch and remember all the wild things
we've done, and laugh about all the narrow escapes.*

*Who knows? But it feels right and it feels solid and that's all you can go
on, isn't it?*

*Anyway, I won't carry on too much now. Plenty of time to bore you
with details. And believe me, I will. I didn't think life could get any better
than it was a few weeks ago. I was wrong. It did.*

Love Kerrie Fahey xxx

Eighteen months after our Belfast engagement, Kerrie and I were
married on 3 March 2001 in a small, red-bricked church overshadowed
by a volcanic hill in the Victorian town of Dookie. Kerrie spent
hours compiling a wedding speech, but by the time everyone else had
rambled on during our reception at the Katamatite bakery, she decided
not to read it out because she didn't want to waste any more of our
guests' time.

This is what she wrote:

It would have taken a keen ear to hear it, but the name of our wedding waltz – well, wedding sway – was 'Playground Love'.

We chose it partly because the other songs that mean something to us are 20 minutes long, 20 decibels too loud or 20 beats per minute too fast to sway to. But we chose it partly because of its title. I don't think I am revealing any strange truth when I say there is a lot of silly little kid in Danny and I still.

We have managed to escape a lot of the burdens and boring bits that come with being an adult. We have achieved not staying in one job for longer than a few years. We have worked hard to be totally financially irresponsible. We have struggled to remain undisciplined, unkempt, unco-ordinated, uninsured and unremarkable. And for that we are fervently grateful and extremely proud. There is a bit of Peter Pan in both of us. And I think deep down we still believe, just like the boy who never grows up, that if we closed our eyes and wished hard enough, we really could fly.

But here we are doing a very grown-up thing: two people who have never committed themselves to anything but their own pursuit of pleasure are committing themselves to each other's care for the rest of their days. It's a playground for two now, and it has to fit in all our families, friends, passions, prejudices. Luckily, it's a pretty big playground, with full bar facilities, gaming room and lost property area, and anyone who knows Danny will know that that last one will always be worth its keep.

I've never met anyone so prone to leaving bits of himself behind.

But then I've also never met anyone so essentially kind and generous of himself.

When I met Danny, I thought he was a bit of a nutter – gorgeous, but a nutter. He'd do these crazy pranks and gags that would have all the boys in the office in stitches. I never saw the jokes. And I thought he was doing it to be a bit of a hero. It was only days later I'd find out that his actions had defused a tense situation, or deflected attention from a character assassination of a colleague, or that it just really cheered up someone who was having a bad day.

Danny has always been willing to be the patsy for the greater good, and it took me way too long to realise that beneath the clown's mask was a pretty compassionate, intelligent and sensitive soul. It took me a long time to realise that here was one of the world's good guys who only said something if he really meant it; a guy who had so many friends not just because he was fun to be with but because he would do anything to help his mates and never look for the favour to be returned.

In fact, it took us both a long time to take each other remotely seriously. We had good fun together, but Danny's eyes were always on a far horizon and mine were always on a book, and usually one that couldn't possibly interest him. There was everything going against us. We liked different music, different television shows, different comedians, different food, different philosophies. But at least it gave us something to talk about. And we haven't stopped talking for five years. Not even when he finally went chasing his far horizon overseas and our unity was tested until it snapped. We raced around our different worlds drinking loads of champagne and meeting hundreds of nameless, faceless, funky, fascinating people in exotic landscapes. And then we realised that it wasn't that much fun without your best friend and staunchest ally by your shoulder to laugh about it all with. And it didn't mean anything being surrounded by that cosmopolitan buzz when it drowned out the only voice you wanted to hear.

So we hurtled back to each other and the bright lights of Katamatite, the world in which Danny grew up – home to him, another planet to me, but one which I have been delighted and honoured to explore under the maternal eye of Danny's parents Peter and Kathy and Danny's multitude of friends. I thank you all for your patient explanations of water rights, rotary dairying, laser grading, artificial insemination, hay harvesting, the principles of irrigation and

multiple system betting. I have learnt more about chemistry, biology,
maths and geography in 12 months at the Katty pub than in 12 years
of a comprehensive Catholic education, but it has probably cost a bit
more, though Mum and Dad might beg to differ.

I have also finally appreciated in 12 months of living with Danny
and his family and friends that I am a very lucky girl indeed. I know
Mum and Dad won't take it the wrong way when I say Peter and
Kathy – along with Louise, Peter and Hayley, and Chris – became like
my own family long before I took their surname. They have always
made me feel cherished and important because of who I am, not just
because of what I represent to their family tree or my relationship with
their son and brother.

And what of their son and brother? This magical man I will laugh
down all the years with? Well, if I close my eyes and wish hard
enough, he can make me fly.

3 March 2003

To celebrate our second anniversary and the successful removal of her
tumour, Kerrie booked a city hotel so that we could behave like we
were meeting in Dublin again. We left Eddie with Des and Elsa so that
we could explore the cracks and crevices of Melbourne's inner-city bar
world. Or that was the plan. Instead, we spent the night playing roulette
at Crown Casino.

Kerrie was excited from the moment she stepped off the train. She flicked
out casino chips like she was feeding the ducks. Her birth date, my birth
date, Eddie's birth date, Grandma Elsa's birth date, Grandpa Des's birth
date and all the birthdays she could remember. She would move to sit down
before a flurry of arms from fellow gamblers placing their bets would flush
her out again – odd numbers, even numbers, single digits, double digits,
whatever numbers took her fancy. By the time the ball started slowing to a
bounce and the croupier prepared to wave his arms across the table and call
no more bets, Kerrie would have covered just about every square available.
And just for good measure she would cover two more.

'Isn't this great?' she said, stopping to drink her bourbon and Coke.

'The croupier probably thinks we're a couple of Frankston bogans,' I muttered.

'So what?'

'I thought we were going to a groovy restaurant and a groovy bar.'

'We were, but who cares? This is fun. And what's wrong with being a bogan from Frankston?'

'Nothing. You're right. Put a chip on number thirty-five for me.'

It was almost a perfect night for Kerrie, until we missed the train home the following morning. Hung over and feeling the rising heat, we had to wait another 30 minutes on a Flinders Street platform for the next ride. Kerrie indicated she was miffed because I had wanted to stop at a TAB. But really we were happy – it was six weeks since I had brought her home from hospital and all the curvaceous women that I had been spying on public transport had become cardboard cut-outs again.

March 2003

Back in December 1999, five months after we were engaged, and living in our cosy Katamatite farmhouse, Kerrie cooked a roast. It was her best effort and it made her mother cry. Grandma Elsa's daughter had become a woman. She was no longer the Takeaway Queen.

Grandma Elsa cried when it was time for her to return to Adelaide; again with happiness. She knew her girl was well enough to cook roasts again. Except Kerrie was going to do more than that, she was going to become the resident chef at 48 Gallipoli Parade. She dusted off her cookbooks and began planning menus for the weeks ahead. In order to improve her culinary skills and impress the customer (me) she wanted to move away from what she knew – suburban Adelaide during the 1970s and '80s. Because of her post-teen predilection for late nights and Chinese takeaway, home cooking had never meant much more than Grandma Elsa's roast dinners, tepid beef curries, and sausages and mash.

'I think cooking is a hobby I could really get into,' she said as she pored over mouth-watering pictures scattered through her recipe books.

'That's great, honey, as long as you don't turn into some food-obsessed hothead, like Gordon Ramsay, and start throwing knives at me and Ed for not peeling the potatoes.'

'Gordon Ramsay? What do you take me for, you fucker? Just do what you're told in my kitchen and you won't end up flipping hamburgers at McDonald's.'

'All right, Gordon, calm down.'

Before her restaurant was open for business, we embarked on an ingredients hunt, spending Sunday afternoon in Coburg Safeway. It was the last thing I felt like doing, but Kerrie's cancer had scared me into these compromises. Plus it made her happy.

I spent most of the time spinning Eddie in a shopping trolley with Kerrie following behind, pausing to study food items for her pantry. One of the main reasons I agreed to a family shopping expedition on a day off was that it wouldn't take any longer than an hour. We'd be back home reading the paper before we knew it. Wouldn't we?

Kerrie's shopping list was a puzzle. Each item needed careful consideration, as if she was deciphering hieroglyphics. She agonised over brands, compared prices and groped and sniffed vegetables. Soon I was fed up.

'I'll go and get the Weet-Bix while you decide which coconut milk you want,' I said, spinning Eddie up the aisle.

'Okay, darl.'

I had time to grab the Weet-Bix ('don't get Vita-Brits') and the toilet rolls ('make sure you get thick, soft sheets') and the pasta ('penne not spaghetti') and spin Eddie a dozen more times before Kerrie arrived at our rendezvous – beside the frozen foods fridge.

'Gee, you took a while,' I said.

'I know, but these things are worth taking time over. I saved money then.'

'Wouldn't it be cheaper to get the no-name brands?'

'Yes, but I tried that when we lived in Cobram, remember, and the quality's not as good. It doesn't pay to be cheap.'

'Well, why are you spending so much time over coconut milk?'

'Because it's important. You wouldn't understand. Go and get the margarine, but make sure it's Olive Grove.'

'I didn't think we were meant to be eating margarine.'

'We're not, but at least it's olive based.'

When it finally came time to escape, Eddie delayed my getaway by charming the woman behind the cash register.

'Isn't he delightful?' she said.

'He is,' Kerrie agreed. 'He's a real sociable little boy.'

Little wonder, I thought, considering the amount of time he spent with his mum. No one else I knew could strike up lengthy conversations with complete strangers like Kerrie could. Not me, anyway. I couldn't be bothered with small talk. I wanted nothing more than to grunt and groan monosyllabic answers, especially at the supermarket.

Besides, I deserved a bet. There would be some horse running somewhere with my name on it, I just had to stop my son being charming so we could get to the TAB around the corner in Sydney Road.

The suggestion flattened Kerrie's mood. Betting on a Sunday wasn't on her list. It wasn't part of her family fun day out like, say, staring at coconut milk for half an hour or extolling our son's social brilliance. Unfortunately, it didn't take long for me to join Kerrie in the trough. My horse didn't win and then came the Sunday night blues: thinking about work, putting out the bins, ironing shirts and going to bed before my wife and son for a 4 am start.

March 2003

When 'Kerrie Ramsay' set about overhauling her kitchen, she didn't give much thought to cutting up slimy chicken breasts. Her rationale hadn't extended much beyond pictures – lip-smacking dishes ready to serve.

Which is why she took umbrage to the main ingredient for her first serious meal, chicken curry. That and the fact she was a temperamental redhead.

'This chicken is gross,' she complained, as I poked my head around the back door. 'It's almost making me ill, having to put my hand on it.'

'Don't touch it,' I offered.

'How else do you expect me to keep it from sliding off the table when I cut it?'

'I don't know. Do you want me to do it?'

'No.'

'I don't mind.'

'No. I'll do it.'

I had poked my head around the back door because a prerequisite of booking in to Kerrie's kitchen was minding the child, or else 'you can eat somewhere else, you fucker'. She was taking this celebrity chef impersonation seriously.

So I was stuck in the backyard playing aeroplanes, zigzagging our son between bushes with his arms outstretched and my arms getting tired. But that was okay. The real problem was not having time to talk to my wife. Occasionally I would drop Eddie into his shell-shaped sandpit and see if the maestro needed help, or would like to chat about my workday, or have a cuddle on the couch, all to which she indicated she was much too busy. Following recipes took concentration, she said. Although I couldn't see what was so hard about browning chicken in a wok, while cutting up asparagus and stirring the rice. But I'd never been much of a cook.

During one of my many kitchen fly-bys, Kerrie was yelling at the recipe book. 'These stupid preparation times are a load of crap. Try pulling all this together in twenty minutes. Cutting up that bloody chicken took ten minutes.'

It struck me then that Kerrie wasn't used to failure. Her life had always fallen into place. Even her first bout of cancer in 1992 was a mere hiccup. She had breezed through school, strolled through newspaper life, conquered cancer and rarely lost at Scrabble. So why wouldn't she be a good cook?

I tried to convince her she would be. And opening night was a success. Despite the incongruous outbursts, the slimy chicken, misleading cooking instructions and a nagging husband, her first chicken curry was a cracker.

'Kerrie, this is great,' I said. 'This is restaurant quality. I give it eight out of ten. One point off for presentation and another off because there's no tablecloth. Otherwise it's perfect.'

'Oh, you're just saying that. The rice is overcooked.'

'No, the rice is great. The whole lot is fantastic.'

'Thanks, honey. But it's not quite right.'

And so it went: Kerrie experimented with her menu, was never quite satisfied with the outcome and as a result rarely finished her meal. She couldn't eat overcooked rice, especially with slimy chicken fingers.

March 2003

Keeping cancer at bay was one thing, pinpointing why it had returned was another. Kerrie worried that pregnancy was to blame. She worried that the strain on her body, the swirling hormones and the demands of motherhood had triggered a relapse. It burned her to think so because she wanted another child. She wanted to complete our family.

'Eddie needs a playmate,' she said.

No specialist would be drawn on a reason. It was inconclusive, they said. So Kerrie was left hanging – should she have another child or concentrate on preserving her life? For me the choice was simple, and selfish. Wait.

Coping with one child was hard enough and I didn't want to lose her again to that maternal cocoon in which she had enveloped herself during the first six months of Eddie's life when I had been reluctantly pushed from No. 1 man abut the house to No. 2. Besides, we hadn't planned on becoming parents in the first place ... not in March 2001, anyway.

We found out Kerrie was pregnant three days before our wedding. As a teenager I dreamed my life-changing moment would be a tap on the shoulder in a crowded shopping mall by a Hollywood agent. 'Give us a call, son, we want to make you a star.' The acting break never came. Instead, my world was tipped vertical by a blue line in a small window on a plastic strip the size of an icy-pole stick.

'How accurate are these pregnancy tests?' I had asked Kerrie after she dragged me into the bedroom.

'About 99 per cent,' she said.

'Gee.'

And I meant, Gee! This was pretty serious stuff. Say goodbye to Peter Pan.

I felt guilty for not clicking my heels, or popping the champagne corks, but more than that, I felt numb.

'Well, what do you think?' Kerrie said, breaking the daze.

'Think? It's great, honey,' I said, trying to convince myself.

'We're going to be parents!' she shrieked.

So just like that I was going to be a dad. No stork, no flashing neon signs, no wife dancing around a doctor's office, just a thin blue line.

It shocked Kerrie, too.

I still didn't believe I could be pregnant, she wrote at the time.

It couldn't be. We'd just quit our jobs. Danny had another one lined up in Sydney, where we were going to live for a year and fritter away the last dregs of our youth at funky clubs. I liked drinking and smoking and staying up late. They were the only hobbies I had.

The Woody Allen dithering started in my head while I waited for the appearance of a blue line in a square window to determine my fate: What will I do without my freedom? I'll never have fun again. I won't be me anymore. I can't cook. I'm not comfortable with kids – we bore each other. I'm not grown up enough yet. We have no home, no assets, no security – and no desire for them. Pregnant now? Absurd.

Well, the little test kit didn't think so. And so while my mum and dad, who had come from Adelaide to stay with us before the wedding, were whirling about the house in pre-wedding pandemonium, I sneaked up to the bedroom to show Danny the evidence: ready or not, we were going to be someone's mummy and daddy.

Danny looked like Wyle E. Coyote always does when a boulder has just bounced off his head and the cliff ledge he's standing on starts to shear away from the cliff and fall into the canyon below. And I think that's probably how he felt, too.

All I could manage was a bemused smile. Funny, Wyle E. Coyote's plans always got buggered up, too. But he survived. So would we. We three.

Three. I was actually beginning to like the sound of that. It was always my lucky number.

But now, two years later, while canvassing the possibility of 'we four', I convinced Kerrie to wait. She decided she would turn her mind towards finding a way to keep out cancer. Doctors had ruled out chemotherapy and radiotherapy, suggesting Kerrie undergo regular scans to monitor her health. Live well, they said, and, hopefully, the cancer would either disappear or at least lie dormant for another ten years.

Her first move was to book in for an Ian Gawler seminar. Apparently he was a guru. I'd never heard of him, but Kerrie explained that he had lost a leg to cancer and had been given two weeks to live. That was more than twenty-five years ago. He was now an industry, writing self-help books, running workshops, holding retreats, and heading up a foundation.

Sure, I said, barely masking my scepticism, sounds like he should have some idea.

She told me she would also look to God.

Great, I said, he should have some idea, too.

March 2003

Out of left field, my career received a boost. I was offered the sports editor's job, meaning later starts, more creative input and autonomy over a section in which to poke fun at Lleyton Hewitt.

While I wasn't an obsessed sports nut – I couldn't name more than a dozen Carlton footballers and they were *my* team – it was the dream job. I was being offered a chance to be slightly irreverent and a break from the mundane. The world was littered with athletes who took themselves far too seriously and were paid far too much – David Beckham; Tiger Woods; Kim Clijsters; her look-alike, Lleyton Hewitt; almost every player who had donned an AFL, league or union outfit; Lleyton Hewitt; sports tragic John Howard; Jana Pittman; Shane Warne; the English cricket team; and Lleyton Hewitt.

If sarcasm and muckraking were the job's perks, co-ordinating staff was the downside. If I knew fewer than a dozen Carlton players, I knew even less of other teams – a glaring absence on the CV in AFL-obsessed Melbourne. I'd have to wing it, tell the guys, 'Of course I fucking know who Adam Simpson is, I was just looking slightly confused when you mentioned his name because I thought I saw someone fall off their chair across the office.' I'd been told that getting on the front foot and dropping an assertive 'fuck' during the conversation was a powerful tool for masking ignorance and maintaining superiority. The chair bit I made up myself.

Anyway, Kerrie said it was a great opportunity.

'You'll be fine, Danny,' she said.

April 2003

Before I started my new role, I had to say goodbye. To the farm. My parents had sold up, retired and were moving into town. After thirty years at Cassidy Road, Katamatite East, they had milked their last cow. 'Thank God for that,' I think Mum said. Dad was more circumspect, but I'm sure it was the right decision because his shoulders sagged less.

Kerrie, Eddie and I spent a week in our old weatherboard farmhouse, helping prepare for the clearing sale. As well as lining up his good machinery, I helped my father drag out and stack three decades of junk. That was the nature of clearing sales, you got rid of the lot – old cars, rusting ploughs, sheets of corrugated iron, mangled bike frames and what seemed like kilometres of crap. Apart from contributing one or two car wrecks, I had no idea where it had all come from, and I'm not sure my father did either.

Kerrie and I drove away the day before the sale, saying goodbye to my childhood bedroom, our backyard cricket pitch, the makeshift football arena, the tennis court and the dreaded dairy and its sludge pit. The only tangible thing I took away from my life on that farm was a blue-and-white sign that been hanging on the front gate, emblazoned with my parents' name.

If someone at work starts behaving differently or acting quirky, chances are they're either having an affair with a colleague or they've been touched by cancer. Peculiarities to appear in my workdays were lunch tins and an aversion to the microwave, subtle oddities that had been introduced since Kerrie's afternoon at the Ian Gawler seminar. Not without resistance, though.

'Kerrie, I can't take my lunch to work in this tin. It looks like a saucepan,' I complained.

'Don't take it then. It's just meant to be less likely to give you cancer, that's all.'

'And how in the hell is a plastic container supposed to give you cancer?'

'By leaching dioxins into the food which are then released into the body.'

'Oh! All right, I'll take the tin, but people are going to laugh at me.'

'So what? Tell them it was your wife's idea because she doesn't want to get cancer again.'

'You know I don't talk about your cancer at work. How am I going to heat leftovers? I can't use a tin in the microwave.'

'Use a bowl.'

'I'll take sandwiches instead.'

Soon I was using the tins, sneaking them into the bottom of the fridge and furtively pulling them out so that I could hide around the corner and eat my cold chicken curry.

Thankfully, workmates who spotted my odd lunchboxes refrained from ridicule, probably because they'd either heard Kerrie had cancer or they thought I was having an affair.

Not all of Ian Gawler's tutelage had swayed Kerrie, however. When Eddie and I had driven across to Camberwell Town Hall one Sunday afternoon to collect her from the seminar, it was a lugubrious Kerrie who slumped in the front seat. She seemed relieved to be going home.

'How was it?' I asked.

'It was okay. Actually, it was a bit disappointing.'

Before then, my money-grabbing radar had been on alert. Now I was more curious than cynical.

'Why was it a bit disappointing?'

'Well, firstly there were a lot of desperate-looking people there. Unwell people, obviously with cancer, who need this guy to be right or else they won't survive. That made me sad.'

'I bet it did.'

'A lot of what he said made sense, and was fairly obvious, but I feel like they expect you to stop and drop everything so that you can change your life. I can't just abandon you and Eddie. Preparing the right environment and the right foods would almost be a full-time job in itself. To absolve yourself from stress, you need to buy a retreat in the bush and for that you need a lot of money. And we don't have a lot of money.'

She didn't say much more, preferring to stare out the window at the clouds as I drove back across the Yarra River.

Apart from avoiding plastic containers, microwaves and fatty foods, Kerrie was anxious to exercise, mentally and physically. She felt an urge to walk. After dinner.

'Where to?'

'I don't know. Around the block, wherever.'

'Why?'

'Because I want to get fit and healthy.'

'Sure.'

Packing Eddie into the pusher, and co-ordinating sneakers for the first time in our married lives (Kerrie had an amazing figure for someone who had rarely broken out of a trot since under-12 netball), we headed around the block.

'This is great!' she said. 'Let's keep going.'

So far, so good. We went around another block, much to Eddie's pleasure. Our little adventurer was exploring his neighbourhood and his vocabulary. Cars he had mastered, but he called helicopters and trucks 'car cars', for dogs he said 'boom booms' and trains were 'tains'. I cracked up laughing when he called a duck 'ga-ga'. It was uncannily similar to his moniker for Grandma Elsa, 'Ga-ca'.

'Is he calling your mother a duck?' I asked.

'Don't be nasty,' Kerrie chuckled back.

Few steps were in silence. We talked about new ways of poking fun at Lleyton Hewitt at work, or Kerrie's day, or people's houses and even people's cars.

'Doesn't this feel great?' Kerrie would say. 'You can smell the cut grass. Ian Gawler recommends that people spend at least fifteen minutes in the sun each day, without sun block.'

'That goes against conventional thinking, doesn't it?'

'Particularly all the warnings about skin cancer. But I don't think he expects people to stand under the sun until they fry. Just ten or fifteen minutes a day to soak up a healthy dose of vitamin D.'

Walking after dinner became routine. Three nights a week we would push out, extending our radius farther and farther, and with each step Kerrie's wellbeing improved, stopping less often to catch her breath on the Gallipoli Parade hill. Eddie was almost always asleep when we reached the front door, saving at least half an hour of bedside lullabies and giving us time to cuddle on the couch.

Early May 2003

If Ian Gawler was the impetus for our walks, Kerrie claimed God led her to the notice board at Coburg Safeway and lifted her eyes to a phone number for yoga classes. She had to enrol.

So Monday nights became yoga nights and she would return home feeling stretched and relaxed and fielding questions from me about the many weird and wonderful poses, including, my favourite, downward-facing dog. Like farts to a five-year-old, it always made me laugh.

What didn't appeal to my smutty sense of humour was my wife's fondness for her yoga teacher, Karl, a tall, slender, handsome guy who had a finger wedged firmly in the spiritual power point. Coincidentally, he also lived in our suburb. After a number of yoga classes this middle-aged, single 'hippy' encouraged Kerrie to further her spiritual journey by learning reiki.

Not in a position to reject therapeutic possibilities, Kerrie had a 'healing session' with Karl, during which he supposedly acted as a conduit for mystical energy by holding palms above her traumatised body and tapping into the 'Divine Source'. She assured poor old paranoid me that no clothes were shed. Only tears. Because when he held his hands above her tumour site (previously unknown to Karl), Kerrie was so overwhelmed she cried. And how do you explain that?

'I think I was meant to meet Karl,' she said. 'Why else would I see the phone number for the yoga sessions, and why else would he live in our suburb? I think it is a sign that I should be doing this, don't you?'

I didn't have an answer, just a gutful of jealousy. The hippy was making my wife happy, and *HE LIVED IN OUR SUBURB*. Unbelievably, Kerrie didn't pick up on my green-eyed vibes and continued to eulogise the benefits of reiki, particularly the 'self-healing' element. Apparently, as she ascended through the levels, and her awareness grew, she would be able to channel energy to repair her body. She justified praying to the 'Divine Source' by saying He was God, just in case her Catholic friends were listening.

So on Monday nights she went to yoga classes and on Tuesday nights she started going to a reiki prayer group. At the hippy's house. A couple of blocks away.

We started walking less often, and I started singing more lullabies.

One night Kerrie returned from reiki, overflowing with elation and love.

'Oh Dan, it was so amazing,' she said, creeping into the room and sitting on the bed. 'You've got to try it. I just feel like I have so much energy.'

'What did you do?'

'We sat around in a group and said the Open Heart Prayer, and then we did individual healings on each other. People were bursting out laughing.'

'Isn't that a bit weird?'

'They say just let out any emotion or feeling you have. Even if you have to burp or fart. Letting yourself go is all part of the process.'

While she was telling me about sitting around, feeling euphoric among this group of fartmongers, I conjured up images of cults and darkened cellars and orgies … oh, I had to stop this destructive mindset. Anything that kept Kerrie's mind from cancer was a great thing, remember. She should be encouraged, not beaten down by a resentful husband.

'This is not some weirdo sex cult, is it?' I asked. I couldn't help myself.

'Don't be silly, honey. There is nothing untoward about the group at all. Come over, you should experience it. I would love for you to share these feelings.'

'How does it work?'

'They encourage you to be in your heart; that all emotions and feelings should be dictated by your heart and not your brain. As you meditate and channel energy from God you have to try and remove yourself from thought, distance yourself from thinking. It is hard to do, but I picture you and Eddie and smile. There is so much love.'

'Are you sure it's not a cult?'

She looked at me with a frown. I was ruining the ecstasy. But what was I to do? I was jealous. It was my job to make her happy, not some bunch of weirdo burpers congregating in our neighbourhood.

'I'm sorry, Kerrie. I'm just jealous that they can help make you feel this way.'

May 2003

Pointing the car south-east and with no real game plan, we drove out of the city, arriving in Cape Paterson a couple of hours and a bakery stop later. It was wonderful. The rhythmic pounding of the waves made us feel more alive. Sometimes you forget about the ocean, and its power, especially when you are locked in a three-bedroom suburban house, or a crowded train carriage or an office block. So we spent most of the afternoon driving from beach to beach and looking at the water, occasionally getting out to film ourselves chasing Eddie up and down sand dunes, or digging holes, or peering in rock pools. At one stage, Kerrie asked me to leave a footprint in the sand.

'Why on earth do you want to take a photo of my footprint next to Eddie's?'

'Because it will make a good photo.'

'I can't see how.'

'Life will pass us by so quickly that soon his foot will be bigger than yours. Sometimes it is nice to have a reminder of where we were. You'll see.'

June 2003

Dear Eddie,

You are developing into the most delightful little boy. And most of it is because your mum is plying you with love.

She has a brilliant knack of memorising words so that you have your own Wiggles member or *Play School* host on call. She has taught you to distinguish between colours and recognise numbers, not bad for an eighteen-month-old lad, but more importantly, she is teaching you to dance, to sing, and to embrace people, even strangers.

The only thing she missed was the bath. That was my job. For a short time you were terrified of water, until we discovered that blowing bubbles and splashing the floor was a hoot – although sometimes Kerrie didn't agree.

It is hard to believe it is only six months since her operation. Sometimes it is hard to believe it even happened. Scans have shown your mum is still in remission, she suffers only mild discomfort, which The Professor says is exercise related, and she is in great shape mentally and physically.

She is still doing yoga every Monday and still traipsing off to the hippy pad for her weekly prayer session, which involves tapping into some divine spirit.

So when you grow up and discover pictures of her dressed in white bed sheets and sacrificing chickens, you'll know why. Don't blame me; I love chickens.

Anyway, she derives peace of mind from reiki and I'd rather that than being chased around the kitchen dodging knives because she can't cope with life, or that she can't cope with my messy habits, such as leaving towels lying around and splashing bathwater on the floor.

Grandma ('Ga-ca') and Grandpa ('Pa pa') were in town three weeks ago and couldn't keep their mitts off you. Although Grandpa found time to sneak outside for surreptitious swigs from a bottle of port, while Grandma Elsa occasionally excused herself to duck off to the pokies.

How wonderful our life seems now and I have to occasionally remind myself of the anxiety we suffered over Christmas, especially so I don't start taking your mum for granted. She briefly thought about returning to newspaper work, but poo-pooed the idea because she enjoys your company too much. She wants to help you grow into a special little man. You should be so lucky.

Love Dad

23 August 2003

'Reiki is not a cult. Reiki is not a cult. Reiki is not a cult. They don't engage in orgies. They don't sacrifice virgins.' My mantra as I dropped Kerrie at a stranger's house in Clifton Hill at 9 am on a Sunday.

'Bye honey,' she said, kissing Eddie in the back seat. 'Thanks, love,' she said to me before walking up the footpath and disappearing.

Reiki was becoming an obsession. She wanted to learn more, practise more, and become so immersed and accomplished in this soul-cleansing meditative art that she would make it a part-time career. This was bigger than cooking.

'I'll be able to help people and maybe make a bit of money on the side,' she said. 'I really feel excited by this, Danny. I can set up a little cottage industry; maybe offer reiki healing sessions a couple of days a week. It will help me feel good, help other people feel good and I'll be able to contribute to the budget. What do you think?'

'That sounds great, Kerrie. Are you sure it's not a … ah, never mind.'

Through the hippy, she enrolled in the Clifton Hill workshop to attain her first level of reiki tummo. She would be tuned and aligned by a spiritual mechanic from Indonesia. All this for a couple of hundred bucks.

'Kerrie, if the idea of reiki is to be in your heart and loving and embracing kindness, why wouldn't you teach people for free? It sounds a bit opportunistic to be charging people for something that is supposedly flying around the ether.'

'I know, I was thinking that myself. But I suppose these people have administration costs and organisational costs and I guess they have to survive. It's the same principle as charging for massage lessons.'

I left Kerrie in Clifton Hill, wondering what Eddie and I were going to do until 4.30 pm, and whether my wife would be in a trance when we got there.

Eddie and I hadn't spent a lot of time alone together, father–son time, just the boys. So I started with the park, pushing swings and zipping down slides (well, Eddie zipped and I shuffled because my arse was too big and kept getting wedged), proving that I was a fun dad to be around. For about 30 minutes. Then my mind started flickering to adult themes such as horse-racing, buying houses and sex in marriage.

I can't pinpoint why I so quickly lost patience with behaving like a two-year-old. Mostly it was because I felt like a dickhead galloping around in view of other more sedate, mature parents. But on this day the park was empty. We walked home and put on a Wiggles video, giving Eddie a chance to expend some more energy singing and dancing while I read the newspaper. Wiggling was not my thing.

When the video ended, we went to another park, this time lasting about twenty minutes before I started mulling over whether I'd be perceived as a failure if I didn't commit to placing a mortgage noose around my neck so that a bank could kick away the chair. We walked home again and I put on a Bob the Builder video, or 'Bup the Builder' as Eddie called him, and realised I was quickly running out of ideas to entertain my son. What did Kerrie do all bloody day without going mad? Actually, how did Kerrie stop herself thinking all day without going mad?

We ate lunch, tried to have an afternoon nap, stacked cars on top of each other and played with stones and wood chips in the backyard while all the time I had to resist the urge to return to the newspaper or put my legs up in front of the TV.

I thought I had done a pretty good job until I arrived at Clifton Hill to collect Kerrie ... an hour early. I drove by the house and, unable to peek through the curtains or detect any activity or sacrificial rituals, decided to take Eddie to another park. By 4.30 pm I was back outside the house, waiting. By 5 pm, there was no sign of Kerrie and I was getting worried, and sick of singing songs (my repertoire didn't extend much beyond 'Wake up, Jeff' and 'Baa, Baa Black Sheep'). By 5.15 pm, I'd had enough.

'C'mon, Ed, we're going to get your mum.'

A gentle, smiling Indonesian guy in his mid-twenties answered the door and said the workshop was still in progress, but that we were welcome to wait inside the house, which belonged to a slightly tetchy middle-aged woman who was prancing around the kitchen looking slightly annoyed and uncomfortable that a strange and noisy infant had suddenly materialised and was terrorising her cat. I tried to distract Eddie from pulling Whiskers' tail, while making small talk with the Indonesian guy and the tetchy woman and a few other strangers wandering around the kitchen. From what I could ascertain they were involved somehow in the reiki workshop, but momentarily not engaged in the free-loving exercise taking place in a spare room and holding up my wife.

I don't know whether it was my desperate looks, or those of the cat-loving householder, but my Indonesian friend decided to fetch Kerrie, and she soon emerged from a side room looking serene, smiling and, I'm glad to say, fully clothed.

'Sorry I'm so late, honey,' she said. 'We were almost finished and I had no idea of the time.'

Maybe it was her reiki-inspired beaming heart, or that smile on her face, or the fact I was no longer a single parent, because, despite myself, I was no longer aggrieved. Just happy to have her back.

'It was amazing, Danny,' she said as we returned to the car. 'I wish you could have done the workshop, too. There really is something to this reiki.'

'What did you do all day?'

'We had our crown, palm and heart chakras attuned so that we could channel energy. I know you probably think I'm crazy, but it really worked. I could feel this ball of energy in my hands.'

'Are you sure it's not all in your head?'

'I don't think so because Sam, another guy at the workshop, wasn't feeling anything and then when our Reiki Master told him to hold his palms just inches apart, he went "whoa" and said he was blown away by the rush.'

Apart from her new-found talent, Kerrie brought away a certificate declaring she had achieved the first level in reiki tummo. Something to hang on the wall.

Kerrie asked a lot of questions of her new prayer group friends. Where does the energy come from? How should it feel? Can anyone be attuned? And, of course, the big one: can reiki cure cancer?

Her friends were as noncommittal as her doctors.

'It depends,' they would say. 'If it is meant to be cured, it will be cured. Recovery and healing are blessings from the Divine Source.'

Kerrie interpreted that as a yes. Almost every night she would sit in the lounge room with her hands resting on her tumour site, channelling healing energy. She said she could feel her palms generating abnormal heat, while I pretended to understand.

At least my work was going well. No one was taking me seriously, and I was given a pay rise.

* * *

September 2003

We kept hitting the road at weekends. On one Saturday I was able to convince Kerrie to drive to Flemington racecourse. The next week she flatly refused to go anywhere near the track. Probably because she lost.

Her tale of woe started near the stables. While I was trying to catch the eye of a winner, Kerrie was chasing after our son and ended up bumping into an elderly gentleman leaning with his arms on a fence. They struck up a conversation and it wasn't long before he realised she was a bright spark, a doting mother and married to that gambling buffoon over there who was winking at a horse. So he offered her a tip.

'He told me to have something each way on Enzed in the next race because he has a horse with the trainer and she says it is going well,' Kerrie told me.

I didn't need convincing. We strapped Eddie into his stroller and hustled around the back of the members' stand to a TAB outlet.

The mail was good. Enzed won. The problem was Kerrie hadn't made it to the front of the queue in time to place her bet. She was steaming. She had missed out because a guy in front of her had monopolised the TAB operator's time, placing a multitude of complicated bets.

'I don't understand why he hadn't put all those bets on earlier,' she complained. 'Why couldn't he just back one horse like everybody else? Next week, we are getting out of Melbourne.'

September 2003

One weekend we didn't go for a family drive. One weekend Kerrie went off alone. She packed a cut lunch, a pillow, pictures of herself as a little girl and left us for an inner-child workshop, disappearing into her past.

Before cancer Kerrie had never disclosed anything about her childhood other than happy memories. There was never any talk of ghosts. But we all have them and I'm convinced that this second bout of cancer, more than ten years after the first, caused Kerrie to doubt herself. Maybe she hadn't properly resolved issues from her youth?

Maybe she had not achieved closure? Maybe her forgiveness of others was not enough?

She never said, but I'm sure the need to pinpoint a reason for her illness, or, more accurately, a need to eliminate reasons for her illness, led my resolute wife to search for her younger self.

When she came home, looking tired but at ease, she told me she had found a vulnerable, innocent girl. A pretty, freckly young pre-schooler sitting defenceless with her hands crossed in her lap, legs swinging, her feet in white sandals. My wife recounted how she placed an arm around this girl's shoulder and offered comforting words: 'I have come to help you. You are no longer alone.'

Together, over the course of a weekend, they courageously calmed their sense of abused trust and injustice.

'Do you think she'll be all right?' I asked.

'I think so.'

'Do you think you'll be all right?'

'I think so.'

With the little girl comforted, told that her guardian angel would remain by her side, Kerrie said she was ready to move on once again. She told me she was okay, so who was I to think any different?

July 2006

Dear Kerrie,

I think Eddie is missing you.

I've sent him to his room for defiantly bouncing, jumping and climbing on the couch despite my persistent demands to stop and he's burst into tears.

I don't particularly care if he clambers over the furniture, but my parents do and they own the house. So I wave the finger of discipline, which causes him to march resentfully down the hallway and slam the bedroom door.

That's when I hear him sobbing.

Drawn to his room, I creep through the door and sit on his bed.

'I'm sad because my mummy has gone to heaven. I miss my mummy,' he says.

Part of me suspects he's using tears to slide out of trouble, but the rest of me believes he's sad because you're not here for a comforting hug. I can't afford to take the risk so I pull him to my chest and rub his back.

'I miss her, too,' I say.

Miss you,

love Danny

August 2006

Dear Kerrie,

Our son has abandoned plans to join the fire brigade when he grows up and wants to be a butcher. He announces it on the road to Yarrawonga. The career change comes about because Pat, who is driving, asks if he is going to play football when he's older.

'No, I want to be a butcher,' he says.

'But you can be a butcher and still play football on the weekends,' Pat says.

'No, I am going to be a butcher and cook sausages all day long.'

So there you are. I'll never want for sausages again. Although if we ever inherit a cat and find it stuck in a tree, I'll have to get it down myself because there'll be no Fireman Eddie on call.

He homed in on the butcher idea last week during an excursion to see how sausages were made. Eddie called the butcher a genius. The butcher, understandably, was thrilled.

'You might think you're an idiot, but really you are a genius,' Eddie said. He tells me he heard this on *Charlie and the Chocolate Factory*, continuing his practice of misquoting lines from his favourite films at bizarre times.

Not all his quips are borrowed, however. He had Shannon and Caroline in stitches down the river on Sunday, asking them if their dog, Ella, was getting married.

'Will she marry a big black dog and have babies?' he asked.

'We don't know if she'll have puppies,' Caroline replied.

'But will she marry a big black dog?' he persisted.

'I don't know. I don't think she'll get married,' Caroline said.

He was happy with that answer, and at least we were distracted and out of the house. No jumping on the couch or tears of frustration to manifest sadness.

Miss you,

love Danny

August 2006

Dear Kerrie,

Eddie wants to marry everyone. When Pa goes to heaven, he'll marry Granny. When Granny goes to heaven, he'll marry his cousin Georgia. When Georgia goes to heaven, and so on and so on …

But he's bewildered when I ask him if he has a girlfriend.

'You know I don't have a girlfriend, Dad,' he says.

Perhaps he'll be more interested at school next year because he's sure to draw attention. I take him down to meet the principal at St Joseph's this morning and he puts on a show. He walks straight into a Grade 5/6 classroom and far from being bashful, he starts with Lightning McQueen impersonations.

'Kachow,' he says, karate-chopping the air as the kids laugh.

And then he starts imitating the teacher, telling the kids to 'quieten down'.

He leaves an indelible impression because the next time he visits St Joseph's, the same Grade 5/6 kids start chanting, 'Eddie! Eddie!'.

So he volunteers to sing a song. Instead of 'Baa, Baa, Black Sheep' or 'Wake Up, Jeff', he launches into 'Life is a Highway', off the *Cars* movie.

The teacher is gob-smacked and, quite frankly, so am I.

Miss you,

love Danny

23 September 2003

As a godmother, Kerrie ticked all the boxes – she was attentive, she loved children, she had an erudite comprehension of Christianity and an unshakeable belief in the Big Guy upstairs. That's how we found ourselves on a ten-hour bakery run, starting in Melbourne, passing through Horsham, stopping in Keith, taking in Tailem Bend and culminating in Adelaide for her niece and nephew's christening. That's a lot of pies and pasties, not to mention toilet breaks and playground stops.

The dual christening was a charming, small, family gathering, made even more memorable by Kerrie dashing up the aisle of Glenelg's Catholic Church because we were five minutes late and the priest was anxious to wet the babies' heads. If only she had made such an entrance for our wedding.

'I couldn't find a park,' she muttered to her brother Brendan while taking up position beside the altar. He looked mildly worried, but hardly surprised. Kerrie was always late.

I flew back to Melbourne the following day, leaving Kerrie to indulge her parents in Adelaide with Eddie. The next time I saw her we were also preparing to go to a church. This time for a funeral.

Kerrie knew her best friend's husband, Daryl, had been battling pancreatic cancer for two years. What she hadn't realised was how far he had slipped. She was shocked to see him dreadfully thin, pale and intermittently nodding into morphine-induced sleep.

Days after the christening he was admitted to hospital and everyone except Daryl prepared for the end. Kerrie said he flatly refused to accept he was dying. He even admonished doctors for saying so. At that time and from afar I could understand the nature of his fight – 'never surrender' – because the mind was the greatest weapon against cancer. Right? What I didn't realise was how his blind hope and the withering nature of his disease tortured Kerrie. Partly because it was so tough on his wife, Linda, and their seven-year-old son, Jakeb, and partly because of her underlying fear: 'what if this happens to me?'

'I just wish he would let go,' she kept telling me on the phone.

While Kerrie was giving me daily updates, I was in a parallel universe. I felt sad for Daryl and Linda, but I had the cushion of distance, not having to live his death hour by hour. I missed my family, but for once I didn't feel the pressure of rushing home to be Eddie's playmate. I could stop and have a couple of beers after work and later flop on the couch and watch normal TV. Three weeks without the Wiggles.

I sympathised with Kerrie and told her she was doing a great thing by spending time with her friends, but beyond that there was nothing else I could do.

September 2003

Strangely, the days after Daryl's death, leading up to his funeral, were cathartic for Kerrie. She spent valuable time with Linda and their friend Margie, leaving Eddie with Grandma Elsa so that the three old school buddies could have sleep-overs, order in meals and open bottles of wine, tempering their grief with their best memories of Daryl and mirthfully reflecting on their childhood mishaps and misadventures.

I think for that reason Kerrie was relaxed when she met me at the airport. Daryl's passing had ended the suffering, now it was time to mourn. I was the same. The spectre of a funeral always left me feeling awkward and anxious, but it was good to see Kerrie. Despite my down time – leaving towels on the floor, socks on the couch and dishes in the sink – I realised how much I missed hugging my wife.

We talked a lot that night – our intimacy heightened by the background of death – but I still didn't correlate Daryl's situation with Kerrie's illness. Why would I? She had been so well since February.

Walking had improved her physical wellbeing, reiki had tuned her mentally and at the worst we still had at least another nine years before the tumour returned.

28 October 2003

Dear Eddie,

Happy birthday, son. Sorry we had to cancel the celebrations, but no one wants their kids around a two-year-old still recovering from gastro. To make matters worse, the Bob the Builder cake has proven a flop because soon after we light the candles and launch into a rendition of 'Happy Birthday', you burst into tears and try and leave the room. Funnily enough, the same thing happened last year. Can my singing be that bad?

At least Granny and Pa are staying with us for the occasion, adding to your pile of presents and helping make a dent in the chocolate cake. Although when your mum slices through the cake and inadvertently lops off Bob's head, you again burst into tears.

It is hard to believe you are already two, but sometimes you act and look as if you've been here before. Your mum thinks you're quite clever for your age, telling me you've become a real mimic, following her around the house and trying to copy every word she says, even to the point of picking up the phone, or a remote control, putting it to your ear and saying 'hiya, Pa'. Parroting is a good and important skill for learning the language. Just don't repeat any of your mum's sardonic lines about me. They're not true. And you'll be in trouble if I hear you say them, especially the one about 'your hopeless father leaving things lying around all over the place'.

While I've been busy at work (oh, for these past six or seven months), Kerrie says you've invented your own colour chart: 'abba' for yellow, 'boo' for blue, 'pod-pool' for purple, 'ger' for green and 'reb' for red. We're also in the process of inventing a new look, because people are increasingly mistaking you for a little girl. And no son of mine will be called a little girl! I prefer manly tantrums such as your

first public display of angst in the Kmart toy section last week. That's
right, son, if you can't get your own way, bung on an act. Although
don't bung them on in front of me because I get terribly embarrassed
in public and will probably give in to your demands or hide behind
the CD section. Your mum is far better at handling these psychological
stand-offs.

So by two you have learned to react to bad singing (of 'Happy
Birthday', anyway), throw tantrums to get your own way, wave bye-
bye to everyone you meet, say goodnight to Mr Moon, hum note-
perfect renditions of 'Frere Jacques', 'London Bridge' and 'Twinkle,
Twinkle, Little Star', and have tapped into your feminine side – which
I'm still not happy about, so you're getting a haircut tomorrow.

Next year, as well as keeping your mother happy, I want you to
concentrate on kicking the football, taking a keener interest in fishing,
learning about horse-racing, and, most importantly, teaching yourself
to use the toilet. I've already had to administer a suppository because
of your refusal to do No. 2s and I don't want to destroy the friendship.
Love Dad

8 November 2003

I was seven when Elvis died, but I don't remember. And John Lennon
was shot dead in New York when I was ten, but the news flash didn't
etch the date on my memory, probably because I was out on the farm
somewhere with my younger brother Chris hitting ants with a stick. Or
kicking the football. Or watching cartoons.

But I know where I was when Shogun Lodge died from a heart attack.
On the highway to Geelong. Kerrie was driving, Eddie was fastened tight
in the back seat and I was in the front, listening to the radio. Shogun
Lodge was dead before he hit the Flemington turf. The sad end of one of
my favourite racehorses and a piece of my past.

I'd first seen Shogun Lodge run while sitting in Kerrie's family home, at
the same time trying to make a favourable impression on her parents. It
was the spring of 1999, two weeks after I had returned from overseas, and

the first time I had met Des and Elsa as their prospective son-in-law. Things were off to a good start, mainly, I think, because Elsa was relieved that her daughter was getting married. But if Kerrie was our common ground, racing became our meeting point – Elsa, an old equestrian, loved horses, and Des and I loved a bet. That was how we all came to be sitting around the TV when Shogun Lodge ran a brave second in the Victoria Derby. He stuck in my mind because jockey Shane Dye unsuccessfully protested the result, and, even more poignantly, it was the afternoon I won Grandpa Des's approval. I'd come a long way from the Belfast phone box.

I'd asked him some sort of small favour, politely of course, and as he strode past my chair he stopped and looked at me with a cheeky grin. He wiggled his fingers like an excited cowboy brandishing six-shooters.

'Of course you can, Danny,' he said. 'Because you are in, son. YOU ARE IN.'

Another reason I felt an affinity with Shogun Lodge was that he nearly always ran second, and I always backed him when he did. He encapsulated my life as a punter. Almost. Nearly. Missed by a whisker. If only. We could have been rich.

For that reason, Kerrie knew his name better than most. And for that reason she was listening to the broadcaster when he said Shogun Lodge had stumbled mid-race and crashed through the Flemington rails.

'Oh no,' she said, staring at the road.

Jockey Glen Boss had been thrown to the ground, four days after winning the Melbourne Cup on Makybe Diva, but appeared to be okay, the caller said. Shogun Lodge had not moved.

'Oh dear,' Kerrie said, still staring straight ahead. 'I hope he's all right.'

By the time we reached Geelong, we knew the horse was dead.

'Oh, that's terrible,' Kerrie said.

It's hard to explain, but it felt like we'd lost a pet. There would be replacement horses, of course, but not one that would remind us of the 'what ifs' or the 'if onlys' or the 'you are in, sons'.

8 December 2003

Kerrie didn't cry during her mother's funeral. She waited until we walked into the reception room for sandwiches and a cup of tea. She waited until two of Grandpa Des's mournful pub friends offered their condolences. George was on a walking frame, struggling with osteoporosis, and Brian hobbled on his numb feet. They had come to a funeral for a woman they had never met, knowing her only in conversation. For two hours a day for almost twenty years 'Elsa' was Des's non-drinking, non-pub-visiting wife.

Kerrie wiped the tears from her eyes as she thanked the lugubrious pair for their thoughts. She said later she cried because of the look on their faces – too many hard years, too many funerals.

I didn't wait until tea and sandwiches to cry. I broke down in the church, sobbing during the requiem Mass as I knelt on the floor, barely able to believe that the woman who had kept me awake for half a night trying to teach my son to sleep was gone. My cheeky, bossy little mother-in-law, who could have passed as royalty, was dead, passing away in the middle of the night because her heart gave way.

Her death wasn't without warning. Less than two weeks before she died, Grandma Elsa had been rushed to hospital and diagnosed with an aneurysm of the aorta, a condition so advanced it was beyond repair. Kerrie had flown straight over. We clung to hope that she would live on, Elsa being Elsa even optimistically trying to convince us she had a good two years left. But those two years didn't last two weeks and like a lot of my bad news I found out on the work phone. I rang my mother, who was in Melbourne looking after Eddie, to see if she'd heard from Kerrie. She was due to fly back from Adelaide that afternoon.

'Didn't Kerrie call you?' Mum replied.

'No, why?'

'Elsa died this morning. She died in her sleep.'

'Shit. Why didn't Kerrie call me?'

'She said she wanted to wait until after your deadline. She didn't want to bother you.'

'Bother me! Bloody hell! I thought they said Elsa was going to be all right for another two years! Shit! Look, Mum, I'm coming straight home and then I'm going to set sail for Adelaide. Can you pack Eddie a bag?'

'You can't drive all that way this afternoon.'

'I'll stop overnight in Horsham. I'll be home soon.'

Except, I didn't go straight home. I sat down beside an artist and mapped out a spread for the following day's paper as if nothing had happened. I didn't want to leave until my work was done. Besides, I could hold back the tears. Kerrie hadn't rung; emotions could wait. Or so I thought, because as I spoke to one of the sports writers about a follow-up story my chin started to quiver and my voice started to break. Unable to hold it together, I turned and walked out. Elsa was gone and I didn't get the chance to say goodbye.

In some ways I think Kerrie convinced herself to be happy for her mother. Either that or she was so exhausted from helping her father and brother organise the funeral, taking phone calls and speaking to family, that she didn't have time to mourn.

'Mum always said she would never make old bones,' Kerrie said. 'She was scared of ending up a geriatric and being dependent on others. She didn't want that; she wanted to die in her own home and be carried down the driveway. She got her wish.'

She also got to play the poker machines the night before she died. Just days out of hospital, Grandma Elsa asked Kerrie to chauffeur her on a button-pushing, reel-spinning tour of the surrounding suburbs. They had a ball and they came home winners, Grandma Elsa with a purse full of dollar coins and Kerrie with her heart full of love. They capped the night off with a cup of tea.

By morning she was dead.

Kerrie laughed during her mother's requiem Mass. When the priest was waving incense around the coffin, Kerrie couldn't help but quip: 'Mum's having her last smoke'. Des looked momentarily horrified, and Kerrie smiled. It was her mother's cheeky sense of humour. A witty remark that would have made Grandma Elsa cackle more than anyone else, particularly because it was made within the stuffy confines of the Catholic Church, where hitherto you were expected to be reverent and maudlinly respectful and not cracking jokes.

After tea and biscuits, we went back to Brendan's house for the wake. It was supposed to have been his day of celebration; Brendan buried his mother on his birthday. So we wished Brendan many happy returns and toasted Elsa's life.

I marvelled at Kerrie, how composed she was at a time of such sorrow. But looking back, I realised it was partly a lie. Later, she blamed her cancer for shortening Elsa's life.

9 December 2003

We left Adelaide the day after the funeral, promising Des we'd be back by Christmas. Kerrie wanted to go home. She was exhausted.

Compounding our grief was Eddie's toilet issues. He had become neurotic about pooing, holding on for days, often throwing himself on the floor, writhing around with clenched bum cheeks to hold back the tide.

Driving to Adelaide for Grandma Elsa's funeral the week before had been particularly frustrating. While I was trying to make sense of losing Elsa, Eddie was moaning in the back seat. I tried feeding him chocolate, raisins, and more chocolate to flush it out, all to no avail. He wouldn't let go and the hour driving into Horsham consisted of Eddie grunting and groaning trying to block the flow and me yelling at him from the front seat to 'just do poos, Eddie, for God's sake'.

We booked into a motel and by the next morning he had still refused to open his bowels. My temper had been increasingly frayed by a sleep-interrupted night, so I laid him on his back, undid his nappy and before he could say 'I love Murray the Red Wiggle' pushed a suppository up his bum. He went wide-eyed with shock and was bloody annoyed, but I was beyond the point of sympathy.

Five minutes out of Horsham, the suppository worked. He didn't have a choice. Gladly, I pulled off the highway to change his pungent, overloaded nappy.

'Good boy, Ed. I bet that feels a lot better.'

If heaven existed, Elsa was up there having a laugh at my expense.

Kerrie, though, chided me when I arrived in Adelaide and told her the story.

'Oh that's cruel, Danny. You shouldn't use those things. The doctor said he would do it eventually. You just have to wait. And pushing him will only make it worse.'

Funny, I was expecting a 'thanks for coming'.

Feeling sorry for myself became a common theme in the lead-up to the funeral because, I guess, my loss wasn't as great as theirs. As Des moped between the lounge room and the bedroom, disappearing to shed his tears and re-emerging to drown his sorrows, Kerrie turned her attention to the funeral. I was left to cook, clean and look after Eddie. Being able to help was some comfort, but I wasn't used to Kerrie being totally distracted. I felt under-appreciated and ignored, and it almost came to a head when Eddie was banished from the lounge room because Des's reverence for a visiting priest made the possible distraction of a child having fun unthinkable. He's just a kid, I thought. And given the choice, Elsa would have told the priest to leave.

I took Eddie outside. He pointed out Grandma's car.

'Yes, Ed, that is Grandma's car. But Grandma has gone now. She has gone to heaven,' I said, noticing a Qantas jet taking off from Adelaide airport. 'See that jet plane, well, it is taking Grandma all the way to God.'

The night before Elsa's funeral we sat on the veranda and Kerrie emerged from her cloud. She reckoned her mother had known about her condition for years but had kept it to herself. Looking back, it made sense. For those three months in our home there were often times when she would have to stop and rest, grabbing at her side like she'd been pierced by an arrow. One day she even snapped at Kerrie for trying to take Eddie from her lap. 'Don't deprive me of these moments,' she insisted.

Kerrie was relieved the funeral was organised and her mum would have a good send-off the following day. It was then she made me feel guilty.

'Thanks for all your help, Danny. I don't know what I would have done without you.'

19 December 2003

Before we drove back to Adelaide for Christmas I had a work party to enjoy. I loved Christmas parties. You uncovered peccadillos and hidden talents, stories that work colleagues had kept secret for most of the year. Quiet people became rowdy, noisy people became reflective. The dynamics changed.

We met at the Standard Hotel in Fitzroy. I told Kerrie I'd be home around 8 pm, probably half-pickled, but at least early enough for a good night's sleep before our ten-hour drive across the Wimmera.

By 9 pm, I was standing on a beer garden table singing 'Hot Potato' to a group of startled onlookers and by 11 pm, because we had been asked to leave the pub, I ended up at a Collingwood nightclub popping pills.

It was 6 am when I crawled into bed, telling Kerrie I'd lost my backpack, but with a couple of hours' sleep I'd be right for the drive to Adelaide.

Kerrie was more disappointed than livid, probably aware that I'd never completely grown into a man. She knew that after a couple of drinks I found it hard to say no. I was remorseful, of course – I always was after a bender – but I fell asleep during the first three hours of our road trip and only when I woke up could I start making amends.

A Christmas without Elsa was almost unthinkable, but there we were in Adelaide doing our best. That's the way she would have wanted it, we all said. And then Grandpa Des fell off the stepladder. He was reaching for the Christmas decorations in the top cupboard when we heard a thud from the lounge room, followed by a groan. Rushing to see if he was all right, we found Des sitting on the carpet, moaning that he had hurt his back. We helped him to his feet, but he hobbled around the house, adding to his misery, and eradicating our hard-nosed intentions of enjoying this Christmas 'no matter what'.

Like all accidents viewed in hindsight, Grandpa Des's tumble could have been avoided. I could have/should have/would have climbed the stepladder for the Christmas decorations and Des would have been fine. It's just that he didn't ask, and I didn't offer. And the only reason we wanted those Christmas decorations was because 'that's what Elsa would've wanted'.

As Des battled pain on two fronts, we didn't foresee the long-term implications of his tumble. Despite ensuing visits to a physiotherapist and chiropractor, Des's back ailment ended his twice-weekly golf game – a vital component, because it was the only component, of his health and fitness regime – and caused him almost unbearable discomfort during daily radiation treatment for prostate cancer.

25 December 2003

Dear Eddie,

Thank goodness you are around to give us some Christmas joy. While I don't think you understand the concept of Santa Claus, you sure did get a kick out of all the presents this morning, marching proudly around the house in your Bob the Builder hard hat and trying desperately not to let go of all the new cars. A kid should have more hands.

There's even a parting gesture from Grandma Elsa – her presents, not presence, a touching reminder that she had been thinking of us all on her last shopping trip before flying to heaven. She gave me tennis balls, Grandpa Des a belt and you a Bob the Builder sleeping bag, something that will come in very handy when we decide to go on our first fishing trip.

Poor Grandpa is still struggling with his back. Not even a few Crown Lagers over Christmas dinner at Uncle Brendan's house do the trick. At least you have fun, chasing around the backyard after Ruby and Zac and the three of you spending hours on the swing. Well, it might not have been hours, but my arms sure feel that way.

Bob the Builder is flavour of the month. We see him at the Cheltenham races on Boxing Day. You follow him around the lawn area like a star-struck fan, even proffering your new toy Ferrari. You must be enamoured because not even Ruby and Zac were allowed to play with that car on Christmas Day.

The house at 2 Waite Avenue is dull without Grandma Elsa, but at least your booming voice is adding some spark and occasionally drawing Grandpa out of his doldrums. It seems strange when I push you on the swing that she isn't talking to us out the kitchen window, but at least we get to see her plane flying overhead, still taking her to heaven.

Love Dad

31 December 2003

Goodbye cruel year. May the stars align for a more prosperous 2004.

My wish was in silence, but Grandpa Des's request was audible above the excited din at one minute past midnight on the balcony of 2 Waite Avenue. Fireworks were flashing over Glenelg, dogs were barking at the sporadic burst of suburban crackers and a party across the road was in full swing, people blowing incessantly on irritating party whistles.

'Let's hope for a better year,' Des said, proposing a toast to Kerrie and me with his glass of red. 'It can't get any worse than the last one.'

And it didn't, for about three and a half months.

January 2004

Back in Melbourne, I hovered around Kerrie waiting for her to stumble. One day, I thought, the sadness would break. And when it did, I would be there to catch her. That's what husbands were for. Or so I thought. But I hadn't counted on my wife's faith in ghosts.

It all surfaced when I became sick of waiting. She looked tired and worn out so I stopped loitering around the kitchen arms outstretched, and asked Kerrie if she felt an urge to cry, whether the loss of Elsa was too onerous for her to carry alone.

'Not really,' she said. 'I can feel Mum's presence and that is very comforting. Don't look at me funny; I really do feel like she is watching over us.'

'In what way can you feel her presence?'

'Well, the other night I was putting Eddie to bed, sitting beside his cot, and I asked Mum to give me a sign. I thought, *"If you are here, Mum, let me know that you are watching over us."* And at that precise moment, Eddie said, "grandma".'

'And you think that was Elsa?'

'I do. They say kids can see ghosts. Why else would he say her name at that exact moment?'

She had me there, maybe it was too freaky to be coincidental, but even so I wasn't prepared to believe in ghosts. That's how I convinced myself not to be scared of the dark. I mean, if Elsa's benevolent spirit was floating around our ceilings, so, too, could a tormented soul such as Jimmy bloody Blacksmith. And that was something I didn't want to believe in. Not when I was going to bed down the end of a long passageway, in the dark, and at least two hours before my wife. I turned the subject off ghosts.

'I think about Elsa a lot,' I said.

'Do you?'

'I do. Sometimes at work she'll just pop into my head, or when I'm on the train home I start thinking about how Eddie probably won't remember her. I can't believe she is no longer with us. That she won't be driving across to Melbourne anymore.'

'Yeah, that makes me sad, too, especially because Eddie won't remember how much she adored him. But I'm coping okay. It's not as if I saw her every day. That part will be harder for Dad. I guess it really hits me when I pick up the phone and then realise she won't be on the other end.'

And with that I stopped following Kerrie around.

12 January 2004

It was a Sunday night when Kerrie's face went white. We had driven back to Melbourne from Cobram after celebrating my father's sixty-third birthday and she was checking the answering machine. She was looking at me, but through me, listening intently to the phone. I thought someone had died.

'What's wrong?' I asked as she put down the receiver.

'It was my doctor. She's been leaving messages all weekend for me to call her. She got the results of my blood tests on Friday afternoon and says my haemoglobin levels are dangerously low and that I could be bleeding internally. The last message says that as soon as I get the message I should go to a hospital emergency ward.'

'Why? What does that mean?'

'I don't know. It's ridiculous because I feel all right.'

Kerrie wanted to wait until morning and preserve our lovely weekend. Eddie had helped Pa blow out his birthday candles and we'd had a boozy night with Chooka and Nicole at the Katty Pub. I wanted to agree. A trip to the hospital would be time-consuming and tiresome; I needed eight hours' sleep. But when I listened to the doctor's messages, it pushed an internal panic button. What if she died in her sleep, like Elsa?

'Kerrie, I think we should go to the hospital. What if you get worse during the night?'

'I feel all right, honestly. I've been fine all weekend and you'll be up late before work and we'll have to take Eddie. I don't think I could be bothered with the hassle of an emergency ward.'

'But your doctor wouldn't tell us to go to a hospital without reason. She would wait until Monday. I think we should go, just in case.'

So Kerrie reluctantly trudged back to the car, strapped Eddie in his safety seat and we drove in to St Vincent's Hospital, Kerrie continually insisting she was feeling well and me quietly praying she was right. When we bobbed at reception, mentioning that Kerrie had been told to come because her haemoglobin levels were 74, the nurse asked where she was bleeding. The figure didn't mean much to me, but it was obviously low.

Thankfully, Kerrie was vindicated. For one night, at least. After it was ascertained that she wasn't in imminent danger, she was allowed to go home.

'I told you I felt all right,' she said.

'I know, I know. Kerrie, I don't like admitting I'm wrong, but on this occasion I'm happy to do so.'

January 2004

We had a mystery to solve.

Why was Kerrie losing blood? Where was it leaking?

Within two days of our phone-message-inspired dash to hospital Kerrie had undergone a CT scan at Peter Mac and been topped up by a transfusion.

The source of the bleeding remained unclear. The scan did not show any abnormalities and Kerrie couldn't remember passing blood. Her condition was puzzling. Her recent tiredness, she thought, was a by-product of motherhood. I told her I thought it was an excuse to bypass sex.

In all seriousness, I wasn't worried by Kerrie's dilemma, largely because she wasn't concerned. Or she didn't look fazed. But I hadn't noticed a lot of things lately, such as her being listless, or feeling dizzy or shunning red meat.

The only cause she could pinpoint for anaemia was the recent absence of steak in her diet. Since Daryl's death she had become semi-vegetarian. A specialist agreed it could be responsible, but suggested she have further tests to make sure.

The behaviour I couldn't ignore, however, was Kerrie's addiction to ice blocks. She chewed them all day long, beginning her noisy crunching soon after breakfast and still chomping relentlessly late at night.

'Kerrie, that's really annoying. Why do you need to do it so often?'

'Sorry, babe. It's a craving. I can't stop.'

It was the Kerrie Russell ice service. She munched through tray after tray. To keep up with demand there were strict company protocols: filtered water only, no tray stacking in the freezer and no plastic, such as a packet of frozen peas, to be left on top of the forming ice. It spoiled the taste.

'Are you sure all this ice munching isn't to blame for your internal bleeding? It hasn't damaged the lining of your stomach, has it?'

'No. I mentioned it to the specialist and he said it wouldn't make any difference.'

The specialist booked Kerrie in for a colonoscopy and gastroscopy, but when they were both clear the search was scaled back. Call off the hounds.

I interpreted the lack of action as a lack of concern. No haste, no worry. Who cared that it would be four weeks before she could see a haematologist? Who cared that we were at the mercy of the health system's wobbly wheels of motion? The blood transfusion would keep her suitably animated until then, we were told. So I didn't bother worrying. I mean, if she were dying, it would be more urgent. Right?

February 2004

If Grandma Elsa's ghost was watching over Eddie's cot, a whirlwind had blown into the spare room. It was Chel. She had returned from twelve months abroad and needed a temporary place of abode.

I said yes, of course, but Kerrie was concerned about sharing our house. What if things didn't work out? What if we needed the privacy? She asked me again if we were doing the right thing.

'Of course,' I said. 'This is my best friend's girlfriend. I would think of nothing else but helping her out. And it will be good for us to have someone different around the house. It will be a break from routine.'

It was less than two weeks before we all found our space, and Chel had swung a sledgehammer through our routine.

- Before Chel we hadn't pulled Eddie's inflatable pool out of its Christmas box.
- After Chel, Kerrie took the plunge, stripping down to her singlet and jocks to escape the heat – we didn't have air-conditioning – with a nude Eddie bouncing off the rubber walls.
- Before Chel I was continually goading myself, without success, to start a fitness campaign.
- After Chel we jogged to the local oval and started running laps. It didn't matter that we overcooked the preparation on our first night, and didn't return for weeks. It was a start.

But the biggest difference Chel brought to our home was time. Since last year's wedding anniversary, Kerrie and I had rarely been out alone. Chel was the impetus for change. As recompense for a bed, Chel would often keep Eddie amused before we put him down of a night. He loved his new playmate. So did I. While she entertained our son, I talked to my wife.

14 February 2004

It was a great feeling to discover a new Kerrie. I saw her emerging from the bedroom, dressed for our Valentine's dinner. She had borrowed a gumleaf-green dress from Chel, which complemented her auburn hair and set off her blue eyes.

We didn't care that it was Valentine's Day. Chel did. She insisted that we celebrate the occasion by dining out. She practically pushed us out the door.

As we caught a taxi to Smith Street, Collingwood, I told Kerrie she looked great. One of those moments when you see your partner in a different light, a nuance you've never noticed before and one that rekindles the spark.

Kerrie seemed taken aback.

'I mean it, Kerrie. You look great.'

'Thanks.'

The downside of our evening was the stifling night. Despite the sun gradually fading, the temperature hovered in the high thirties, made worse by a fire on the wind that scorched your cheeks. Smith Street was practically deserted.

'Where is everyone?' I asked. 'I thought it was impossible to get into a restaurant on Valentine's Day. And it's a Saturday night.'

'It must be too hot for people to leave their houses. Or they've all left the city for the weekend. Look at what they're missing,' she said. And that was saying something because normally Kerrie detested the heat.

We picked a bar to escape the steaming footpath and sat in a booth, cooled only by a ceiling fan. The first drink set us talking and we didn't stop until the time nudged 10 pm. We hadn't eaten so we walked along Smith Street, turned into Johnston Street, returned to Smith Street and could not agree on a place we liked. Tired of walking, tired of reading menus, we settled on a box of chips from KFC and returned to our little bar. There was more drinking to be done, conversations to share and beauty to admire.

1 March 2004

Seven weeks after her bleeding alarm, the public health system remembered Kerrie. She spoke to The Professor and he doubted cancer had returned.

'He said he would be extremely surprised if I had another tumour,' Kerrie said. 'The scans were clear. He sounded a bit annoyed that I'd phoned him, actually.'

Despite the cranky reception, the news helped me breathe easier. Bleeding we could deal with, cancer was unthinkable.

For that reason, I was confident Kerrie was okay. The January scan was clear, she was continuing to gain weight, she was taking a daily interest in my newspaper pages and she was grateful for Chel's high-energy interaction with Eddie.

She was referred to a haematologist and I decided to tag along, re-establishing our association with Peter MacCallum Cancer Centre and igniting our dilemma with the three bears.

15 March 2004

As Kerrie and her haematologist considered the puzzling culprit behind her internal bleeding – possibly a lack of red meat, possibly heavy periods, possibly pregnancy and thirteen months of breastfeeding, or possibly something else – my incorrigible son and I bickered over three huge, stuffed bears residing in the hallways of Peter Mac.

As Kerrie's haematologist explained the extra vim and vigour associated with an iron infusion, Eddie insisted the biggest bear, about the size of a well-fed sumo wrestler, was the mummy. I argued it was the daddy. He wouldn't yield, even when I used Goldilocks as a reference point.

As Kerrie emerged from her consultation room with three plastic jars and the distasteful suggestion she had to fill them with stool samples, I was refusing to play with our son.

'Kerrie, this is ridiculous; he thinks you are the biggest bear and he thinks I'm the mummy bear,' I complained.

'That's understandable. I loom larger in his life at the moment so he equates me with the biggest bear.'

'But I want to be the daddy bear. Doesn't he know that daddies are bigger than mummies?'

'Well, obviously not in this case,' she laughed.

Not convinced, I walked over to Eddie and told him to give the daddy bear a hug, playfully admonishing him when he went for the wrong one.

'That's the mummy bear,' I said. 'The daddy bear is the big one.'

No luck. If the bloody manufacturers in Teddy Bear Land had given the middle-sized bear breasts, I would have swiftly ended the frustrating debate, but there was no female anatomy to latch on to, so to speak. Kerrie laughed again.

'Honey, he's not going to change his mind,' she said. 'You're just going to have to accept that I'm the most important person in the family.'

Despite her jesting, I felt a tiny pang of jealousy that Eddie didn't see me as the protector, or the breadwinner or the 'man' in our lives.

Kerrie was kind enough to massage my jilted ego. The next time I feigned hurt at being labelled the mummy bear, she bolstered my pride until I was the star at the centre of her retro solar system – I was slicker than Humphrey Bogart in *Casablanca*, more loveable than Jimmy Stewart in *It's a Wonderful Life* and funnier than Peter Sellers in *The Party*.

April 2004

Significant changes blew into my life. Eddie started calling big red trucks 'big red cocks', meaning trips into the public arena were loaded with shock reactions and embarrassment whenever we saw a fire engine. And the newspaper, under a new editor, was pushed in a more serious direction.

I was told this meant I could no longer superimpose footballers' heads onto cows' bodies or pretend we had access to a ouija board for channelling dead Hollywood stars for their take on modern-day athletes and their acting talents. It felt like I could no longer have fun. I interpreted the change in focus as dull and a step backwards. I felt superfluous to requirements.

I unleashed the grumbles and gripes at home. That's what husbands do, I thought. Kerrie listened to me complaining about staying back on Tuesday afternoons to ghost a footballer's column, trying to coax something beyond 'we're taking it one game at a time' from his week. She tolerated my bitching at having to dedicate half of our Sundays to watching sports review programs, reading newspapers and catching the nightly news so that I knew who won a volleyball match in Europe. She felt the brunt of my lack of humour at having to eschew humour at work.

As usual, and despite her continuing lack of energy, Kerrie tried to pump some air into my confidence.

'You don't have to eliminate humour,' she said. 'There's always a place for abstract observations, particularly in sport. Maybe you just have to be more clever in the way you deliver it.'

'Like how?' I whinged.

'Find out things that people don't already know. That's what I want to read about sportsmen or sportswomen. Not who they play next week.'

'But you know what footballers are like. When's the last time you heard one say something interesting?'

'Well, it's the job of the reporters to extract humorous or interesting anecdotes from athletes. I can't do that for you.'

Kerrie also suggested I might need a holiday to freshen up. So we went to Adelaide for Easter. And on the road I felt myself unwind, shedding stress each time we passed a 'big red cock'.

Easter Saturday, 10 April 2004

My father has a knack for fishing. I think it's patience. He doesn't twiddle or twitch or feel a need to reef the rod or incessantly reel in the line to check bait like I do. He can sit quietly, almost serenely, and wait. That's why he caught three mullet off a bridge at Victor Harbor before I'd even had a bite. That and he threw his line right in the middle of another angler's berley patch.

My parents had been touring around South Australia and Dad and I left Kerrie back at the caravan for a sleep. She was exhausted after a week of sorting through her mother's possessions. She cleared knick-knacks from cupboards, packed clothes into garbage bags and filled boxes with odds and ends.

'Dad will leave all these things here forever, otherwise,' she reasoned. 'Mum is dead. You can't leave the house as if she is still living in it. You have to move on.'

The big clean-up served as a belated grieving process for Kerrie. Her fingers walked through the past, scrunching and grabbing at dresses, caressing statues of unicorns and sliding over pictures of rainbows. She sat and wept re-reading her mother's letters.

Sadly, I didn't understand. My depth of appreciation of Elsa extended back only four years and I liked her things around the house. For that reason, I struggled to comprehend how Kerrie could remove herself from me mentally and physically during this letting-go process.

'Kerrie, this is meant to be a holiday. We can have sex, you know,' I complained.

'Danny, I'm not in the right headspace. I want to concentrate on clearing out Mum's things, and when I've finished we can have sex. I've got to get this done for Dad.'

Kerrie worried about Des. Not about his Christmas back injury, although it was stopping him from playing golf. Not about his prostate cancer, because the radiation treatment had seen his blood tests drop to safe levels. She worried that he would keep on living as if Elsa was in the house, still slipping out for a grog.

'Bring the drink inside, Dad, for goodness sake. Mum's dead. You don't have to hide it anymore. I don't mind.'

But after a week of purging, Kerrie wasn't ready for intimacy. She needed to rest. She fell asleep in a chair beside my parents' caravan at Victor Harbor. My mother agreed to mind Eddie while Dad and I went fishing.

And that's how we found ourselves on a footbridge over an inlet with my dad stealing fish from under another angler's nose. The fisherman didn't seem to mind that my father was reaping the benefits of his methods because he even offered us a bag of ice to keep the catch cool. I admired his generous nature because I would have been pissed off.

Dad shrugged off my concerns when we walked to the car. He didn't feel like he'd done anything wrong.

'Weren't you worried that he might get annoyed?'

'What do you mean?' he grinned.

'You dropped your line right in the middle of where he had spread all his berley,' I said.

'Did I?'

We packed up and left him cleaning his fish.

11 April 2004

Dear Eddie,

I love Woofa. I never met the dog because she died when your mum was a teenager, but she is a legend. A wiry little 'bitsa' about the size of a Jack Russell terrier, smelling incurably like a manky, wet rag, Woofa is the dog that stole Easter.

She ate Kerrie's Easter eggs. The ones she had scattered throughout the garden to create a treasure hunt for Grandma Elsa. Kerrie had even designed a treasure map. 'But Woofa ate the lot before Elsa had the chance to start looking and I burst into tears,' Kerrie said.

The only remnant was a trail of shiny tinfoil wrapping.

'So the next day I bought Elsa a little chocolate bunny as a replacement, which she hid in a cupboard in her bedroom,' Kerrie said. 'But while Elsa was on the phone one afternoon, Woofa snuck inside and went up the passage. She never came inside! And she never went up the passage!

'I was sitting in the lounge room watching TV when Woofa re-appeared looking very pleased with herself, wagging her tail and leaving a trail of foil behind her. I yelled, "Woofa!" and then burst into tears again. I was devastated. I think Elsa chased Woofa outside, but she couldn't help but laugh at the absurdity of it all.'

There is no Woofa to sniff out our treasure at Port Willunga, Eddie, only possums or rats. Because when you, Ruby and Zac hunt around the lawn with Mum, Uncle Brendan and Aunty Jane in tow, it becomes apparent a number of Easter eggs have been spoiled by bite marks. Or so I'm told because I'm still struggling to lift my head from the pillow courtesy of a bourbon-fuelled finish to the night.

About midnight we had ventured out to spread the booty. It was my first time as Easter Bunny and was to be your first treasure hunt as a son. I wanted to be crafty, make you three sweet-tooths search long and hard for the treats. I tiptoed around the yard, tucking chocolate surprises deep in the forks of bushes and practically burying them in the garden bed. I was quite pleased with myself. Until …

'What the hell are you doing?'

It was Brendan.

'They are barely three years old, they'll never find them in there. They will struggle to find them sitting on top of the lawn.'

'Oh,' I said. 'I just thought …'

'Nah, don't bother. It will take forever otherwise.'

So I crawled back into the bushes to retrieve the hidden treasure and started again, following Brendan's lead of quickly scattering eggs around the perimeter of the yard before ducking in for another drink.

Thankfully we have plenty of chocolate because not even the possum population of Port Willunga has appetite enough to finish the stockpile we've amassed. There's plenty for three avaricious kids to smear across their faces and even enough left to provide hung-over parents with a sugar fix. The lesson of Woofa has been learned.

Love Dad

April 2004

Eddie is a song and dance man, always belting out snatches of his favourite tunes, with a bit of arm-waving and stamping thrown in for emphasis. He is two and a half now and so much fun. He's really talking and interacting, noticing things around him and bringing them to my attention. Make that EVERYTHING.

'Yes, darling, that's a bird. And yes, darling, I know that's a red car with a trailer. That's right, there's a white plane with two engines, wings, a tail, wheels, lights, windows ...'

His enthusiasm for the mundane makes it un-mundane, if you know what I mean. I guess that's the beauty of children. They make us remember how wonderful the world around us is if we don't look at it through tired eyes. Or some philosophical bullshit like that.

Kerrie

May 2004

Kerrie and I had our night at a flash restaurant, only it wasn't the Flower Drum. It was Pure South, an ambitious new restaurant at Southbank. And I didn't need to collect on the horses to pay the bill. The owner said he would pick up the tab.

Phil was a guy I had played football with more than twenty years ago and I arranged to review his new venture in our newspaper. That's how we circumnavigated our minuscule budget: restaurants provided the grub, and journalists provided the review. Kerrie thought it was a great deal. I thought it was hard work.

She walked out of the house bubbling with excitement; I dragged my feet with apprehension. What if the waitstaff expected me to behave like a bona fide 'food critic', some culinary guru who knew what he was sniffing for when he put his nose to the wine glass?

Admittedly, I had done some homework, using a cheat sheet to jot down the vernacular of serious food columnists, noting chic words such as 'drizzle' and 'sliver'. But these guys knew what they were talking about. They knew why a dish tasted sublime, or why it missed the mark. They knew what had gone wrong or what had been left out. I didn't. I knew the difference between rare and well-done. At least Phil would be able to steer me in the right direction. Except he wasn't at Pure South when we arrived. He had taken the night off.

'What if he hasn't told anyone about the bill arrangement?' I said to Kerrie as we were led to a table near the chic gas fire.

'Just tell them.'

'I don't think I can. I'm too embarrassed.'

'Don't be silly.'

I was nervous. Shifting in my seat, sweating and when a waiter floated by our table and started reciting the specials, I replied in a funny voice. I tucked my jaw back into my chin, turned my wine glass incessantly and my intonation wavered between Tiny Tim and Dr Julius M. Hibbert, physician to The Simpsons. Kerrie asked me why I was behaving so oddly.

'I'm trying to act like a serious food critic,' I said.

'Don't be ridiculous. Just enjoy the meal.'

'I'm too scared to ask about the meaning behind these dishes. I'm meant to know this stuff.'

'Danny, are you serious? Just enjoy the experience and worry about the review later.'

'But what about the décor and table setting? Stephen Downes always remarks on the setting. I'm a sports editor.'

'I'll handle the décor. It will be a joint review, okay? Now relax a little bit and stop talking in a funny voice.'

So we ate. I had seared calamari served on an eggplant puree with a salad of artichoke, tomato and olives; Kerrie had saffron angel-hair pasta with rock lobster, ocean trout, lemon, chilli and chives. Then we got to the mains. I had lamb and Kerrie had a 350-gram Cape Grim rump served with King Island double-cream mash, red wine sauce, watercress, red onion and radish salad.

Her steak was so succulent you could have sliced it with a letter-opener. Hey, I was getting used to this food critic stuff. A couple of wines helped me relax. I was even engaging in banter with the waiter and not sounding like a twat.

Until it was time to take care of the bill.

'I can't tell him, Kerrie. I'll just pay the cashier and chase it up tomorrow.'

'Don't be silly. You won't get the money back. You cleared it with Phil, just tell them.'

'I can't, I'm too embarrassed.'

'I can't believe you're too embarrassed. You're the guy who loves getting naked after a few drinks and you can't speak to a waiter. I'll go and tell him.'

'That's not fair. I haven't been nude in years.'

Kerrie marched over to our waiter and confidently told him, 'Phil's taking care of this.'

I held my breath and looked through one eye.

'No problems,' he said.

I felt so relieved I whipped out some cash and gave him a tip.

14 May 2004

I stirred in the middle of the night. I thought I heard coughing.

I did hear coughing. And gagging. And dry-retching.

I rolled over to see Kerrie sitting up with her head bowed forward, wiping her lips with a tissue.

'Kerrie, are you all right?'

'No, honey. I've got terrible stomach cramps.'

'Do you want to go to hospital?'

'I think I should.'

Kerrie was checked into St Vincent's Hospital after almost two days on an emergency ward trolley. She was diagnosed with a bowel obstruction. A subsequent MRI showed she had a tumour. It wasn't good. If the January scan had shown up clear, the tumour was growing at a rapid pace, which meant the cancer had taken on a more aggressive form.

Once again, the best way of tackling the tumour was surgery. Only this time The Professor had reservations. He was worried about scar tissue and adhesions from her past operations.

'It will be a jungle in there,' Kerrie was warned. 'Removing the tumour might not be possible.'

With Elsa gone, my mother moved to Melbourne to take care of Eddie.

When she arrived, I snuck off and locked myself in the bathroom. There was nowhere else to cry.

2 September 2006

Dear Kerrie,

I'm at a function in St Kilda with about 200 people. It's a benefit, pulled together predominantly by Brian, Whit and Macca, with help from Marns, Bluey and Mike. They've organised the room, the band, the grog, the food and everyone's having a cherry ripe afternoon.

The humbling part is that the benefit is for Ed and me. I don't know how to thank them so I keep it to myself. I hope my smile is enough.

To love is a great thing, but sometimes to feel loved is even greater.

Miss you,

love Danny

September 2006

Dear Kerrie,

I find it hard to visit your friends.

It's not the arrival, it's the departure.

When it's time for us to drive away, despite their hugs and warm goodbyes, it's like we are leaving a piece of you behind. I drive away half a person. There's no talking about the day's events, discussing our hosts or the things we should've or shouldn't have said. There's just Eddie and me in the car and sometimes I'm too distracted to want to play make-believe and I snap at him as a result.

The melancholy strikes again when we drive to the Dandenong Ranges to visit your aunties. I've never been here without you. Instead, there's just Eddie and half a person to run down Aunty Annette's back garden for a glimpse of Puffing Billy and his waving passengers.

I like talking to Annette, she's warm and she understands death and she allows me to unravel, but despite the many spiritual paths we traverse, we can't fill the empty chair in the corner.

Then Eddie and I visit Aunty Marion, who says she still feels your presence, as if you've never left. But I can't feel it. Not me. Every direction I turn I notice your absence.

Miss you,
love Danny

8 October 2006

Dear Kerrie,

Eddie bursts into my room because he's besotted with a documentary on the Discovery Channel.

'Dad, did you know that prairie dogs bark when they see a coyote?'

'What's that?'

'They go, "yelp, yelp, yelp" and then they dive in their tunnels before the coyote can catch them and eat them up.'

'Who does?'

'The prairie dogs.'

'That's great, son.'

'Dad, pretend you are the prairie dogs and I'll be the coyote coming to get you.'

So he growls and snorts and I have to 'yelp, yelp, yelp' and bury my head under the doona. Satisfied with my impromptu performance, the coyote scoots back up the passage to watch some more TV.

Even bedtime books have taken on a new bent. Tonight Eddie stops me turning to the next page of *The Lion King* because he wants to study the zany faces on the dastardly hyenas. He tries to imitate each screwball expression, scrunching his nose, baring his teeth and then sticking out his tongue.

'Okay, Dad, you can turn the page now.'

I turn out the light and make to walk off when he asks, 'Dad, can you sleep in my bed for five minutes?'

DANNY RUSSELL

'All right. Five minutes, but then you have to go to sleep.'

'Dad, we forgot to kiss Mum goodnight.'

So I grab our wedding photo off his bookcase and hold it up to his face so he can kiss your picture goodnight.

Then we 'yelp, yelp, yelp' and bury our heads under the pillow.

Miss you,

love Danny

11 October 2006

Dear Kerrie,

We're at the sports club having lunch and I'm halfway through a spiel about who will win the Gold Nugget at the Ballarat races when Eddie interjects and asks if all mums get cancer.

'No, they don't,' I say.

'How come?' he asks.

'Because … (and here's the uncomfortable pause because I don't know why) … because that's something God decides,' I manage.

'How come God gave Mum cancer?' he persists.

He's good, this boy of ours. He asks in such a casual manner as if he's pondering something meaningless such as why do bowling greens have ditches, which he asked Pa earlier that day.

I don't know how the question came about, but I'm stuck, trying to make sense of why God fingered you and not some other kid's mum.

'God needed Mum by his side so that she could be with Grandma,' I say.

It's an answer not hard to believe, because if I were God, I'd want you by my side, too. But there's little time for further contemplation because Eddie has another question.

'Well, how come God didn't want Mum when I was three ?'

'Because Mum needed to spend some time with you before she went. She needed to teach you things about life such as good manners. That's why you have such good manners,' I say.

Then Pa chips in: 'She was a good mummy, wasn't she?'

'Yeah,' Eddie says, but his thought pattern has been shattered because he's no longer asking the questions and he bounces off on a tangent, challenging us to a lemon squash skolling competition. And as he blows bubbles through his straw, I breathe a sigh of relief.

Miss you,

love Danny

28 October 2006

Dear Kerrie,

It's Eddie's first birthday without a mum.

He's not sad, I am. I remember the day he was born like it was yesterday. And I bet you are the same.

My God, he's so helpless. So tiny. So perfect. So … unlike his parents.

That's what I thought when solemn-faced, dark-haired Eddie Russell came into our world on 28 October 2001 and promptly turned it upside down and inside out.

I've become a cooing, clucking fusspot who can't remember what day of the week it is and Danny's getting interested in superannuation and organising household budgets.

But Eddie is blissfully ignorant of the wonderful mayhem he has wrought in our home since his seven-hour delivery, which was less traumatic than I imagined it would be (thank you pethidine).

One minute I was gritting my teeth through the contractions thinking this whole pregnancy thing was a very bad idea indeed, the next Eddie was being popped on the scales (8 lb 12 oz/4 kg – phew) and doing a magnificent arc of wee all over the midwife, who deserved a medal instead of a wet blouse.

And we've been oohing and aahing over – and occasionally been quite alarmed by – his bodily functions ever since.

He fascinates me. I find myself staring into his face for great measureless gobs of time, then I wonder where my day has gone. Of course, it has gone in feeding, changing, burping and adoring him.

Only new mothers understand how exhausting this can be, and how challenging it is to learn how to be a mum without stressing your way into the funny farm.

I wake up thinking he's in my arms and the doona's smothering him. I worry he's too sleepy, then I worry that he's too alert. Am I being a bad mother using disposable nappies? Have I fed him enough/ burped him long enough/overhandled him and made him unsettled? Is his jaundice going? Is that a blocked tear duct or conjunctivitis?

It's a surreal twilight zone, this motherhood game. Life is a fog of sleep deprivation and NapiSan fumes, snatched naps on the couch after Good Morning Australia *and delight at Eddie's growing delight with the world.*

He's a curious little chap, and it grabs my heart when his surprise at all his new discoveries is played out on his angel face (do angels get milk rash?).

There are troughs with the peaks, of course, such as constant low-level anxiety about his health and development. Every rash becomes meningitis, every gurgle a serious gut complaint. Eddie's grandparents, without whom we would be lost, assure us these fears will ease in oh, say, fifty years.

And there's drudgery. The endless laundry. The social isolation of breastfeeding. Being dressed exclusively in tracksuit bottoms and vomit-streaked tops. Watching the diet. (Still no grog!)

Yet I'm so grateful for it all it makes me cry. One long and hazy night when we were still in hospital, I was watching the television news with Eddie asleep at my breast. The newsreader was delivering messages of misery about the war in Afghanistan, murders and car crashes. I cried then. I cried because my world was warm and sweet, right then and there, a bubble of innocence. I was crying a thank you to God for letting me experience that moment of perfect peace.

Well, here I am five years later, standing to the side of the kitchen as Eddie unwraps his presents, thanking Grandpa Des for *The Incredibles*

DVD and the *Cars* characters before turning to me and asking about his birthday party.

This is a problem because I haven't organised one, despite him spending the year inviting all his friends. We've just been in Adelaide for two weeks with Des, and Granny Kath's incapacitated because she broke her wrist on a golf trip.

But none of these things make me feel any less inadequate as a dad. 'Nobody is coming around today, Eddie. I'm really sorry, but I thought I explained that to you, mate. We didn't have time to invite them,' I say.

'Why not?'

'Because we were in Adelaide. (Quick, somebody call a spin doctor.) Remember we had a little party with Ruby and Zac in the park? We'll do the same today. We'll have chocolate cake with Pa and Granny and Grandpa. And we'll have party pies, sausage rolls and lollies.'

'Yeah, I can eat anything I want because it's my birthday.'

'Well not anything, but you can have a lot of treats.'

Crisis averted.

Eddie's happy because he believes his birthday entitles him to eat whatever he wants, say whatever he wants and do whatever he wants. Another victory for spin. Relieved, I grab Grandpa Des after the cake and renditions of 'Happy Birthday' and we duck out for a couple of hours to watch the Cox Plate.

Eddie loves his day, playing with new toys, reading new books and eating fistfuls of lollies. He asks me again why we didn't have a party, but I say we'll have a ripper next year instead. Then as I tuck him into bed, he asks me to sing 'Happy Birthday' one more time.

Miss you,

love Danny

May 2004

My sugar levels dropped if I didn't eat every two hours. I became semi-nauseous and irritated, barking irrationally at anyone within biting distance until the metabolic balance was restored.

So I simply couldn't comprehend Kerrie's headspace: it would be two weeks before The Professor could squeeze her into the schedule for surgery. That meant a fortnight without food, unable to eat because her blocked bowel wouldn't allow a safe passage of food; two weeks listening to the desperate, grumbling demands of her stomach.

I would have curled into a foetal position and buried my head in a pillow.

Kerrie didn't give up. She was disappointed at the delay, annoyed that she had dropped her guard and allowed cancer's re-entry into our lives, but instead of sulking she distracted herself by making friends with the 'inmates' who were intermittently wheeled in and out of her ward. She also became addicted to pictures of food, obsessing over the cooking sections of women's magazines. She made me look at photos of lamb tikka, Thai beef salad, grilled salmon and kumara salad, chicken and corn vol-au-vents, ham and zucchini pie, Cajun-style blackened fish with green rice, French onion soup and even cakes.

'This is my pornography,' she said.

With the same voyeuristic appetite as a teenage boy, she couldn't get enough.

Instead of reading smutty stories and sniggering, 'They did it for how long?', Kerrie was flipping through recipes and marvelling, 'They cooked what, with what, for an hour!'

She also made me look.

'Doesn't this walnut cake look delicious?' she fantasised.

I almost felt dirty, peeping over her shoulder, carefully avoiding the gaze of other patients and their visitors until I was able to reason that what we were looking at actually was JUST A CAKE.

'Kerrie, aren't you torturing yourself by looking at all this food?'

'Not really. I'm going to feel hungry regardless. And I like daydreaming about all the wonderful things I'm going to eat when I get out of here.'

Kerrie further fed my guilt by feeding me. When the tea trolley rolled by she would order a cup of coffee and accompanying biscuits, despite the prominent sign above her bed: Nil by mouth.

'They're for my husband,' she would whisper with a conspiratorial grin and a wink of the eye as if inviting the trolley person to join her band of merry men.

While Kerrie claimed she felt 'like she was on drugs' and too spaced out from a lack of food to succumb to negative emotions, my thoughts were betraying me. I started to believe she could die. While I was sitting on the train, I considered life without her. Where would I go? What would I do? What about Eddie? Would I meet another woman?

And it was this last thought that disturbed me most. It was perverse, but intriguing, imaging a new life. I thought about the missed opportunities of the past and the possibility they might present themselves again in the future. If she were to die, would I marry again?

And that's when the internal tug-of-war began.

I can't be thinking about another woman.

You just did.

I know, but it's wrong. Kerrie's alive and she can make it through this latest setback.

Let's be realistic, she is in a precarious position. This is her third tumour. You and Eddie will be alone. How about someone like that dark-haired woman across the carriage?

Stop it. My life is with Kerrie. I don't want to think about another woman.

You just did. I saw you look at that dark-haired woman.

All right, I looked, but that doesn't mean I want to sleep with her or get to know her. She might be a compulsive/obsessive, or she might listen to Celine Dion, or she might hate horse-racing.

Okay, okay, let's forget about looking at dark-haired women for now. But you and Eddie are going to be alone.

Because I worried about Kerrie dying, I also worried about her funeral. Despite the total inappropriateness of this train of thought, it persistently bugged me, the possibility of getting it all wrong. I experienced Kerrie's stress in the days after Elsa's death, trying to match her mother with the 'right' songs, readings, flowers and even her last outfit. I couldn't do these things for my wife. What was her song?

I wanted to ask her these things, have her write them down and then lock them away in a vault so that there was one less thing to worry about. Thankfully, these morbid thoughts abandoned me as soon as I saw Kerrie in her hospital bed. She always looked pleased when I walked through the door.

'Hello, darling,' she would smile while flipping through a magazine. 'Come and have a look at this cake.'

May 2004

Dear Eddie,

You don't see St Vincent's Hospital as an oppressive building filled with sick people, even when we pass emaciated patients on walking frames or sitting in wheelchairs out the front taking ironic drags of their cigarettes. You see it as a playground.

There are gift shops with chocolates. There are lift buttons to push, corridors for running, and Kerrie's bed to clamber over. Except I stop you from clambering over the bed. Mum is too sore and tired and I don't want the nurses to boot us out. Not yet.

I'm so glad your Mum has agreed to see us. I hate being torn between the hospital and home, abandoning one love to be with another. This way we are complete. I know you'll be bored in twenty minutes and I'll be flustered trying to restrain your curious hands from grabbing for inappropriate places, but at least we've got a little time together to hug and kiss Mum and to climb over chairs.

It is a grand view from the TV room out over Melbourne's eastern suburbs to the Dandenong Ranges. And the way your mum sits and stares out those windows with a longing in her eyes, I think she is hearing a voice.

'Come home to us, Kerrie,' the ranges call. 'Come back to our trees and our sunsets and our cool mountain nights, sitting by the fireplace. Come back to your mother's home. Come back to your roots.'

Then again, maybe it's just that spaced-out feeling.

At least she's been given a leave pass this Saturday and will be able to breathe some fresh air. We might go for a drive, or sit in a park or show her some of your tricks. I am glad she wants you to visit. She wants to stay in focus. Not like last time when she came home from hospital and felt you'd forgotten she was your mum.

But I don't think you forget. You change when she's away, there's no doubt, refusing to go to the toilet, clenching tight in a subconscious protest against her rotten deal, but I think you'll always know she's your mum.

You'll be leaving in twenty minutes, but not before you've checked out the gift shop, pressed the lift buttons, run up the corridors and cuddled your mum. At that time Granny Kath will take you home and I'll remain, reassured we are still a loving little family.

Love Dad

May 2004

For one day a week, at 7 am on a Tuesday in 1996, I pretended to be a taxi driver. I used to crawl foggy-minded out of bed, take a phone call from

Sport 927 radio station and act as if I was an eavesdropping cabbie with all sorts of weird and wonderful gossip, plucked from the many sports folk I had supposedly ferried from A to B while tearing around Melbourne in my taxi. Basically, I made the lot up. After two months my imagination was left fallow, harvested once too often, and my paid segment was unceremoniously cut the day I had my housemate shove a wheelie bin into our tin fence, yelling and screaming with shock, pretending the commotion was my cab ploughing into former Hawthorn great Dermott Brereton in the middle of St Kilda Road. Despite the unexpected mock carnage, the breakfast show hosts, Kevin Bartlett and Dr Turf, somehow managed to hold the segment together until a commercial break, my housemate and I rolling around the ground pissing ourselves laughing, at which time the phone line was cut. They never called back.

Here I was eight years later drinking with my old housemate at the Rob Roy Hotel, having walked around the corner from St Vincent's Hospital, leaving Kerrie to sleep and killing time before a dinner-suit engagement at the Crown Palladium Ballroom. My white shirt hadn't been ironed and while we sat on a beer my old buddy conjured up ingenious ways of getting it pressed: we'll sneak into the hospital laundry; we'll waltz into a flash hotel, like the Hyatt, and pretend we're guests; we'll ask to test run an iron at an electrical goods store.

'You don't by any chance happen to have an iron?' I asked the barman.

'An iron?'

'Yeah, an iron. For ironing this white shirt.'

'Sorry, mate.'

'Oh, okay. Two beers, thanks.'

After five beers and no solutions our time was up so I slipped on my crumpled shirt, hoped no one would notice it under my second-hand jacket and crutch-crunching pants, and went to the Casino, plonking myself on a media table at a racing industry dinner.

Well, what a surprise! I was sitting next to Dr Turf, the former radio host, eight years after the St Kilda Road–Brereton incident. We'd never met – part of the radio persona deal I'd struck with the radio show producer in 1996 was a condition of anonymity – and as a result I'd waited years for this moment. I'd watched him on ABC's *The Fat* and admired his caustic wit.

I decided to introduce myself, relieve Dr Turf of almost a decade of second-guessing as to the mysterious identity of the hilarious taxi driver. I just wished my pants weren't so tight.

Wouldn't he get a shock on turning around, once he stopped talking to those self-important, albeit higher-achieving, members of my profession on the other side of the table, to meet his old sparring partner, the cabbie. Once he knew who I was, he'd never look back … to the other side of the table, to the formerly more important types.

Remember me? Of course you do, I'm the cabbie. Imagine, after all these years we finally come face to face. Who would have thought we'd end up here?

No, no, that wouldn't do – he's no Eddie McGuire and I work for a newspaper that no one's heard of. Cut the self-importance, and play it a little more subtle, ease into the conversation.

'Hi, Dr Turf,' I said, when he finally turned around, 'I'm Danny Russell.'

'Hi.'

'We used to …'

But before I could finish, someone called him back. Bugger, I'd better have another glass of wine. Maybe two.

I caught his eye again.

'Hi, Dr Turf. We have some history,' I said. History? What did I mean by that? Did I mean *history* history or just normal history? Damn, I was getting confused.

'Oh yes?' he said. Phew! He's interested in history. I hadn't blown my chance.

'Yeah, I used to be the cabbie.'

Blank face.

'The cabbie! When you did the 927 breakfast show with Kevin Bartlett, I used to call in with the rumours …you know, the cabbie?'

'Ah yes, the cabbie. I remember.'

Phew, again! He remembered. The mystery had been solved. Imagine the poor man's relief.

After all these years, you cheeky bastard. Man, did our listeners love you. And what about poor old Dermott Brereton (click of the finger, haw, haw, haw).

Except he didn't say those things. He turned back to the other side of the table and started talking about Channel 7's forthcoming coverage of the Athens Olympics.

Hmm, that didn't go to plan.

I needed to bring in the heavy artillery; tell him the Bomber Bill story. No racing fan could resist my wedding-suit anecdote about Bomber Bill. Except Dr Turf.

'You'd never guess, but the only reason I could afford my wedding suit and my best man's wedding suit was backing Bomber Bill in a running double at Moonee Valley and picking up a thousand bucks,' I told him.

'Great,' he said, eyebrows slightly arched.

To Dr Turf's credit, he introduced me to Bomber Bill's trainer, Robert Smerdon, who was seated at the next table, before returning to the Olympics.

At least Smerdon enjoyed my story.

'He's a lovely old horse,' Smerdon said of my wedding-suit cash cow, 'why don't you and your mate come down to the stables one day and see him?'

'I will,' I said. 'I bloody well will.'

Although I barely registered a speck on Dr Turf's media career and he'd probably heard a thousand more uplifting punting stories, I was disappointed not to be his new best mate. Maybe I wasn't that funny. I turned my attention to a bottle of red. We got along famously and after a waiter uncorked the red's friend they convinced me to stagger around the ballroom and collect autographs for my hospitalised wife.

Part-time radio announcer Keith Hillier was my first victim. Keith and I went way back, spending at least 40 of the year's 52 Saturday mornings together. Keith's dulcet tones piped into our bedroom via the clock radio, cajoling his horse-racing panel to deliver desperate punters, like me, a bunch of winners for the day. Except very few of them won. Regardless, Kerrie didn't appreciate our relationship.

What better way to cheer her up than get the man's autograph?

'Sign here, Keith. Can you make it out to my wife, she's an avid listener,' I said.

'How do you spell her name?'

I went blank, inexplicably thrown by the simplest of questions. What did he ask again, my wife's name? I could picture her face, picture her reading a glossy magazine in her hospital bed, smiling despite being cut off from three-course meals, bottles of red and casino ballrooms. But what was her name?

Kerrie Fahey, that's it. No, Kerrie Russell. We're married. Kerrie Russell. Kerrie with an 'ie' not a 'y'.

'She is your wife? You do know how to spell her name, don't you?' Keith interrupted, standing with his biro poised, ready to write.

'Yes, she's my wife. Of course she's my wife. Ho, ho. Ha, ha.'

I staggered outside and caught a taxi home, trying not to slur my words or mention Dr Turf and Keith Hillier. You never knew who was listening.

25 May 2004

My third tour of duty. Operation Jungle Tumour. And I knew the drill. Kerrie was wheeled off to theatre by humourless orderlies in shower caps, while I moped off home, thinking of The Professor as a safari suit-wearing explorer, complete with pith helmet, hacking his way through a cluster of vines and crocodile-infested swamps in search of cancer. Good luck, old chap.

Granny Kath and I did our best to stay occupied. I knew well enough not to expect imminent news so I took Eddie to the park, sitting him on my lap and cutting belly-tickling arcs on a swing. I don't know if it was the pendulum motion brushing Eddie's stomach, or the sheer thrill of flying, but during one of our downward curves he suddenly shot me a look of unconditional love. It was the look he usually gave Kit Kats and it caught me by surprise. Our eyes locked and it felt like a warm flannel was gently washing my soul. So this was what it was like to be a dad. This was what Kerrie meant. I smiled back, the clock ticked, gravity pulled at my outstretched feet, Eddie turned his head and the moment passed. But I hung onto that feeling for the rest of the afternoon. I couldn't wait to tell my wife.

With hours still to kill, I pushed Eddie to the corner store, pointing out dogs with their noses pointing to the ground and straining against leashes while taking their owners for a walk. We spied an arrogant black cat perched on a brick fence, nose pointed in the air, mocking the dogs. Ice-cream in hand we returned home to watch *Thomas the Tank Engine*, passing the same cat, watching the passing of different dogs. Then we played in the backyard, then we revisited the park, back to the corner store for another treat and home to watch *The Wiggles*. Three hours of killing time. When I ran out of ideas and options, I handed Eddie over to Granny Kath and sat near the telephone, waiting for the call.

Despite jumping at the first bell, I let it ring four times before answering, standing to gather my composure. It was The Professor. I let him do the talking. He said the operation had been tedious, picking through the adhesions, and there had been complications, such as removing a section of Kerrie's small intestine that had been attached to the tumour, but ultimately it had been a success.

'That's great,' I said. 'What do we do now?'

'We wait for the bowel to start working,' he said.

Thousands of questions all led back to the same answer: we wait. So I didn't bother asking. The Professor was a busy man and he probably needed to change out of his blood-spattered safari suit.

I left Eddie with my mother and drove to the hospital, navigating the streets, roundabouts and traffic lights from memory, my mind focused on seeing a bloated, traumatised wife.

Sometimes it was hard to be polite to hospital staff. Sometimes I bit my tongue. Sometimes I stopped myself from blurting out, 'Put yourself in my wife's shoes if you want something to grumble about.'

Kerrie wasn't a demanding patient. When she was in pain, she asked for painkillers. When she felt nauseous, she asked for anti-nausea drugs. She was hardly attached to the buzzer. She treated her job of getting better seriously. And it annoyed me when others didn't do the same.

Like yesterday. A blundering nurse was so preoccupied about finishing her shift and getting home for a house inspection that she accidentally yanked on Kerrie's drainage tube, pulling at the stitches in her skin and causing Kerrie to yelp in agony and me to jump wide-eyed out of my chair. While my wife didn't say anymore, I could see the tears of pain and frustration in her eyes.

At least her yelp yanked the nurse's attention back on line because she apologised profusely and stopped grumbling about inconsiderate housemates, overtime and rosters. She fussed over Kerrie to make sure she had her medication and was comfortable. She even fluffed her pillow.

That wasn't so hard, was it? I thought to myself.

Kerrie had to suffer all types of pricks. Needles, intravenous drips, and even a young doctor. He was inconsiderate and over-ambitious, stirring my ire by digging around in her arm trying to find a vein. He became exasperated at not hitting the spot, practically ignoring Kerrie's attempts to absolve him of blame. 'Everyone says I'm hard work,' she said.

There's an art to difficult veins. Only certain types have the skill – known in the trade as vampires. They don't have sharp teeth and they don't emerge at night, but they have an uncanny knack for tapping blood. A couple of slaps on a patient's arm, a quick jab and they're in.

Kerrie, growing tired and sore of being pricked and prodded, suggested she could wait for a nurse. But this doctor was reluctant to admit defeat by abandoning the job and handing responsibility to a subordinate. He said so himself: 'I don't like to fail.'

Kerrie was quick to respond.

'Welcome to humanity,' she replied.

I loved her for this comment – he'd studied medicine, she'd studied life. I loved it in the lift, I loved it on the train and I told Mum and Des when I got home.

'I hope it makes him a better doctor,' I said.

30 May 2004

God must have seen the roof at 48 Gallipoli Parade in the autumn of 2004, homing in like a Google Earth satellite on our suburban abode, catching sight of Eddie charging around the backyard. There's no way He could have missed us. Each night before sleep I was asking for Kerrie's swift recovery, Grandpa Des was praying in the spare room and my mother, who was sleeping on a makeshift bed in the study, was constantly wishing for her beloved daughter-in-law's return to health.

Our prayers were answered. Kerrie improved rapidly. Within days of the operation she was sucking on ice and tolerating fluids. The first complication was not her digestive system, but the menu. She couldn't stomach the hospital's recommended steps up the food chain – jelly and broth.

'The broth is awful. It's tasteless. It's basically flavoured hot water and not very well flavoured at that. The jelly? The jelly makes me gag,' she said.

So she stuck to icy-poles before progressing to toast. The drainage tube had been removed, her wound had dried and she was looking to get home. With her father, my mother and Eddie all in the same house, she was missing all the fun. Besides, God had other roofs to watch.

June 2004

Hope was a two-edged sword. We had to believe Kerrie could live, which in turn made us susceptible to a myriad of alternative 'cures' – apricot kernels, vitamin C injections and special tea leaves. The spruikers were at our door and the elixirs were endless. Everyone had a story about a relative or a friend who had survived. And every story had a website. While I listened to these theories with a sceptical ear, I knew they were told with the best intentions and at least they sounded better than chemotherapy.

But before Kerrie could move forward or even start logging into websites she needed a reason. She fingered the stress of two deaths. Prior to Daryl and Elsa passing away she had been fit and healthy and mentally strong.

By the end of the year she had let reiki lapse, she had slipped back into eating fatty foods, we'd stopped walking and she'd lost two people dear to her heart. She reckoned that was enough incentive for cancer to gatecrash.

This time, she said, her recovery would be different. This time she'd maintain the regime, and it would be 'easier living in the Dandenongs'.

I stopped reading the paper.

24 July 2004

Dear Eddie,

What do I know about chemotherapy?

I know people's hair fall out. I know it is associated with cancer patients. And I've been told it's hell.

Six years ago I was sitting with my legs dangling in a Hungarian lake, listening to an Australian nurse talk about her rounds at a London cancer hospital, soaking in a calm, cloudless day, thinking that I didn't have many worries, and the water, despite being icy, was pleasant on my skin. It was not until she mentioned the word 'chemo' that I felt a shiver.

'Chemotherapy is hell,' she told me, her eyes lucid with experience. 'I've seen it too many times. People go through hell. They basically kill your body and then bring you back to life. And most times it doesn't work. I don't know if I could go through with it if the odds weren't stacked firmly in my favour.'

She had seen cancer patients mortgage their houses and sell their possessions, buying any hope they were sold, and ultimately dying with nothing.

'People see doctors as these supreme beings,' she said. 'I get really pissed off.'

I often think back to that conversation and never more than now as your mum sits on a hospital bed waiting to be injected with poison by a nurse who looks like she's dressed for a nuclear power station. They have warned us about the potency of these chemicals – 'no unprotected sex, and always flush the toilet'.

And here I am beside her, my legs dangling over the bed, a murky grey lid on Melbourne's sky, and I'm shivering inside. I want to buy hope and so does Kerrie. Despite weeks of doubt, we have to believe in the oncologist, that there is more reason to trust what he says than his charming disposition. He says the chemotherapy has a 30 per cent success rate with leiomyosarcomas, the new form of Kerrie's cancer. He also says there's a 30 per cent chance the tumour won't return. Kerrie reckons this gives her 60 per cent – 'better than any casino'. For this reason, she says, it will be worth the suffering. That and we come to the conclusion we don't have a choice.

I wait to see if Kerrie's face changes colour or if her hair starts falling out while the chemicals slowly enter her system and when I'm convinced she is going to be all right, for now, I excuse myself and search for a newspaper.

As I sit and flick through the pages I wonder what ever happened to that lakeside nurse. I wonder if she ever left her London cancer hospital and came back to Melbourne. I wonder if she got married or stayed single or even ended up here in Peter Mac. But most of all, Eddie, I wonder if she has changed her mind on chemotherapy. I hope that in six years things have improved, medicine has advanced and it is no longer hell. For your mum's sake.

Love Dad

August 2004

'Welcome to Danny's Juice Bar'. The sign was pinned in the corner of our kitchen, beside the cutting board, underneath the power point and slightly to the left of the toaster. It had been there since Kerrie came home from a body and soul expo with a marvellous little panacea – a juice handbook containing more than 50 different potions claiming to cure anything from flatulence to cellulite.

The recipe pinned on our wall would combat cancer. It was a doozy – among the ingredients were spinach leaves, shiitake mushrooms, garlic and raw beetroot.

In preparation for the first batch I filled the cupboards with fruit, vegetables, bulbs and fungi, although the shiitake mushrooms were hard to find. And hard to pronounce in front of a greengrocer when you're slightly embarrassed and prone to becoming tongue-tied.

Nevertheless, it would be my wizardry and my potions, not my enunciation, that kept cancer at bay. And, hopefully, flatulence because it had become an unpleasant side effect of the chemotherapy – and I thought the nurses wore protective clothing because of the chemicals.

It took a while to dust off the juicer, used once since our wedding, but Kerrie didn't mind the wait. She was happy to have her own juice bar. It was another investment in the new 'us'.

Since chemotherapy, I had joined her renewed pursuit of reiki, closing my eyes and crossing my legs and asking for energy and enlightenment from their divine source. While I hadn't been attuned and didn't share her 'buzz' or feel the same charge of energy coursing through my chakras and my mind whizzed around like a five-cent poker machine, Kerrie was glad for the support. She even took me to her prayer group, proudly introducing me to her fellow members, some of whom looked like they had floundered at a difficult crossing. I was polite and understanding and opened my eyes only once, peeking to make sure none of my new colleagues were disrobing or engaging in lascivious acts while we supposedly had our minds closed in prayer.

I tried to lock out cynicism until we headed home.

'Actually, Kerrie, I think there would be more normal people at a swingers club.'

'I know,' she laughed. 'They are a strange lot. But they are warm and caring and we all need reiki for one reason or another.'

Kerrie didn't laugh when I poured my first juice. Instead she objected to the overbearing fragrance of minced garlic. I chose to ignore her protest.

'Drink up, drink up,' I said. 'This is good for you.'

Not convinced, she took a mouthful and her face contracted like a deflated balloon. She took a moment to gather her composure. I moved in closer, awaiting the verdict.

'Well?'

'I suppose it's not too bad,' she offered.

'Not too bad? It's magnificent. Forget your regular juice bars, this batch is the work of a druid. Go on, have another drink.'

Kerrie couldn't reciprocate my irrepressible enthusiasm.

'All right, but the taste of garlic is pretty strong.'

'I thought you liked garlic.'

'I do, but I usually prefer it in a stir-fry.'

So I took taste-testing upon myself, placing the mug to my mouth and skolling the lot, all the time trying not to gag.

'See, that wasn't too hard,' I spluttered.

Kerrie shook her head. She tried another mouthful – mainly to placate the mad professor staring from across the table – before placing the cup in the fridge and promising to return for more … later.

'In the meantime, maybe you could make me an apple and celery juice?' she said.

'But it's not in the book … but apple and celery aren't in the section under cancer … but … oh, all right.'

Despite ignorant expectations and glimmering belief that Shiitake mushrooms and a host of other nasty-tasting food types could cure cancer, the second night at 'Danny's Juice Bar' was less successful than the first.

After I had once again shown Kerrie I could swallow the lot without vomiting, she took a mouthful before putting the cup to rest.

The third night was worse than the second, pushing me towards a petulant storm. I was wasting ingredients. And my time.

'Kerrie, you have to drink this. I'm making it for your own good. Apple and celery juice is not the recipe for cancer patients. This juice is. Here, it's not that bad. I can drink it.'

The time for humouring me was over. Kerrie flared. Her eyes burned like a lioness about to lose a cub. I waited to be chastened, for her paw to strike.

'I don't like it,' she said forcefully. 'I don't want to drink it.'

'But it's good for you.' I'd taken a backward step, but I wasn't beaten. There was a crisper filled with papaya worth fighting for. Why else would we keep a fruit that smelled like vomit?

'Danny, for God's sake, you can't make me drink this juice. It's awful. I appreciate your sentiments and your efforts, but there's no way I'm going to drink this shit. It smells putrid and it tastes worse.'

'Fine. Make your own fucking juice.'

Two could play at getting annoyed, although my childish ire would come in the form of silence, picking at my wife's defences by refusing to answer her questions with anything more than an ignorant grunt. I retreated to a lounge chair and ignored her, bubbling inside, feeling sorry for myself and frustrated in the way a shop owner might feel when their business goes belly up. I had only been doing my best, trying to help. The one thing I could do, make juice, and she had refused. Darkness followed me around the house, cloaking me in an impenetrable shadow as I prepared lunch for the following day's work, laid out my clothes and went to bed. The relentless drumming of my perceived injustice kept me from sleep.

Why was she pushing me away? Look what happened the last time she wandered from the script, allowing Friday night fish and chips, pizzas and takeaway food to creep back into our diet.

And that's when the cloud lifted, raised by my own malicious thoughts. I felt cold and unfaithful.

How could I be so facile? Cancer wasn't a vicarious illness. I couldn't force my will on her tumour; it would only force us apart.

This was Kerrie's journey.

I made a mental note before drifting towards sleep: chuck the stinky papayas out on bin night.

August 2004

While waiting for chemotherapy to kill her cells, my curious wife started staring at a yellow dot. She brought it home one afternoon, no bigger than a twenty-cent piece on a white sheet of A4 paper, an unremarkable yellow smudge, looking like the work of a five-year-old kid and a highlighter.

'Here, have a look at it,' she said, thrusting the paper in my face.

'What am I meant to do with it?'

'Stare at the dot, and tell me what you see.'

'Nothing. I don't see anything. Just a yellow dot.'

This bloody thumb-sized smudge was giving me nothing.

'Can't you see anything else?' Kerrie persisted.

'Nothing. What am I meant to see? A dog? A horse? Two people engaged in a bit of funny business? Help me out here, Kerrie.'

'A purple haze around the circle's edge.'

'A purple haze? Oh … oh, wait … yes, hang on a minute … yes, I can see a purple haze. There's a purple haze around the yellow dot. What do I win?'

'Peace of mind.'

'Is that all?'

'Purple calms the mind. Professor Sali explained it to me as a doorway to meditation. If you are finding it hard to close your mind, this is a simple way of relaxing. Stare at the yellow dot and when you see the purple halo, close your eyes, retain the colour and your mind will relax. When I do it, I get the same feeling as reiki.'

So my idea of a five-year-old's art project was Kerrie's idea of peace. She watched it like an episode of *The Bold and the Beautiful*.

Professor Sali was a new influence in Kerrie's life. After reading of his growing reputation in newspapers and later on the internet, she had organised a consultation at his Melbourne office. She liked that as a pioneer of integrative medicine he had a foot in both camps, using a joint approach to combating cancer: agreeing that there was a need for aspects of modern medicine, such as surgery, but also a need to complement this by treating your mind and body like a temple.

She liked the importance he placed on exercising the mind: have a confidant; disappear into a movie once a week, particularly a tearjerker; write every day, but be sure to destroy the evidence; meditate; and, above all, be nice to yourself by playing music, gardening or getting a pet.

'It makes sense to me, like creating your own little pressure valve to let off some steam. Psssssst,' she said, twisting an imaginary knob behind her ear.

Then there was his diet. Dark, bitter chocolate, nuts without salt, food without salt, tea without sugar, bread without butter. Life without flavour.

Kerrie wanted to give it a go. But chemo didn't give her a chance.

Friday the 13th, August 2004

I didn't look at the date. I was too preoccupied with my own misery. I should have taken the day off. It was an omen.

While Kerrie reluctantly prepared for her second round of chemotherapy, which would be more potent than her first, I was letting work get me down. I left the office in a foul mood. It was the opening night of the Athens Olympics and I had watched as someone else handpicked the stories and co-ordinated the pages. I was annoyed because as sports editor I thought this should have been my job. Instead, for the next two weeks during the sporting calendar's biggest event, I would be looking after football. No Olympic stories for me.

Rightly or wrongly, I took it as a vote of no confidence. I was sports editor and I thought it was my job to handle the Olympics. The thing that annoyed me most was that I wasn't given a reason. Not even a 'you're struggling to make deadline' or 'it works better this way'.

Once again, Kerrie was left to pick up the pieces, while wearing a hospital dressing gown and waiting for a nurse to wheel in a bucket of nuclear waste.

'Don't worry about it. Maybe they thought you needed a break while I was having chemotherapy. Don't take it so personally,' she said.

'I know, but at least I could have been given a reason.'

Once again Kerrie didn't need the hassle, me stuck in a mental gutter for the unloved, her trying to latch onto my ego and hoist me out.

Ten days after driving Kerrie home from her weekend treatment, indulging myself to think 'this chemotherapy isn't so bad after all', she fell ill. She couldn't eat, she couldn't hold down water, and she lacked energy. Mum and I suggested a doctor, but she insisted she would be okay and the nausea would pass.

'I don't need to go to hospital. Wait until tomorrow, I'll be fine.'

But she wasn't fine. By the following day, Thursday, there was no improvement and on Friday morning she was worse. My mother and I were becoming anxious and yet Kerrie still rebuffed any suggestion of hospital.

When I left for work, I felt like I was abandoning my wife. I didn't know what to do. By the time I arrived at the paper I was feeling bitter. I couldn't see how far I had slipped, unable to recognise the beast bubbling within, making me sneer and jeer when I'd normally offer praise. There was no sharing in national pride as the office cheered our Olympic heroes. The only time I smiled during the Athens Games was when rower Sally Robbins lay down her oar before crossing the finish line. I surreptitiously applauded because she had the audacity to give up, the nerve to let it all go, throw away years of hard work and toil because she didn't feel like fighting.

I wanted someone to call me weak, threaten to throw me in the river. Anything was better than going home and seeing Kerrie suffering.

And I almost got there. I almost broke down and wept, letting the whole office in. The beast's growl turned to a whimper and my chin started to tremble when I was told to change a headline. A stupid bloody headline on a story that didn't matter: 'Walker, Lexus ranger'. I was told it didn't work. I was told using Lexus was a free plug for Collingwood Football Club's major sponsor.

I felt worthless. Not because of the headline. The headline didn't matter. But because I couldn't do anything right. I felt like giving up. I was powerless at home, why not succumb at work? It would make things easier. Lay down, Sally.

Except I couldn't lie down. Some innate pride kept me upright, held my cracking façade in place. I left my desk and sat in a toilet cubicle, willing myself not to cry.

People would talk. He's the guy who cried over a headline. He's the guy who couldn't take the heat. I wasn't ready to drop the oar. Not yet.

I left the cubicle, caught the lift downstairs and went for a walk along the Yarra, sucking in the greasy wind ripping off Melbourne's dirty river. Anything was preferable to the oppressive air that had worked its way up eleven floors of air-conditioning.

I knew there was no time for a walk. Deadline was ten minutes away. I just needed someone to turn me around, someone to clear my head so that I could return to the computer and put the paper to bed. That someone was Roger, a former workmate who saw me picking through the pedestrian traffic and stopped for a chat. I liked Roger. He spoke openly, he took time to listen and he almost always laughed, even when I didn't make sense – like that mad, rambling morning. His eyes smiled and didn't judge. His mellifluous deep, throaty chuckle helped calm my frayed nerves.

* * *

When I made it home, Kerrie made me forget about work. It's not what she said, rather how she looked – pallid, dull-eyed and vague. I'd come home a mess, but she was worse. She needed to go to hospital and was too feeble to argue. I walked her to the car, my arm around her waist, practically lifting her feet like a puppeteer. She was scrambled, her speech audible but disjointed. I left her in the passenger seat, saying I'd be back in a second. I needed to grab the house keys off Mum. But when I returned, her mind was gone – her head lolled across the seat, mouth agape, nothing but the whites of her eyes.   My arse closed and my guts shrank.

'Kerrie, wake up. Kerrie.'

I straightened her head, gently squeezing her shoulder.

'Kerrie? Are you all right? Kerrie, wake up.'

Slowly her pupils rolled forward, finding the horizon and fixing on my face, bringing back her mind.

'Call an ambulance,' I demanded of Mum, heartbeats kicking at my ribs.

'I don't think we're covered,' Kerrie whispered.

'Jesus, Kerrie, I thought you were dead.'

23 August 2004

Time machines were too complicated. One twiddle and the ripple became a tsunami. I'd seen it in movies: interfere and people ceased to exist. No, what I needed was a revolving door; one that could swing me out of trouble.

I'd gone to visit Kerrie, an unsuspecting victim. Her sights were trained the moment I stepped into her ward. Not even an, 'I'm fine, thank you.'

'We've got to take control of our lives, Danny,' she said from a chair beside her hospital bed. 'I need *YOU* to take control of our lives. One of us has to be more assertive, make decisions. We can no longer drift along. I don't like Pascoe Vale. I can't live there anymore, it's treeless and bleak and depressing.'

She was feeling better then! No longer severely dehydrated, a platelet transfusion had helped restore her energy, but worst of all it appeared Dr Phil had been giving her relationship counselling. Fucking Dr Phil. I needed to cut the cord on her midday TV.

'When I get out of here, we need to make changes,' she continued. 'I need *YOU* to drive them. Otherwise we'll never break out of our rut. You know what we're like. You could cut down to four days a week at work and we could move up to Emerald. I feel a connection with the hills, I would be close to my aunties and it would be a good environment for Eddie. We could have a wood fire. Maybe I could work one or two days a week.'

'Okay, Kerrie,' I said.

Okay. That's all I could manage. Okay. Okay. Okay.

But I knew with or without decisions cancer had me by the balls. It was the reason we needed to move, and the reason we had to stay.

We needed the fresh air, but we needed to be close to the cancer institute.

A new environment would be invigorating; moving house would snap me in half.

I could do with less time at work, but not a four-day pay packet.

Kerrie needed me to make decisions, but she had to maintain her independence.

'Okay, Kerrie. Okay.'

28 August 2004

The Dandenongs!

I felt claustrophobic, hemmed in by towering trees as we navigated the steep, winding roads looking at rental properties. I started clicking my jaw to unblock my ears.

'This house looks okay,' Kerrie said, switching off the car.

'Where are we?'

'Belgrave Heights. This is where Mum grew up. This is where her parents had their corner store. This is where I spent my holidays as a kid, flying across from Adelaide to visit Nana Edward, spending time with Aunty Annette and girl cousin Jenny.'

It was the fifth address we had scanned that day. Five times the feeling of dread as we swung into driveways, me silently begging the spirit of each house not to tug at Kerrie, lull her into a sense of belonging that had decided our houses in the past.

I didn't want to move to the Dandenong Ranges. They were too far from the city. It would mean almost three hours a day on public transport. But I couldn't tell Kerrie. I knew I had to make sacrifices and share her enthusiasm, but I couldn't take control of our lives.

September 2004

Back in 1996, not long after my twenty-sixth birthday I walked into Edward Scissorhands off Balaclava Road and asked the burly Russian barber to shave my head. Baldness wasn't a decision, it was a matter of time and I wanted to steal a march on my receding hairline. While Kerrie thought it looked and felt great, rubbing her palm over my stubbly noggin, my work colleagues weren't convinced. Some of them were shocked. They shouldn't have been. My cover had been disappearing for years, the deforestation program revealing unsightly tracts of scalp, making me look older, and isolating wispy strands of hair so they blew across my forehead.

I didn't have a spare couple of grand for a transplant and Bert Newton put me off wigs so shaving was my only option. Besides, the positives outweighed the negatives.

Upside: no bad hair days, money saved on hair products, dandruff-free jackets, and no more shower caps. Okay, I never wore shower caps in the first place, but there was certainly no need to buy them in the future.

Downside: cold nights.

Kerrie always laughed when I slipped under the Doona during winter months, my body suffering mini-tremors because I couldn't keep the top of my head warm. My scalp acted like a conduit for cold and the chill ran to my toes. I reacted like a warm foot being licked by an icy ocean, except there was no running up the beach to safety.

Kerrie always reckoned I overreacted.

'*FOR FUCK'S SAKE, I CAN'T BELIEVE HOW BLOOOOODY COLD IT IS,*' I yelled, flipping around the bed, searching for a hot pocket of air.

It always made her laugh.

'Oh, you poor thing,' she twittered, unsympathetically.

Little did she know eight years later the tables would turn.

I showed slightly more compassion than Kerrie when she decided to steal a march on chemotherapy by having me run a set of clippers through her hair, watching great clumps of womanhood fall to the lino. Thankfully, it suited her smooth, rounded skull, high cheekbones, strong ears and soft face. Even her fading freckles sat kindly.

'Brrrrrrrr,' she complained, slipping under the covers and trying to nestle her scalp under my armpit.

'I think I'm owed an apology,' I twittered, unsympathetically. 'I told you it was cold. Didn't believe me, did you?'

'Okay, okay, you were right, but I'm not apologising. Hand me your beanie.'

Apart from the colder nights, Kerrie slipped seamlessly into baldness. I thought she carried the look with the same poise and power as Sinead O'Connor. Not until her prominent, dark eyebrows started dropping like autumn leaves did she lament her appearance. She found it harder to leave the house, suffering mild attacks of paranoia when she went for a drive, when she went shopping or when she took Eddie to the park.

'I feel like a freak,' she said. 'People stare at me and it's terrible. I was walking down the street today and this young woman just kept staring at me. I felt tiny.'

I tried to temper her fears.

'Everyone stares,' I reasoned. 'I find myself gawking at people each time I cross the Yarra River footbridge near work, but not because I think they're freaks. People are curious. They might actually think you're beautiful with your shaved, Sinead O'Connor head and want to check you out.'

'I don't think so.'

'At least people are looking at you. It would be worse if they tried to avoid your gaze. What about that girl at Carmel's party? She said you looked great.'

Kerrie didn't look like a freak; she looked like a cancer patient. Even with scarves and hats, it was unavoidable. And yet I don't think her feelings of inadequacy and waves of self-consciousness stemmed entirely from her look. Her sinking energy levels were also to blame. She felt like she had a permanent dose of the 'flu. For two months she had been unable to shake lethargy, struggling to feel alive.

'I'm sick of feeling sick,' she complained.

Spring 2004

Dear Eddie,

I must be cracking up. I've started to believe in a horse.

Northerly, a horse that has won me money on racing's biggest stages: Cox Plates and a Caulfield Cup.

Since trainer Fred Kersley announced his great champion was returning from a serious injury that many had considered career threatening, I have surreally linked it to your mum's health. If Northerly can win again, then Kerrie can beat cancer.

She thinks I'm slightly mad, but I point out her history with clairvoyants. 'You've got to invest your faith in something, right?' I say. 'I mean, you've been staring at a yellow dot.'

I always laughed when people likened Phar Lap to a bright light during the Depression. After all, he was only a horse.

But now I need a horse. Now I need Northerly. Grandma Elsa loved him; he's an unfashionable thoroughbred with a giant heart and has run and won during the greatest moments of our lives – our wedding day, during our honeymoon, the day before you were born. If he is coming back from injury, surely it is a sign?

What is so wrong in believing in a horse?

Love Dad

October 2004

'Listen, can you hear that?' my mother asked.

'What?' I looked up from the paper.

'Singing. It's coming from the bathroom. Kerrie is singing.'

We stood there listening, like farmers hearing heavy rains on their corrugated iron roofs during a drought. Her voice seeped through the walls.

'She is singing,' my mother marvelled, almost as if she expected me to pinch her. 'She must be feeling better. I haven't heard her sing for a long time.'

It was true. During four cycles of chemotherapy and two miserable months I had not heard her hum. This was heavenly.

When Kerrie walked from the bathroom, a towel wrapped around her torso, and marched down the passageway to our bedroom, she was oblivious to our gaping mouths. We continued to stare after her, spellbound. We were reaching the other end. Kerrie was feeling better. She was singing again. She was no longer sick of feeling sick.

'What's the matter?' Kerrie asked when she re-emerged.

'Nothing's the matter, Kerrie. Nothing's the matter at all.'

7 October 2004

'Where's that yellow dot, Kerrie?' I asked.

'It's on the fridge door, underneath a magnet. Why?'

'I need to look at it for a while.'

'Anything the matter?'

'Yeah, Northerly's comeback is over. He broke down during a training gallop and has been retired.'

'I'm sorry, honey.'

'So am I.'

October 2004

Riding my bike became a great distraction; 16 kilometres to unwind along a path from work through the suburbs to home. It also allowed me to set a goal: Around the Bay in a Day, a 210 kilometres organised ride circumnavigating Melbourne's Port Phillip Bay. Brian and I had done it before and we planned on doing it again, phoning each other daily for motivation and support.

'I haven't ridden at all this week, what about you?'

'Nah, me neither.'

'But I'm going to go for a couple of rides next week.'

'Yeah, me too.'

This conversation played out like a broken record until I began to fear we wouldn't breach the city's outskirts when it came to the big event. So I started riding home from work, using Kerrie as inspiration.

Each afternoon when I switched off the computer and felt like catching the train, embarrassed at being seen by colleagues in my lycra riding gear or exhausted at the prospects of a head wind or a cold day, I thought about Kerrie.

Because of my wife I had the nerve to consider riding 210 kilometres in a day. Because of Kerrie I didn't make the start.

She picked up a virus and I needed to stay home and look after Eddie. Sadly, Kerrie felt like she was letting me down, despondent that her health was once again sabotaging my dreams. She was wrong. I felt relieved not to ride and so did my arse.

'Kerrie, you have saved me a great deal of pain. Our training was barely enough to get us halfway around. It would have been a slog. I'm more relieved than disappointed, so rather than blame you, I say thank you.'

Meanwhile, Brian rose to tackle the cycling marathon alone, changing into his padded bike shorts, packing parcels of food and wheeling his bike down three flights of stairs only to discover a puncture. Back up the stairs and half an hour later, he, too, decided to stay home. We promised to tackle the event the following year.

'And this time I'm going to start training early and get a lot of miles in my legs.'

'Me too.'

23 October 2004

Why did I get home at 5 am?

Where do I start?

Winning $500 on Bomber Bill in the third race. Drinking a production line of Crown Lagers because of the win. Flirting with a woman from the office after she informed me, 'I'm single now.' Or mingling with 40,000 gregarious racegoers planning for party land while I contemplated returning to a suburban house and toy trains by 7 pm.

They were all to blame. One led to another. Euphoric from successful gambling and beer, I was prone to misinterpretation, susceptible to beguiling lines. Instead of 'I'm single now' inviting normal conversation and slotting in with reels of other inane comments and dull observations, to me it sounded like a suggestion.

Oh, the power of suggestion.

Party land or wooden trains by 7 pm?

A woman I loved deeply who was temporarily removed from physical intimacy because of a horrible illness or a single woman from the office?

For a moment, or the many moments it took to make up an afternoon, I lost myself.

I had flirted with this woman at work, teased and even imagined, but there was never any depth to our interaction. Until now. On Cox Plate day. In the members' stand. Dressed up, drinking Crown Lagers. A pity to waste an opportunity. And, for once, my conscience agreed.

Me: *Charming behaviour isn't cheating behaviour, right?*

My conscience: No. But I'm not sure you are capable of charming.

Well, forget charming, but what's the harm in soaking up a woman's touch each time she grabs your arm in response to a corny one-liner?

No harm at all. Everyone's fully clothed, public arena, nothing untoward here. But try and ramp up the one-liners, champ. Falling a bit flat at the moment.

Sure. Will do my best. Should we buy 'I'm Single Now' a drink?

Definitely. Get her friends one as well. Don't want to be too forward.

What about backing Lad of the Manor in the next race?

Shit. Almost forgot. Must back Lad of the Manor. There's a TAB outlet next to the bar.

What about Kerrie?

Kerrie? Oh yes, Kerrie. She'll be fine. She's got Grandpa Des at home and it's only flirting.

That's all?

That's all.

So, home by 7 pm?

You've got to be joking.

Courtney and I grabbed a six-pack of beer and sat down to dinner at an Indian restaurant in Collingwood, swapping yarns about those we loved and loathed at work and laughing about our absurd luck at the track. I even felt relaxed enough to talk about Kerrie's health, betrayed only by my bloody rickety chin. I had to get that chin fixed. Maybe spray it with starch.

Apart from my editor, Courtney became the only person at work whom I confided in about Kerrie's cancer. Probably because he was more than a colleague; he was a mate.

And he, too, was to blame for my 5 am finish. Well, sort of.

'Let's go for a drink,' he said after we paid the bill.

'Sure, why not.'

We met up again with 'I'm Single Now', but by then I recognised my delusions for what they were, dropping the corny one-liners and ceasing to hold out my elbow for her hand. She was still sexy and single, that was for sure. I also recognised she had no interest in me. And even if she did, I had curry breath.

24 October 2004

Kerrie hated my wild nights. She hated that I never called. She felt jilted because I was out in pubs and clubs filled with nubile women, paranoid I was no longer attracted to a wife who felt sexless and limp. No words came when she left the bedroom, less than three hours after I made it home.

Feeling like a lump of shit, I reckoned the only way out was to get out. I crawled from bed, grabbed Grandpa Des and hitched a ride with Brian to the Kilmore trots, topping up on beer from the night before.

By the time we made it home I knew winning wasn't everything. Sometimes winning was losing. After drinking all day Saturday, dining out, drinking until 5 am and spending Sunday afternoon at Kilmore trots, I still had $50 from my $500 windfall. But I would have been a better person had I lost in the first place.

28 October 2004

Dear Eddie,

Happy third birthday. Home from work and Kerrie is fussing around the table, waiting for heavy-headed Grandpa to arise from his afternoon bear cave for candle-lighting duties. Despite her aversion to public appearances, your mum has braved shopping centres and their toy stores, using beanies to hide her 'chemo features' while searching for birthday gifts. She has also forgiven my drunken dalliances. What a great woman. I love your mum. Maybe getting Mark Ricciuto's autograph at the races was a saving grace.

The Thomas the Tank Engine trains are a hit, being wheeled in and out of a chip bowl as I throw my overladen backpack into a corner and kiss you on the head. Feeling better, thank you, it took only four days to get over my binge weekend. Not that you've noticed my prolonged hangover. Henry, the big green engine, is the centre of your affections, usurping Gordon, the big blue engine. Good choice, son. Gordon is an insolent old snob anyway, always bragging about his carriage-pulling abilities.

We reckon you'll be a train driver when you grow up, although there's a predilection for trams to contend with. Before Kerrie's fourth and last round of chemotherapy the three of us took a trip on Melbourne's city circle tram and before long you started imitating the conductor, telling people to 'move up, move up, watch your step' as they queued for a ride. Most of the pasty-faced commuters looked perplexed being ordered around by an ostentatious three-year-old, but the conductor was so amused and grateful for assistance she offered you her job.

'Maybe he can drive instead,' I said.

What a couple of months we've had: Mum being dragged through hell, me losing the plot, Granny Kath and Pa helping hold us together. We even had a visit from the Paddle Pop Lion. Much to our amusement and your joy, he showed up at the front door with Chel, barely fitting his gigantic head under our porch to say hello. Poor Lion. After handing you a bagful of ice-creams, giving you a giant cuddle and playing tug-of-war with his tail, he almost fainted from the heat, and we had to usher you back inside before you were traumatised by an eight-foot lion pulling his own head off. Miraculously, Brian arrived at the door minutes later … in a lather of sweat.

Oh, and another thing. While we're on the topic of oversized beasts, during your mum's chemotherapy you started calling the biggest bear at Peter Mac daddy bear. But I don't mind, honestly. You can call him mummy if you like.

Love Dad

November 2004

I loved telling people the story about my poor mother being hit in the head by a golf ball. It illustrated the illusion of luck.

My mum was left stunned and bleeding from a wound on her forehead after her playing partner laid into a fairway wood and the ball ricocheted off a tree before she had time to duck. Taken dazed to the hospital, Mum was further confounded by the doctor's response.

'You're lucky,' he said as he stitched the cut, 'the ball could have hit you in the eye.'

'I don't feel very lucky,' she replied.

For one week I enjoyed dialling my TAB phone account just to hear the automated voice announce, 'Your account balance is one thousand dollars.'

Despite Northerly breaking down, robbing my spring carnival of an amulet, the winners had kept coming – Elvstroem in the Caulfield Cup, Makybe Diva's second Melbourne Cup, Takeover Target in the Salinger sprint, and Oaks winner Hollow Bullet.

While Kerrie knew I was winning by the good moods and bouncy steps, she didn't ask how much and I was reluctant to divulge profits in case she whipped out her avaricious credit cards.

One week of back-patting bliss, and then the ambulance bill arrived. More than $700.

'But I thought we were covered,' I moaned.

'There's a two-month waiting period for pre-existing illnesses. It says here on the bill. I didn't join early enough,' Kerrie said.

How could she be so calm? Especially after the paramedics insisted there was nothing to worry about when they loaded her in the back.

'But they told you not to worry,' I said.

'I know. They obviously didn't want me to worry.'

'But chemotherapy is not an illness. It's fucking torture.'

'I know, honey. I know.'

'What bullshit is a two-month waiting period? Are they trying to encourage people to take risks, drive a sick person to hospital because they can't afford an ambulance? I'm going to fight this.'

'Don't, Danny. Let's just pay the bill.'

Sitting down for a coffee, I expected Brian to load my guns. He had a strong sense of injustice, capable of turning common sense into a diatribe to hammer home a point. Together we would bring the ambulance service down.

As he listened intently, occasionally shaking his head in disbelief, I expected he was compiling a case in our defence. I certainly didn't expect his benign response.

'Look, fight it if you want to, but whatever you do, don't make it Kerrie's problem. She doesn't need to worry about this right now.'

What? Not Kerrie's problem? She was the one loaded into the ambulance. Her eyes disappeared into her head. Her name was on the bill. How could he say it wasn't her problem? Here was my socialist mate, the guy who had argued over tram tickets, telling me to play it cool. Didn't he know there was a TAB phone account at stake?

'Yeah, yeah, Brian, I won't make it Kerrie's problem. But I'm going to fight this. I'm telling you, this is unfair.'

I missed my bedtime compiling a letter of complaint. I argued that Kerrie needed an ambulance because of an overdose of chemotherapy drugs, which was hardly a pre-existing condition. If anything, the doctors had stuffed up. Therefore we should be exempt from paying the bill.

'Kerrie, can you read this for me and see if it makes sense?'

'Sure, honey. What is it?'

'It's …' I looked at her bald head and missing eyebrows and I heard Brian's words.

'It's nothing, Kerrie. Don't worry.'

My letter was futile, eliciting little more than a 'sorry Mr Russell, but you have to pay'. Your wife has cancer, she wasn't outside the two-month waiting period, and you have to pay. Pay. Pay. Pay. Pay. Pay.

So I took my winnings and paid the bill, heeding Brian's advice by cursing the bastards under my breath and not in front of Kerrie. But I needed a doctor's perspective: was I lucky to have won the money in the first place, or unlucky it was gone?

* * *

Kerrie didn't need to tell me. I knew she was again probing her past. I knew she was again hunting out ghosts, putting herself on trial, playing God to determine whether in some perverse way cancer could possibly be a punishment or a self-induced sore. Why else had she booked in for an inner-child workshop last year? Why else would she decide to see a hypnotherapist?

'Kerrie, I hope you don't blame yourself or anything from your past for what you are going through now?'

'No, I don't.'

'Because you are a good person. You don't deserve this.'

But sometimes no amount of assurance is enough. Kerrie met with a hypnotherapist after deciding she had shaken the debilitating chemotherapy hangover.

She came away from the session feeling washed from the inside out, having shed tears and purged repressed anger. It helped, but not in the way I expected.

'You'll be glad to know I didn't blame you or Eddie,' she said after explaining her liberating afternoon on the couch.

'I didn't realise you considered blaming me and Eddie.'

'I didn't. You just don't know what is going to come out.'

'What did come out?'

'Bobby, among other people. I thought of Bobby and I was really angry with him. Bizarre because I haven't thought of Bobby for a long time, it was strange that he popped into my head.'

'What did you do?'

'I cried. I cried about a lot of things.'

So Bobby was partly to blame. I wouldn't have guessed. Kerrie had a crush on Bobby soon after her first operation in 1992. They'd interacted and connected, but in the end her expectations had been punctured. While I thought their relationship was largely a non-event, mainly because that's how Kerrie had painted their brief liaison more than twelve years ago, I guess she'd never shaken the feeling of rejection.

The exercise proved cathartic and Kerrie was able to postpone the trial, no longer feeling the need to play judge and jury with her past.

'I feel so much better,' she said.

'I'm glad. But are you sure you don't blame me and Eddie? Because I'm a little worried now.'

'Honey, I'm sure.'

10 November 2006

Dear Kerrie,

I'm still feeling blue after a mammoth session three days ago at the Melbourne Cup so I'm driving Eddie to the cemetery to visit your ashes. It's his first time so I explain we are taking some flowers out for 'Mummy'.

'But Mummy is in heaven looking down on us,' he counters.

'That's true,' I say, 'but she left us some special ashes and they are kept behind her picture so we'll put some flowers in a vase for her. How's that sound?'

'Okay.'

They're not your only ashes, Kerrie. I'm afraid you've been split in three. It all sounds a bit macabre, but it was all part of your wishes and mine. First of all, Eddie and I spread some in the Murray River at the bend you gazed so fondly upon while living at my parents' house. I didn't know what to use so I grabbed a tablespoon from Mum's drawer and we took turns of scooping you out and tossing you in the water. Ed had no idea what we were doing, but he thought it was a hoot and I'll remind him of the significance in years to come.

The rest of you I sent to Adelaide in a Moccona coffee jar to be spread at your childhood beach at Seacliff. I'm sorry about the jar but I was short on urns and ideas. They wanted to seal the plaque at the cemetery and I was running out of time, and … well, I panicked.

Anyway, we're at Cobram cemetery now and Eddie has discovered the infants' graves and wants to play with the cars and trucks that have been carefully placed around the headstones. I tell him to leave the toys and come and say hello to you first. He runs up to your plaque, looks at your picture, says, 'Hi, Mummy' and then runs off.

'Don't take any of those toys away, will you?' I call after Eddie.

'How come?'

'Because they belong where they are.'

After a short time he wanders over and asks me to count while he runs around a line of graves. When he gets back he wants to run farther and asks me to count again, oblivious to who or what he is running around.

Next, he says it's my turn. My initial reaction is to say no. People don't visit cemeteries to conduct time trials. They go to place flowers, reflect and pay their respects. Don't they?

But then I think, what the hell, you won't mind if we run. I take off, retracing Eddie's steps as he counts to ten and beyond.

'Fifteen … sixteen … seventeen … eighteen. Eighteen! Good one, Dad. My turn.'

Thankfully, the cemetery is deserted and we run until we're exhausted and it's time to say goodbye. We kiss your picture and I feel incredibly serene. I don't know if it's the exercise, laughing with Eddie, the calming vista of orchards and river gums or that you've gently touched me on the shoulder.

Either way, we're doing okay.

Miss you,

love Danny

16 November 2006

Dear Kerrie,

At least you're in heaven; I'm just a dad. Not like Makaylah's father, who's an ambulance driver. I can't compete. Not in Eddie's eyes. Not since he's been comparing notes with other kids.

'She's very lucky because he drives an ambulance. You're just a dad,' he says.

'Oh! Do you wish I was an ambulance officer?'

'No, I wished you drove a fire truck,' he says.

I try to talk up the stocks of a single parent who dabbles in writing, but I don't have a uniform and Eddie's not impressed.

'Yeah, you're a writer. So is Granny, she wrote a story about the Teenage Mutant Ninja Turtles because I told her to,' he says.

So there you are, I'm just a dad and no better a writer than Granny, even though she's being told what to jot down and her words look like chook scratches because her wrist is still broken and she's holding the pen in her left hand.

At least when her wrist mends and she can pick up a paintbrush again, I'll consider her a good artist. And that's more than 'just a mum'.

Miss you,
love Danny

22 November 2006

Dear Kerrie,

Our son has started to crawl. As you know, this is no video-camera-worthy event. Eddie is five. It's hard to take because Eddie was such an early bloomer, walking since his first wobbly dash from the coffee table to the TV as a ten-month-old. We gave each other high-fives.

So how did we arrive back at crawling? I am equally confused.

There's the bee incident. The one when he was stung on the foot while shooting flowers with his water pistol. The one when the scream sounded like he was being dragged down the driveway by a crocodile.

But that's two and a half days ago now and surely a kid recovers faster than that?

Admittedly all this comes on the back of a nasty, week-long cold that has sapped his tolerance and resistance levels, but no matter how many bribes I offer in return for a shuffle, or the numerous amounts of placebos I convince him to swallow, he remains steadfast that his foot is too puffy, too swollen and too sore to put on the ground.

Instead he's resorted to hauling himself out of bed and around the floor on all fours.

From my experience, boys grow into predominantly two types. Those who career headlong into trees, light poles or brick walls only to shake their heads, pick themselves off the ground and charge towards the next inanimate object. Then there are those who believe the appearance of a droplet of blood means their death is imminent, such as Eddie.

Of course, then there is Josh. Josh is an identical twin who suffers from cerebral palsy, needing a small walking frame to move around. He goes to Eddie's kindergarten and the entire class knows he's different. They might ask his adult carer to open their stubborn, air-tight muesli bar packets, or remove a persistent yoghurt lid, but unlike Josh they don't need her help for basic things such as getting to and from the toilet.

And it would be reasonably safe to assume that Josh knows he's different, too. He just doesn't seem to care. He can play practical jokes, interact during game time, interrupt the teachers at inappropriate moments and he probably cries when stung by a bee. But there is one big difference between Josh and Eddie: Josh refuses to believe he can't walk.

Ever since we've known him, Josh's movement has improved. So much so, that he sometimes discards the walking frame and makes an unaided dash across the playground. It is not without its staggering, teetering moments, but it makes the other kids so excited they cheer.

As for our son, I'm becoming so worried that I ask him whether he will ever stand on his own two feet again.

'No,' he says calmly.

So I ask him how he will cope crawling for the rest of his life.

'I'm going to stay inside,' he says calmly.

So I ask him what he will do inside for the rest of his life.

'Play with my trains. And play with my cars. And do some drawings. And do some prophecy. And turn the fan on to keep people cool. That's what I'll do,' he says.

I have no idea what doing 'some prophecy' means and the competitive father side of my nature – the part that wants Eddie to be faster, higher, stronger than his peers – is becoming increasingly annoyed by his lack of willpower to overcome the pain.

I am tempted to yell at him, despite being told by my own parents that when I was Eddie's age I ran around my grandfather's backyard screaming that I was going to die after being stung by a bee. I am tempted to yell because I'm fairly confident that back then I was walking within the hour.

But, I didn't lose my mother to cancer when I was five. So I guess I don't really know his pain. And as a result I don't yell. Instead I try and stay true to your compassionate nature, probing my brain for a solution and starting to feel a little helpless.

I keep thinking what it must have been like for Josh's mother to learn that one of her twins would always be less capable than the other, that he would need special care.

How she must feel when one son runs to the gate, and his twin struggles along behind.

And then I remember that she doesn't talk to Josh any differently than she talks to his brother. That's the key.

I realise that despite his own loss, Eddie barracks just as loudly as his classmates when Josh takes his great steps forward. He might not yet have the courage to overcome pain, but he can recognise it in others. And there's something special about that.

Actually, I think I can him hear him getting off the floor. Excuse me while I go and cheer.

Miss you,
love Danny

5 December 2006

Dear Kerrie,
We are ten minutes late for school orientation day and because of your son's social confidence there's absolutely nowhere to hide. He waltzes

into reception and before I have a chance to quietly ask for directions he's announcing to Rosemary behind the counter, 'I'm Eddie Russell and I'm five years old. Are you my teacher?'

Then he marches through the staff room, which is filled with rookie parents having a calming cup of coffee and dealing with 'separation anxiety', and announces, 'Hi everybody, I'm here.'

Next, it's into the classroom, striding confidently through the door to meet his Prep teacher for next year. A menacing shape suddenly blocks my view. It's the school principal, acting like border security: no parents go in and no kids come out.

'He'll be all right,' she says. 'You can go and have a coffee if you like; meet some of the other parents.'

Normally, I wouldn't worry, but Eddie's only been awake for five minutes. We've just arrived from Melbourne and he's been asleep in the car. And he hasn't had any breakfast after rejecting McDonald's muffins. And his hair is a mess. I want to make sure he's okay, but I don't have a choice. The border security is too tight.

Which is probably just as well because Eddie is in the classroom blabbing to his teacher about being tired and short of sleep. Thankfully he omits the part about no breakfast.

Later the teacher tells me Eddie shouldn't experience any problems fitting into school, and I agree. But I'm not so sure about myself. He's not as clingy anymore. There's no more dropping everything, followed by a running hug. I'm becoming superfluous to needs.

I'm thinking about this growing independence in the uniform shop when a woman takes pity on me because I'm a father and look like I need help. Without prompting she picks out shirts, shorts, a jumper and a hat. She tells me to try them on Eddie. I tell him to strip off, but have to restrain him before he dashes around the room in his jocks.

'You won't be able to wear red shirts next year,' I say.

'Yep, I know,' he says.

It looms as the biggest hurdle. All the loves of his life are red: Murray the Red Wiggle, Lightning McQueen, the Sydney Swans, the red Power Ranger, even a red pillow.

Maybe he misses your hair.

I know I do.

Miss you,

love Danny

18 December 2006

Dear Kerrie,

Happy birthday, darling.

It's hard to believe you're not here.

Sometimes shaking my head in sad disbelief is all I can do to stop myself crying.

Miss you,

love Danny

22 December 2006

Dear Kerrie,

Hashim is not doing his job.

You know Hashim? Our World Vision sponsor kid from Ethiopia.

His father is a peasant farmer. No, not ringing a bell?

Anyway, his picture sits on Eddie's bookcase as proof of the vast chasm existing between the haves (us) and the have-nots (Hashim's family). The sponsorship's my way of paying homage to my parents and their impotent mantra when, as kids, we refused to eat our vegetables: 'I don't care if you're not hungry, children are starving in Africa.'

But to better illustrate the point I've put a face to the suffering. When Eddie starts prattling on about the long list of goodies he wants for Christmas, I point to the picture and remind him that Hashim doesn't have any toys. Not that it matters to Eddie.

'Well, we'll send him some toys and some more money,' he says.

'I'm afraid that's not how it works.'

'How come?'

'Because we don't have that much money.'

While I'm trying to teach our son to reach a higher level of understanding, I'm not really helping matters because I've already filled the cupboard with his Christmas presents.

At least he's eating his vegetables.

Everyone wants to spoil Eddie this Christmas. You can hear the compassion in their words, see the concern in their faces and recognise their desire to help by the size of their gifts. Well, I feel it. I'm not sure Eddie does ... yet. And that's what people don't quite understand. Eddie's too young to fully grasp the enormity of what he's lost. No amount of books, jigsaw puzzles, toy guns, cars and trucks will make a five-year-old comprehend the Kerrie-sized hole in his life. He's too focused on the gifts.

But I appreciate the kindness. I wish I could gather their benevolence and place it in a bottle, keep it for the future when Eddie is struggling to cope without his mum – as a teenager wanting to talk about girls, when he gets annoyed with his dad, at his twenty-first, when he gets married, and when he has children of his own.

Because I'm scared that when he matures and needs you most, there'll no longer be people with presents queuing at the door.

Miss you,

love Danny

Christmas Day, 2006

Dear Kerrie,

The morning starts in a whirl. Eddie rips apart the wrapping on his first present to reveal a Lightning McQueen racetrack. His eyes brighten.

'How did Santa know this is what I wanted?' he says.

The gift is enough. It's all he wants. I could have saved on shopping and wrapping paper. In fact, we have to convince Eddie to unwrap

some more. They don't have the same impact, but he's happy
nonetheless.

And so am I until we drive to the cemetery for a Christmas beer
by your plaque. Tears catch me unawares. As I wipe them away I
remember your words: 'Danny, I think the key is not to avoid sadness,
but surrender to it now and again. No one can live without sadness. If
they have, they haven't really lived. And if you don't get sad, against
what other emotion can you measure your times of happiness?'

We arrive in Adelaide two days later with two presents under the
tree and no Des. He's in hospital with a cooked bladder, the nasty
side effect of his prostate radiotherapy. Apparently he spent two days
unable to pee and was at the point of bursting before ringing Brendan
and being rushed to hospital.

He still managed to leave Eddie a *Cars* clock and a Lightning
McQueen lunchbox under the Christmas tree. The house is barren
without him, although we've brought my parents over for extra
support and we'll endeavour to visit him each day.

Miss you,
love Danny

29 December 2006

Dear Kerrie,
If this letter has an aggressive tone it is because I can't believe you
slept with a German. Well, not that I have anything against Germans,
they're good people in my experience; a little too punctual, but good
people. I just can't believe you slept with another man, who happened
to be German, under my watch. Well, not exactly under my watch,
but certainly at a time when I knew you, and had not dismissed the
thought of someday rekindling our relationship. And maybe you didn't
even sleep with him in the first place. But that's what I was told.

'What about the time Kerrie stayed with that German bloke in
Munich?' Linda said.

German bloke? What fucking German bloke?

Two things surprise me about this conversation: I can't believe someone ACTUALLY told me about the German bloke, and two, I can't believe I'm so gutted.

I keep thinking, why didn't Kerrie tell me this story?

My paranoia mechanism has switched into overdrive: What else didn't you tell me about your life? Who else did you sleep with on my watch (all right, it wasn't my watch, and maybe you didn't sleep with him, but maybe there was someone else on my watch)?

It doesn't matter that we weren't an item at the time, or that we'd broken up because I was pursuing my own selfish dreams, or that I was sleeping with a Swedish girl. It matters that the whole episode feels like it happened two weeks ago. It matters that you're not here to put the story into perspective.

Despite trying to sedate my emotions with common sense, my twisted gut keeps writhing so bloody much that all I can bring myself to do is go back to your father's house, get drunk and smoke a packet of cigarettes.

It's two days later, my throat is still raw from the fags and you can forget about the German. I'm over the German. I've decided you didn't sleep with him and if you did, who cares? I mean, I was no angel, right?

Besides I'd rather focus on Des. He hasn't made it home from hospital to welcome in the New Year because he's still struggling with his waterworks. Although I'm hoping it might be a blessing that he won't be able to grandstand on the balcony at five past midnight and wish for a better year ahead 'because it couldn't be any worse than the last one'. For three years now this wish has been ignored.

The celebrating has been left to my parents and me, although I did call down and see Brendan and Jane for a couple of beers earlier on. It's now 10 pm, Eddie is asleep after feigning mild interest in the Brighton fireworks and I make Mum and Dad promise they won't put the mozz on 2007 by wishing for a better year ahead.

Mum stays true to the promise because she's gone off to bed in disbelief after Dad and I argue that we did our fair share of work during the preparation of Christmas dinner, namely pop the champagne bottles and drink them, while she was stuck with the cooking and the cleaning up.

Content to have won the verbal stoush, Dad and I sit back in our chairs, stretch out our legs, listen to Johnny Cash, sip at our glasses and count down the clock.

It's midnight, the end of 2006. Fireworks explode over the city, light up Glenelg jetty and appear intermittently across the bayside suburbs.

'Happy New Year,' I mutter, giving Dad a hug and wanting to change the subject.

'Let's hope for a better one ahead,' he says.

Miss you,

love Danny

25 December 2004

Dear Eddie,

Mum is no longer a wavy redhead. Her hair is growing back, but straight and dun-coloured. It looks fantastic. Her skin has a healthy lustre and her insides must be glowing, judging by the number of times she breaks into song. I have never seen her more beautiful.

Her recent scans have been positive and she announces we are no longer moving to the Dandenong Ranges: 'I actually don't mind living here. I love the Dandenongs, but it's not very practical.' What a relief!

I am enjoying work, we are enjoying being a family and you will be starting childcare next year.

Our life is back and I pray that all our Christmases will be so happy.

Granny and Pa are excited to have us all home in Cobram – Uncle Chris, Uncle Pete, Aunty Hayley, Georgia and Johnny – helping surround their Christmas tree with more gifts and filling their lounge room with more excitement. The dinner table is crammed with food, drinks are overflowing and we are filling the house with noise.

For once, Eddie, I am not hung-over on Christmas Day, eschewing the Cobram tradition of flocking to the Top Pub on Christmas Eve and boozing it up with old friends. There's one enormous benefit to having a clear head: I'm able to make it off the couch to share your excited face. Presents galore. Lego sets, bouncy balls, play dough. You've got it all. And there's more to come. We're heading across the Mallee tomorrow to spend a week in Adelaide with Grandpa Des.

Love Dad

1 January 2005

We were out of money. After Christmas presents, drinks, food and a week in Adelaide we barely had enough petrol cash to make it back to Melbourne. Then Kerrie gave it all away. She left it at church. In a collection tin. For tsunami victims.

'How in the hell are we supposed to make it back to Melbourne now, Kerrie?'

'We can use the credit card,' she said, without malice.

'But there's no bloody credit left on the credit card,' I countered, with malice.

'God will provide,' she said.

'You can believe whatever you bloody well like, Kerrie, but I'm pretty sure that God doesn't pay off fucking credit cards. Nor will he stop to pick us up somewhere on the Western Highway between Nhill and Kaniva because our car has run out of petrol.'

'We'll make it home.'

I didn't think I was being unreasonable. Of course I was moved by the catastrophe, shocked and saddened by the widespread carnage and enormous loss of life, but I could stand two steps removed. For that reason I would never have tossed our petrol money in a collection tin. I would have at least waited until our next pay packet. And, besides, where was God when the tsunami hit?

Kerrie was different. She bled and wept for the moment. She felt the pain across oceans and continents. There was no option but to give. And for that reason she didn't care whether we conked out around the corner, on the outskirts of Melbourne or anywhere in between.

I gave thought to her perspective and it didn't stop me seething.

How could she? How dare she? After all her suffering, and our suffering, and disruption to our family life, causing me to notice other women and wrestle with guilt, how could she think she was fortunate? How could she think we were lucky to live in this country? For God's sake, she had cancer. It didn't matter where she lived.

2 January 2005

8.30 pm, Mobil Service Station, Bell Street, Pascoe Vale South, Melbourne.

Around the corner from home. Eating humble pie.

Kerrie: 'Can you duck in and get some bread and milk?'

Me: 'Sure.'

Kerrie: 'I can't wait for a cup of tea.'

I didn't mention the petrol, the drive home, the sandwiches we had at Bordertown or the tsunami. I didn't even congratulate Kerrie for somehow conjuring money out of her credit card.

But I enjoyed the cup of tea.

23 January 2005

Excited parents' milestone No. 1: Eddie had his first cinema experience, *The SpongeBob SquarePants Movie* at Airport West. We also took his cousins Georgia and Johnny, spending a trolley's worth of groceries on popcorn and drinks. But that didn't matter because Eddie and his cousins were bouncing around in anticipation and I had waited for this moment. More than baiting a fishing hook or kicking a football. I loved the cinema. I loved kids' movies, and I loved SpongeBob SquarePants.

So I was gutted when Eddie announced that the popcorn box was empty and he wanted to go to the toilet, five minutes from the end with the film perched on its climax. He couldn't wait.

'I'll take him,' Kerrie said.

'No, no, I'll do it. I'll take him.'

When we returned, the credits were rolling.

'What happened?'

'SpongeBob saved the day,' Kerrie said.

'Of course he saved the bloody day, but how? How did he stop King Neptune from frying Mr Krab? What did they do after catching a lift back to Bikini Bottom with David Hasselhoff?'

'I'll tell you in the car.'

Well, there was always our first fishing trip.

27 January 2005

Excited parents' milestone No. 2: Our son started childcare, freeing up Kerrie for two days a week and providing him with a regular diet of three-year-olds' companionship. He also started spending the day without nappies.

We were making real progress.

'What are you going to do with your spare time?' I asked Kerrie.

'I'm thinking about going back to work. Maybe doing half shifts in the afternoon on the daily so that you can come home and pick up Eddie.'

'Why in the world would you want to go back to work?'

'To be among adults again. To use my brain. To earn my own money and feel like I'm contributing. To get out of the house.'

3 February 2005

'I am certainly no saint, but mythologise away if you want. It's not often one is on the end of those kinds of compliments.' – Kerrie (September 1998)

I'd always placed Kerrie on a pedestal, admiring her wit, her social graces and her generosity. She was always offering up her shoulders – one to elated friends who needed to drape their arm around someone and say how much they loved the world, the other for crying on. I also bragged she gave away our petrol money to the tsunami appeal. But she needn't have worried about the mythologising because I'd seen her drive. She was fiery and petulant and taught our son to swear.

It happened on the first afternoon I collected Eddie from Mary Poppins Child Care Centre. I was concentrating on the traffic, turning from a side road onto peak-hour Bell Street. I revved the car, looked anxiously to my right and bunny-hopped before hitting the accelerator and swinging onto Bell Street in front of a stream of cars. Before I could admonish myself for panicking, Eddie piped up from the back seat.

'For fuck's sake,' he shouted. Just like his mother, in traffic, under pressure.

No matter that I swerved from laughing, causing concerned motorists at my rear even further alarm, Kerrie was in for a spray, albeit tongue-in-cheek.

Wait until she gets home from work tonight, I thought.

For years we'd argued over profanities and their place in society.

I reckoned social commentators and prudes overreacted to blue language because, after all, they were just words and often taken out of context. To me it was far more damaging for a vitriolic tongue to call someone fat or useless or worthless rather than a person jesting about a buddy being a fucking idiot.

Kerrie disagreed. Not about belittling a person, but the need to use foul language in everyday speech. She thought it unnecessary.

'How would you feel if Eddie went to school and started swearing in front of his teacher?' she said.

I suppose she thought the car was all right.

But I missed out on my fun, censuring my wife over our son's potty mouth. Instead, I had to say sorry. Sorry for ruining her first night at work.

'It's nothing serious, but I've taken Eddie to the Royal Children's Hospital,' I told her over the phone.

'Why, what's wrong with him?'

'Nothing. He's just gashed his knee and will probably need a couple of stitches. Don't worry, we'll be fine. I'll see you at home.'

'How did he gash his knee?'

'On the metal strip across the passage door. Don't worry, we'll be fine.'

Eddie and I had been home from childcare for less than 30 minutes, hardly into the swing of our boys' night together, when he tripped over, gashed his knee and screamed hysterically at the sight of flapping skin and leaking blood.

He needed a Band-Aid and fast. Except I couldn't find one. Or a patch. Or any-bloody-thing. Where in the hell did Kerrie keep our first-aid kit?

I removed my work shirt, picked up Eddie and told him not to cry because, 'everything will be all right. I'm just looking for a band-aid'.

The best I could do was a fistful of cotton wool thrust across his wound and held tight by a metre-long tatty bandage that I managed to hold fast with electrical tape. Blood out of sight, Eddie's hysteria was reduced to sobs.

When Kerrie walked through the hospital door, I'd rarely felt more relieved.

'What are you doing here?' I asked.

'I've come to see if Eddie is all right,' she replied.

'He's going to need a couple of stitches; we're just waiting for a doctor. I'm glad you're here.'

My tremulous phone voice didn't appear to correlate with Eddie's condition because he was climbing over playground equipment, enamoured with Nurse Sarah who had not only dressed his cut, but was chasing him down a slide.

Eddie followed Nurse Sarah into a tiny suite – I think he would have followed her anywhere – and lay back on a trolley while she placed a mask across his face and pumped him full of happy gas.

'Do you reckon they'd give me a go at that?' I whispered to Kerrie.

'Probably not, but I could do with a whiff myself.'

Eddie had become a giggling mess, laughing at the roof and making Kerrie and me feel more relaxed. Everything was hilarious. Hilarious, until they used the needle.

'Hey, what's that?' he complained, swapping mirth for tears.

I grabbed his arms and held him still until the anaesthetic took effect and the doctor sewed three stitches into the cut. As bad as I felt restraining Eddie, I felt worse when I glanced at Kerrie and noticed the worry across her face.

For fuck's sake, I thought.

11 February 2005

Excited parents' milestone No. 3: Eddie did his first on-toilet poo. Halleluiah. For months he had been sneaking off to the computer room to do his business in a nappy. For months he had been sneaking away to the play-centre ball pit while Kerrie and her friend Di drank coffee. For months he had been tearfully resisting our prompts and bribes to sit on a potty. We were growing impatient and anxious, even in the face of contrary advice from books and doctors. He was three years old and he could say words such as 'disappointed', 'ridiculous' and 'despicable'. So why wasn't he pooing away like his peers?

Sure enough, without warning, Eddie decided it was time. Good lad. Next I would teach him to read the newspaper.

3 March 2005

So I looked like an Oscar-winner. Not Russell Crowe, although my older brother does bear some resemblance. Not Geoffrey Rush, although I too have jumped nude on a trampoline like his piano-playing character, David Helfgott, in *Shine*.

No, apparently, I looked like animator Adam Elliot, Academy Award-winning creator of Harvie Krumpet.

I was accustomed to doppelgängers because people basically likened me to any man under 180 cm with a shaved head. Kerrie made the Adam Elliot connection, draping her arms around our shoulders and saying: 'My two husbands.'

Elliot looked scared, his partner Dan looked amused and I felt embarrassed. Admittedly Kerrie had downed a few champagnes. But so had everyone else. They were on the house. This was the biggest party in Melbourne, a who's who of the city's celebrities – the launch of Red Bull's Formula One team on the eve of Melbourne's Grand Prix. Organisers had hired and refitted a Docklands warehouse at great expense for the glitzy occasion, and because the joint was so vast they needed nobodies such as Kerrie and me to fill the gaps. We didn't mind. It was a great way to spend our fourth wedding anniversary. Red Bull even flew in pop star Pink, although I missed her four-song repertoire because I stepped outside for a cigarette.

I happened to spot Adam Elliot earlier in the night and went over to say hello. We'd never met, but he'd written a piece for our sport section about his cricketing days at Haileybury College. I think he played once. I went over to tell him how much I enjoyed the piece, as it was obvious he didn't have any great affection for the game. Rather than dismiss me as another champagne-fuelled freeloader, he engaged me in conversation. Soon I was introduced to his partner, Dan, and soon I introduced them to mine.

Kerrie told them it was our wedding anniversary and they seemed genuinely pleased for us. Adam told us that Dan was looking to open a restaurant and we were genuinely pleased for them.

We bailed them up for a good hour and not until Kerrie affectionately referred to her two husbands did they decide it was time to move on and socialise or network or whatever it is celebrities do at launches, lunches and awards nights.

But they'd made our anniversary. For a brief moment we'd felt like part of the celebrity circle, and it was not until I crawled out of bed after three hours' sleep and stumbled puffy-eyed and arid-tongued into work the following morning that I reconsidered our statement heading home in the cab, 'one of the best nights of our lives'.

6 March 2005

We shared our last weekend of freedom with Puffing Billy.

Kerrie let me win the toss and take Eddie on the train, dangling our legs out the carriage window, clinging like sloths to the iron bars, occasionally and prudently lifting a hand to wave to cars stuck at intersections or people lining the track.

I don't know why Kerrie let me go. She knew how much our son loved trains. She knew how much he would love Puffing Billy. Maybe it was because I missed the end of *SpongeBob SquarePants*. Maybe she considered it boys' time. Whatever, Eddie and I had a blast.

When Puffing Billy pulled out of the Emerald Lakeside Station, Kerrie and Aunty Annette drove ahead, stopping their cars at crossings and cuttings to shout and scream as our carriage rolled by. It was a family tradition to race the train, Kerrie following the path worn by her mum and her mum's mum. Once, apparently, her grandmother finished waving to the grandkids on the train, returned to the car and jumped in the back seat. It was a minute before she realised the pair in the front were strangers.

We must have passed Kerrie and her aunty a dozen times before our journey ended at Menzies Creek.

'How was that, darling?' she asked, although she could read the joy on our faces.

We left Aunty Annette at Emerald and returned to Pascoe Vale South. I was content, happy and unaware. By the following weekend we would never again be free of cancer.

Labour Day weekend, March 2005

Kerrie knew the tumour was back. She didn't need to consult a doctor or undergo another scan, she was expert at reading the signs.

She revealed the diagnosis on Saturday morning, failing to mask her fear and frustration, smack bang in the middle of what was meant to be a fun weekend – I was starting two weeks' holiday and had invited Courtney and his friends to stay at my parents' house for a tennis tournament. We would play tennis during the day and celebrate at night.

Instead, Kerrie treated our houseguests as strangers, like she was blaming them for her woes. Every time someone entered the kitchen, she walked out. She only spoke to my parents. When I followed her to the bedroom she insisted everything was okay, and disingenuously suggested that I should go off and enjoy the company.

The news hadn't shocked me. Deep down I'd never allowed myself the latitude of believing Kerrie was safe. But this was the first time it created a mini-rift between us.

'Kerrie what do you want me to do? These people are here at my invitation. I can't tell them to leave or go and stay in a motel unless you allow me to tell people you have cancer. Mum and Dad like having people in the house. Don't worry about them. And try not to worry about yourself. I know it's an impossible ask, but let's at least try and enjoy the weekend.'

Which was exactly what I did. By keeping busy, playing tennis and going out at night. I was able to temporarily repress the ramifications of Kerrie's discovery. It was hardly the arm around the shoulder she deserved, but I didn't know what else to do.

By the time the long weekend was over, our houseguests had departed and my focus returned to Kerrie, the tables had turned. She didn't want to go straight back to Melbourne.

'What should we do, then?'

'Enjoy the holidays. You were right. There's no point rushing back. I know what they are going to tell me. Let's enjoy the break.'

For two weeks, between Cobram and Adelaide, she was true to her word. Neither her family nor her friends could have guessed she had cancer again.

14 April 2005

I didn't want the phone to ring. Not then. It was too early.

'We couldn't get the darn thing,' The Professor said.

And that was as crude as surgeons allowed themselves to be when they told husbands or wives or fathers or mothers their loved one was on death row.

'The darn thing.'

Was that all cancer deserved?

What about, 'the fucking tumour'?

Something to spit and snarl as it spewed out of your mouth.

At least The Professor sounded glum and remorseful as he explained any attempt to remove Kerrie's tumour could have resulted in her bleeding to death. Her operation had been an open and shut case. Literally.

Everything about that last procedure had been different: they allowed me past the sliding doors; they allowed me to stand by Kerrie's trolley bed as the wisecracking anaesthetist explained his part in the coming operation; and, while they didn't exactly lead me into theatre, they told me I would be kept posted. They were true to their word. I felt like I had barely made it home when the phone rang.

We knew the operation had more chance to fail than succeed, but I'd hoped, clutching on to my imaginary Lotto tickets right until the final ball. Oddly, when the numbers turned out wrong, the world didn't end. Kerrie started walking, eating, laughing and within four days she was home.

Above all things, she wanted to be normal. She wanted to keep working her eight hours a week, editing copy, writing headlines and meeting friends for coffee. It made her feel independent. She wanted to hold on to the old Kerrie for as long as she possibly could.

In the process, Eddie and I played a bi-weekly game of tug-of-war, acting like a pair of three-year-olds competing for her attention when she emerged from the train.

We were buddies when I picked him up from childcare – 'Daaad,' he yelled before a running jump into my arms.

We were buddies when I took him home from childcare – 'Do you want to play aeroplanes, Dad? I'll be the plane, and you carry me'; 'Do you want to play trains, Dad? I'll have Henry and you can have Gordon'; 'Do you want to watch *Thomas the Tank Engine*, Dad? You sit next to me.'

We were buddies when I cooked dinner – fish fingers, potato, corn and pumpkin (don't know how I maintained the friendship).

Our feud started when we sat at the train station waiting for Kerrie, elated when she spotted our car, waving with shrugged shoulders and a cheesy grin. Her reaction always set his legs kicking. I didn't have the room.

We verbally attacked her, babbling inaudible nonsense like star-struck fans lining the red carpet, desperate for a glance or a hint of recognition. Flustered, Kerrie would turn her head, wanting to listen and answer both her boys at the same time. But Eddie always won. No matter how hard I tried, no matter what fizzing anecdotes I had up my sleeve, I wasn't a three-year-old.

I refused to play trains when we made it home, and the sulking intensified when I presented Kerrie with her evening meal (something more fancy than fish fingers).

'Oh thanks, honey, but I'm not hungry. I had a garlic pizza and a cup of coffee at Blue Train before work.'

17 May 2005

What did Kerrie Russell and Kylie Minogue have in common?

Cancer. Correct.

That was all it took for Kerrie to feel worthless. That and eight pages of the *Herald Sun* dedicated to Kylie and her breast cancer and all the first-class treatment she would receive. Kerrie was at work when the story broke.

My wife depicted flatness better than a marble slab when she slumped into the car, unable to turn her head and respond to the chattering monkeys.

'Kylie Minogue has breast cancer,' she said. 'The *Herald Sun* has devoted eight pages to the story. I feel like nothing. I feel like no one cares.'

These stories turned newspaper offices into ant nests, sending journalists and sub-editors scurrying around the room like they were preparing for a storm. A circulation bonanza.

Kerrie wasn't mad at her work colleagues. How could she be? She hadn't told anyone she was terminal. And besides, we knew how newspapers operated. And how could she be angry with Kylie Minogue? It wasn't Kylie's fault. No, her issue was with our growing culture of celebrity – obsessing over movie stars, TV stars, models, sportsmen, sportswomen, the rich, the famous and those famous for being famous, while the rest of us, even the cancer sufferers, could go and get stuffed.

But in a way I felt sorry for Kylie Minogue.

Could you imagine a superstar such as Kylie going to Myer on Mother's Day and struggling to contain her joy after buying a $300 leather jacket?

Could you imagine Kylie hugging herself in that jacket, staring in the mirror like a kid with a lollipop, before nervously and politely asking the shop assistant, 'Can I wear it out the front door?'

'I've never spent this much on an item of clothing before,' Kerrie said. 'I can't believe how good it feels.'

Can you imagine Kylie walking across Bourke Street in her $300 jacket into the Pancake Parlour, smacking her lips at the menu and excitedly pointing out to Eddie a picture of pancakes, ice-cream and chocolate topping?

That's why I felt sorry for Kylie Minogue. That's what I had to convince Kerrie.

June 2005

Of course, cancer wasn't allowed to lurk in the background unattended. Kerrie took the tumour to a radiotherapy clinic for regular zapping, hoping it would shrivel like a walnut and grant her more time to write headlines, and be a mother and a wife.

But while radiotherapy delayed the tumour's growth, it couldn't disguise Kerrie's hobble. She had lost her swagger.

But my wife rarely complained. She masked the pain. I knew this because I found a typed message on the computer.

Dear Dr Yelica,
My name is Kerrie, and I am a 35-year-old woman in Pascoe Vale
South in Melbourne, Australia with recurrent cancer problems. I am
a level 3 reiki tummo practitioner, but have not been able to dedicate
myself to self-healings as thoroughly as I should because of surgery,
treatment and chronic pain. I heard about this distant healing through
other Melbourne reiki alumni and have asked for your help last year. I
was cancer-free then and felt fabulous, but I have since grown another
tumour in my pelvis that is very painful and cannot be surgically
removed. Please could you help me? I would be so grateful for
anything.
Thank you and bless you,
Kerrie

20 June 2005

I was used to bombshells at home. I just didn't see one coming at work.

Staff were assembled in the editor's office and told we would be producing a Sydney edition of our paper within the fortnight.

Sydney's editorial staff would be coming on line in a week. That is, we would be putting out two papers in the time we had previously put out one.

'Are there any questions? Because if anyone has any queries, now is the time to ask.'

Any questions! How were we expected to compose our thoughts in a couple of minutes? We'd been hit by friendly fire. I was too stunned to talk. The possible fall-out on my home life was catastrophic: longer days under more pressure and less time with my terminally ill wife. Unless, of course, I lost my job.

Any questions? Hang on, oh yeah, I get it. Any minute now and someone would barge through the door and yell, 'Gotcha!' or 'You've been caught on *Candid Camera*!' Wouldn't they? I mean, that's how these gags worked. Didn't they?

'No questions? Good.'

Okay, no *Candid Camera*.

Time and secrecy, we were told, were of the essence, essential to trumping our chief rival. Planning had been in the pipeline for months, and now we were entrusted to keep the news under wraps.

It was hard to swallow because we hadn't been trusted in the first place. As a result I didn't buy the line about the announcement being a reflection of our abilities. I didn't believe it when we were told we should feel honoured to be involved in such a groundbreaking project. I think everyone felt flat.

I was nervous and scared. The news was still ringing in my ears when I stumbled through the front door.

'So what does this mean for you?' Kerrie asked.

'I don't know. I didn't compose myself in time to ask.'

A week later the next bomb was dropped. We were told, via email, that our days would be starting an hour earlier. For me this meant 5 am. Unfortunately, the email wasn't tagged with 'any questions', because by this time I was ready to ask a million.

'I'm starting an hour earlier next week, Kerrie,' I mumbled.

'How come?'

'Because Sydney will go to press an hour before the Melbourne edition. We were sent an email with our new starting times today. An email! I'll be going to bed before Eddie again.'

22 June 2005

As the Sydney project drew closer, I complained to Kerrie every chance I could.

'I've got no idea where I stand. I don't know whether to take charge of the Sydney sports section or if I'm meant to be at the Sydney sports editor's beck and call, and what's more, I'm sure he's none the wiser either. We could be on completely different tangents. Either no one knows what's going on, or someone would prefer me to sink than swim.'

'Ask.'

'It's too late. We've been given the chance to ask questions.'

'Well, ask again. You have a right to know.'

'You'd think I would have been told.'

'It's typical of middle management to leave everyone in the dark. Make them accountable.'

Dark was the operative word. Getting up before daybreak would be another seismic shift in our lives. Everyone was screwing with our time.

How Kerrie found it within herself to carry me through I do not know. Every night she read my pages, generously giving me the thumbs up.

'It looks great, darl,' she would say.

It must have been hard. She was going through menopause. Hot flushes at 35.

1 July 2005

When Kerrie signed up for chemotherapy, menopause was in the small print, alongside infertility and soul-destroying. Easy to miss when you're focused on the big, bold words: **sign here and you could be cured of cancer.**

So to say we weren't warned of possible side effects would be incorrect. To say we were prepared would also be a lie. Kerrie didn't expect to feel old before her time.

'Look at you,' she said to my mother. 'You're 60 and fit and healthy. My body is useless.'

Contributing to her fits of self-loathing was a lack of libido. Chemotherapy caused menopause, I was responsible for the sex guilt. Not that I talked about it anymore. For months I had been able to separate my headspace from physical cravings, realising that Kerrie wanted and needed me no matter how few times we made love.

Unfortunately, my early bickering had left a scar. So she sought help, asking a radiation oncologist specialising in women's health to restore her to a middle-aged woman again, one who felt vibrant, sensual and sexy. The answer was hormone replacement therapy.

Kerrie was given back her libido ... for a time. HRT masked the flushes and provided an energy boost.

'Look out for the white pill,' Kerrie warned. 'When Mum used to take the white pill, she would turn into a monster. Dad and I knew well enough to leave the house.'

But I didn't complain about these hormone-fuelled, irrational outbursts. She was thinking about sex again.

August 2005

Dear Eddie,

I think you are the reason cancer hasn't consumed us. Every day you change, say something new, smile in a different way. You are growing so fast.

Your mum is proud you have upgraded to a single bed, kicked nappies for good and have taken to answering the phone.

'Danny, it's your dad,' you say, holding out the receiver.

I don't see a lot of you during the day – less now because we're putting out an extra edition at work – but Kerrie tells me she is at her happiest taking you to the airport. Together you sit at observation points, eating ice-creams, watching jets take off or land, Mum telling you the airline and model of each plane. You are going to be a planespotter, Eddie, whether you like it or not. It's in your genes. Grandpa worked at Adelaide airport for 40 years and that's where he met Grandma, who was working as a stewardess. Kerrie grew up watching planes. She sees it as romantic, a sense of escapism and adventure as people come and go. Sometimes you visit the terminal, roaming among passengers, checking out knick-knacks and model aeroplanes, and almost always ending up at Hungry Jack's. From there you can watch the planes, waiting for a jumbo to land.

'Aren't they beautiful?' she says. 'They are so big and graceful. And safe.'

Paradoxically, Kerrie has flown only three times in the past five years. She fears flying, even now in the face of death.

People at work laugh when I tell them Kerrie is a planespotter. But what can I say? She is different, your mum.

Love Dad

August 2005

Kerrie tried to live for the moment. She tried to concentrate on the time at hand. At weekends she very nearly succeeded.

We started moving again. Sometimes we drove to the outskirts of the airport, stopping at the north–south runway observation point, hoping to time our arrival with Mr Whippy or a jumbo, but most times we kept going, arriving in Lancefield, Kyneton, Kilmore or Mount Macedon. We stopped at cafés for lunch, choosing our venue for the toys in the corner more so than the menu. This way we had enough time to enjoy a coffee before Eddie lost interest in the toys. Then we bought him a biscuit or worked in shifts – one would take Eddie for a walk, while the other ate. We rarely stopped in one place more than half an hour. Replete with country air and Eddie's little legs stretched, we rolled on to the next park or the next café or the next roadside lookout.

We stopped at Hanging Rock to watch teenage anglers pull trout from the lake; we stopped for tea and scones; and then we drove to the top of Mount Macedon.

'This is beautiful,' Kerrie said as we walked through the bush with only the occasional mountain bike rider for company. 'I don't know why we don't come out this way more often.'

We didn't walk far before Kerrie's right leg ached or my shoulders could no longer bear their infant load, but it was distance enough to feel liberated, freed from cancer's cage.

Our moods only differed on the road home. Whereas Kerrie was dreamy and fulfilled, I began to dread each kilometre because the bitumen dragged me closer to Monday and a week of work.

2 September 2005

What else? Oh, Danny got shat on by a bird on his way to work yesterday. It was that bad he had to come home and have a shower. It was no ordinary shit. Danny said it was like having a cup of vomit poured on him. The smell made him retch. It got him in the face and splattered over his suit (the one he wore to our wedding) and bag. So he came home and in his haste to have a shower and get to work, he put the suit jacket in a bucket of cold water in the laundry. It wasn't until he came home that night that we realised the bucket had bleach in it.

So the poor boy was quite upset about the suit. He said he wanted to hand it down to Eddie because of its sentimental value. His mood wasn't helped when I pointed out that if it was so bloody precious to him maybe he shouldn't be treating it as an ordinary work-a-day business suit. Then we both agreed that being shat on from a great height was not a feeling we were unused to in a metaphorical sense, opened a bottle of red and watched the trots. Well, what you gonna do? It could be worse. We could be in New Orleans. Man, is that an apocalyptic vision of hell or what?

Love Kerrie

29 September 2005

Dear Eddie,

What the fuck am I doing? Your mum is dying and I've become a slave to work. And what's the point? I'm only running on pride.

Each day my failure to make deadline, perpetuated by a colossal workload, my inability to say no to requests, and reluctance to delegate, squeezes harder. I'm becoming sour and humourless.

The workload of putting out a second paper has poisoned the atmosphere. I don't know if I'm seeing clearly anymore, but fewer people seem happy. There's a sense of being patronised, like 'we're all in this for the greater good', when really we're all in this because we don't have a choice – other than to leave. I feel guilty if I'm not working twelve-hour days to make this project work. Which is not right because we can't all work twelve-hour days.

Everything has become harder. My life is a ticking clock: morning alarms, train timetables, newspaper deadlines, getting home to my family and going to bed early in preparation for the following day. I don't want Kerrie becoming any more tangled in this web, feeling aggrieved when I flop in the front door after work, tired and hungry and ignoring her excitement at seeing another adult.

'What's the matter with you?' she asks.

'Nothing. I'm just hungry.' Or, 'Nothing. I'm just tired.'

We are working to live, and I'm turning to vinegar. I'm beginning to hate a lot of things: my job for robbing Kerrie of all the good I have to offer – humour, joy, love and time – utilities, landlords, grocery bills and even the idea of God.

I can't go on like this. I've got to spend time with your mum. She's just come out of hospital after another vomiting attack, and I'm scared the next time she won't come home.

When I sit her down to speak of my decision to quit work, relief washes across her face.

'I think we should move back to Cobram and live with my parents,' I say.

'Do you think they will be okay with that?' Kerrie asks.

'They are. They said so. They've been spending so much time with us already, they've been waiting for us to ask.'

So pack your bags, Ed, we're getting out of the city.

Love Dad

7 October 2005

I baulked at the last minute. Instead of handing in my notice, I acquiesced to Kerrie's pressure and asked for twelve months' leave without pay. It gave her peace of mind.

The asking wasn't easy. I never found it easy to talk about Kerrie at work, and that day was no exception. My editor knew Kerrie and knew she was terminal. She probably suspected what was on my mind, but I still found it hard to hold back the tears.

'How long has she got?' my editor asked.

'I don't know. Kerrie doesn't want to know and nor do I.'

'What if they ask me upstairs?'

'For the sake of paperwork, let's say twelve months.'

Everyone wanted a time line. That's how cancer played out. People were given six months, and lasted two years. People were given two years and lasted six months.

Two months, six months, two years. Time, time, time.

What did it matter? Kerrie was going to die.

The editor and I agreed on an end-of-October finish. Three weeks to go.

When I walked away from the office that afternoon my right eyelid stopped twitching, my left shoulder stopped aching and my feet stopped dragging.

If there was any sense of regret, it was for not making the decision earlier.

I overheard Kerrie's relief while she was talking to a friend on the telephone.

'We are going to move in with Pete and Kath, for a while at least, and going on disability and carer's pensions!' she said.

(Pause)

'Don't panic, I'm feeling fine, it's just that we haven't been enjoying our lives lately – Dan's working too hard and I'm sick of suburbia – so we're taking this chance to be lazy river bums. Dan can write to his heart's content and we can spend as much time in Adelaide as we want with Dad and my brother's family. It just makes so much sense. As soon as Danny suggested it, we couldn't believe we hadn't thought of it before.'

15 October 2005

Brian and I made it around Port Phillip Bay on our bikes. Kerrie was there to see it all. She woke at 5 am to see us off, she arrived in Sorrento four and a half hours later with Chel and Eddie to ensure we caught the ferry to Queenscliff, and the three of them were waiting for us when we pedalled, exhausted but elated, into Melbourne's Docklands after 210 kilometres and more than ten hours in the saddle. I think that ride meant as much to Kerrie as it did to me.

16 October 2005

Kerrie emailed her farewell to the *Herald Sun*.

Herewith written notice that I reluctantly remove myself from the subbing roster, effective immediately. I am sorry to have mucked you around but I was trying to avoid making it so final! Continuing health problems make it impractical and unenjoyable to continue, and I'm sure the standard of my work has been slipping as a result. So I'll bow out gracefully now with a big thank you for indulging me my half-shifts and the (very generous) pin money it brought me. Getting back into the workforce really did wonders for my self-confidence, and you can't put a price on that, so thank you again. I really had fun.

Now my hubby, little boy and me are heading for a lazy life on the Murray. I'll read the Herald Sun *in a very leisurely fashion front to back every day with fondness (but for crying out loud, will they put*

*the sudoku, word scramble, crosswords et al. on facing pages, a la
Daily Mail 'Coffee Break' section? For some reason, it's annoying that
they're not together!)*

Thanks again,

Kerrie Russell

19 October 2005

I'm so excited about this (move), the joy has affected me physically.

*I feel better than I have in ages, despite starting a new chemo
regime. It takes one hour to shove into my veins every three weeks and
so far haven't had any side effects (knock on wood). My doctor says
it's unlikely to be very effective, but also unlikely to knock me about,
so I decided to give it a go.*

*I know I don't talk much about my health and I know that
frustrates some people because they don't know what's going on with
me, but I find the whole thing really tedious. And there's nothing to
tell. I have cancer and can't get rid of it. End of story. I don't want this
illness to define me. I don't want anyone to dwell on it because, believe
me, I don't. I'm here now and I'm feeling good at the moment and I'm
like a footy player and just taking it one game at a time (and pleased
to get the four points, obviously).*

Love Kerrie

28 October 2005

Dear Eddie,

Happy birthday to you, happy birthday to you … Mum has thrown
a party and you are among a bunch of kids gorging lollies and cake
when I step out of a taxi with a birdcage and a pair of budgies.

Don't worry, they're not for you. They're mine. Today was my
last day at work and the birds are a going-away present from my
colleagues. Not quite the bottle of whiskey I was expecting.

So what's with the budgies? Remember when I copped a liberal dollop
of bird shit from a great height?

Never mind, I'm free. In two weeks' time we will be packing our life into a removal truck and pulling out of Pascoe Vale South forever.

Grandpa Des has come over for the celebrations, although he's retired to the bear cave for a spell because the screaming and general excitement have tested his decreasing levels of patience. I might put the birds in there, too.

Not Kerrie, however. She is beaming, handing out bags of lollies as a parting gesture to your buddies, content she has put on a good show for her son.

I can't believe how different we feel. It is like someone has blown away the dark clouds.

Love Dad

1 November 2005

Makybe Diva won her third successive Melbourne Cup. I stood in Flemington's overloaded public arena with a group of friends, grabbed a mobile phone and rang home.

'Kerrie, did you watch the race?'

'I did. Isn't she just amazing?'

'It's incredible. The crowd is going mad, listen.'

I held the phone to the heavens as Glen Boss rode the mighty mare back past the finish post and trotted her in front of the screaming throng, continually pointing at Makybe Diva in disbelief at the historic moment.

Kerrie didn't want to go to the Cup. Not with 100,000 people, being buffeted and bumped, knocked around like a pinball each time she needed to place a bet or buy a drink. But we shared the moment in our own special way.

It wasn't the first time I had cheered home Makybe Diva that spring. Chris and I had watched ten days earlier at Moonee Valley when she dragged a wall of horses into the final straight and then kicked away, leaving the wall to crumble as she won the Cox Plate. I'd backed her then as I did in the Melbourne Cup. Winning made it easier to fall in love with horses. But the big difference this time around was me. I had grown. I stood in line with Chris after the races and when a taxi stopped, I bade him farewell. There was to be no party in the city nor a 5 am finish for me. I wanted to go home.

And it was the same after the Melbourne Cup. As my group of friends danced and swilled at a Flemington pub, I snuck off into the night.

When I crawled into bed with Kerrie, she kissed me gently on the cheek.

'Hi honey,' she said. 'You're home early.'

'I guess I am.'

'I'm glad you shared that moment with me, today.'

4 November 2005

Kerrie cried when I said I was staying home. For her, it was one cancellation too many.

'I don't think having a farewell drink with me is that important, Kerrie. The work guys will understand,' I said.

'But I won't. Every time you plan on going somewhere I get sick. Not this time. You are going to those work drinks.'

'Kerrie, I've been to the Cox Plate and the Melbourne Cup. I've been to plenty of things. This is just another excuse to have a piss-up. They'll probably be doing that anyway.'

'It's not for them, it's for you. You need to go.'

For the past two days, Kerrie had been feeling unwell. For two days she had been willing herself better. If anything, the anxiety made her worse, twisting her stomach in knots at the thought of ruining my occasion.

'I'll be okay with Eddie. Get in the car and I'll drive you to the station.'

'Are you sure? I really don't mind staying home.'

'I'm sure. You're going.'

10 November 2005

Taking a pair of budgies to Cobram was going to be an issue. After more than thirty years on a dairy farm with cows, dogs, cats, chooks, turkeys, ducks and the occasional pig, my mother was adamant that when she retired there would be no more pets. Thankfully, the crisis was averted. Kerrie told it best:

> *I seem to recall you asked about the budgie story.*
>
> *Well, on Dan's last day of work, he was presented with a pair of budgies as his going-away present ...*
>
> *But we got the last laugh. A week after getting them, Eddie thought they might like a fly outside and opened the cage. Bye-bye birdies. Then, just when we were wondering what the hell we could do with the birdcage, seed, toys etc that came with the unfortunate and unloved little fellas, a lovely lady we had hired to do our 'vacating the premises' clean-up told us she had just bought some parakeets for her kids and needed a bigger cage! Bingo, no more cage (it was pretty big).*
>
> *We didn't really even tell Eddie off for liberating the budgies. I told him that they would probably be killed by big mean birds out there in the wilds of Pascoe Vale South, and he had the decency to be a little taken aback by that information ... for five minutes. Then he happily recounted his crime to anyone who would listen, including the fact they were 'killed-ed' by nasty birds. No real animal lover, our boy.*

While it was my noble intention to shield Kerrie from the laborious chore of moving house, I needn't have bothered. She didn't show any inclination. She hired a cleaner, who we paid in cash and budgie equipment, and left the cupboard clearing, box packing and furniture moving to me.

My biggest problem was not lack of help, it was lack of a game plan. I double-handled everything. After packing away the cutlery, assiduously wrapping china tea cups and soup bowls in newspaper, I realised we would still be eating for another week and for that we needed plates. I unpacked the box.

I moved the lounge chairs into the computer room, before dismantling the computer, clearing out the bookcase and moving the lot, including chairs, into the spare room.

While taking rubbish from the spare room to the wheelie bins, I would pass the laundry and remember the cupboards needed to be cleared. Cupboards done, I would forget what it was I was doing when walking past the laundry and have to return to the spare room. Except I wouldn't make it past the bathroom because the pot plants needed to be taken out back, which was where the bins were, which reminded me of the rubbish I was removing from the spare room in the first place.

Loading the truck went more smoothly. Thanks to a couple of mates. Coatesy supplied the truck. We didn't even ask. He left his Cobram bar at 3 am, picked up Chooka from his Invergordon dairy farm on the way, and the pair arrived at Pascoe Vale South soon after 6 am. After two hours' sleep and the second half of Australia's World Cup soccer qualifier in Uruguay, we started clearing the house. By this time Brian, Chel and Courtney had arrived to lend a hand.

We were on the road by 12.30 pm, leaving Kerrie and Eddie to stay with Brian in Melbourne because they had to drop off house keys the following day.

Before I climbed in the truck with Chooka and Coatesy, I pulled Brian aside and told him to stay close to Kerrie.

'She gets tired very easily and with her stronger painkillers can get a bit vague,' I said.

A good hour out of Melbourne on the Hume Freeway the phone rang. It was Brian – Kerrie couldn't find the keys to our car or the house.

I had them in my pocket.

November 2005

We've settled in very nicely in Cobram. It's wonderfully relaxing and I love being around Pete and Kath, though they're out most days being dynamic, creative and community-minded (or avoiding us?).

*Eddie is enrolled in kindy for next year and occasional care two
days a week at the moment because he patently needs little-boy fun we
just can't (and don't wanna) provide.*

*His kindy class is more than one-third Iraqi kids, so he may end up
being a little bilingual, too. It'll be handy to know how to say 'you're a
wee-wee head' in Arabic.*

*Oddly, there are only four girls in the class of 25. Poor, poor little
things. Whoa. All that pre-testosterone. If he ends up gay it won't be
because of living up here.*

*Oh the river, I really get now why people paint it. Definitely feels
like we made the right decision. Danny goes fishing every day and his
punting has fallen right away. Don't know why. I thought it might get
worse with all this time on our hands.*

*But we have joined Sporties again. Well, it's an institution. And the
one and only time we have been in there since moving up, I won $150
in the club jackpot. Now don't worry, this isn't the start of a slippery
slope. But once a month is fun. We're even considering going to bingo.
My metamorphosis into a 63-year-old is almost complete. I just love
the pace, the empty roads and the mothering great sky. Yep, definitely
the right decision.*

    Kerrie

Late November 2005

Two significant things happened in Adelaide: shopping and a trip to the
cinema.

Buying clothes was a great sign. Kerrie almost pranced out of her
limp as she moved between outlets looking for an outfit for her best
friend's wedding. The swagger was back as she strode out of change
rooms, twirling on the balls of her feet so that all manner of ensembles
lifted and fell, asking for my opinion while Eddie played hide-and-seek
among the clothes racks. When she settled on a dress, the buying didn't
stop. She compiled a summer wardrobe. I'd never seen her buy up like
that before.

Linda's wedding was a special day, and not solely because she was starting life again after Daryl's death. No, her marriage to Brenton helped Kerrie and me to further straighten out our creases and iron out our frowns.

Seeing Kerrie laughing with her friends and being able to join in the conversation was almost like being in a fairytale. And while there was no hiding her compromised health and the fact we had dropped out of mainstream life, none of us could have imagined she would be dead in less than six months.

A cutting reminder of Kerrie's ticking clock came days later when we took Eddie to see *Chicken Little*. Kerrie was in a bad mood as we left the cinema, finding it hard to contain her distaste. She said the movie portrayed a bad message. Eddie and I didn't go so deep. We thought it was fun.

'It was crap,' she said. 'I can't stand this new-age philosophy that it is okay for kids to continually question their parents or disobey adults like his baseball coach. That's not the sort of message I want imparted on our son.'

'If Chicken Little didn't disobey his baseball coach, he wouldn't have hit a home run.'

'That's not the point.'

'I don't think Eddie will play baseball.'

'You know what I mean.'

'Kerrie, it was just a kids' movie.'

'Well, it was a bad kids' movie.'

'All right, you don't have to like it, but there's no need to spoil Eddie's fun.'

Kerrie fell silent.

I was bamboozled. Kerrie could fly off the handle, no doubt. I'd heard her yell at deceitful politicians on TV or bang her fist on newspaper articles over what she perceived as injustice. Once she rang up the frozen food company McCain's and complained about their juicy corn commercial. She said it was insensitive to farmers battling drought. She later blamed her reaction on pregnancy hormones. But this was different. This was a kids' movie.

'Are you all right, Kerrie?'

'I'm in a lot of pain, that's all.'

Early December 2005

I drove the entire trip from Adelaide to Cobram. Kerrie shifted uncomfortably in the passenger seat or slept when her painkillers took hold. We had promised Grandpa Des, as he waved goodbye from his driveway, that we would be back in three weeks for Christmas. Deep down I wasn't so sure.

December 2005

Not resigning from work turned out to be a mistake. Because I had eight weeks' leave to fulfil, I was still on the payroll and couldn't claim a carer's pension, which meant I couldn't pay out our loan. Fretting about money was such a waste of energy, but I couldn't help thinking that Kerrie's remaining time would be much more enjoyable if we were loaded. I kept my anguish to myself.

Kerrie was distracted elsewhere. Three words and she burst into tears.

'I have cancer.'

It was her first consultation with a Cobram doctor, brought about because her right leg had been swelling and causing discomfort. But it was evident she needed more than respite for lymphoedema, she needed to get things off her chest.

Kerrie's cries for help always caught me napping, probably because she worked so hard at protecting everyone else's feelings. I didn't expect to see her emerge from Dr Chrissie's room with red eyes.

'I had a cry,' she said. 'I feel so much better.'

I was finding it harder to be open. Each time I ran into a familiar face or an old school buddy in Cobram's main street, I danced around the real reason we were home. I said I had taken twelve months' leave without pay and had moved in with my parents for 'some time out'. Kerrie set me straight.

One afternoon we drove out of town and stopped at the Big Strawberry (yes, Cobram's on the 'big' map) for a coffee. The owner, an old schoolmate, stopped for a chat, asking what I was doing and what was going on. I launched into my prepared reply, when Kerrie stomped in mid-sentence.

'I have cancer,' she said. 'Danny's taken time off work so he can look after me.'

So there you are. That's why I was back in my home town.

Kerrie explained her intervention in the car.

'Danny, you sound like you are being evasive. It all sounds a bit suspicious. Just tell the truth.'

21 December 2005

Dear Eddie,

Don't cry. I hate needles, too. Believe me.

I didn't want to bring you here. Mum is too tired and her swollen leg is too sore.

Here, have a look at this book. See the elephant? Do you know what noise an elephant makes?

Come on, mate. Don't cry.

I didn't want to hold your arms. I didn't know they were coming at you from both sides. I didn't feel the pricks that made you cry, but I can feel your pain.

'Why?' you ask.

'Why what, mate?'

'Why do you have to have needles?'

'You need to have needles so that you don't get sick in future.'

What a hollow answer. Don't ask me about diphtheria, tetanus, pertussis, polio, measles, mumps or rubella. Don't ask me why needles haven't helped your mum. I don't know about any of these things.

Eventually you calm down and the nurses allow us to leave, satisfied you are not having any adverse reactions to the shots. When we arrive home, you insist on re-enacting the needle scenario, time and time again. We take it in turns to give each other imaginary shots, insisting 'this will make you feel better'.

Kerrie smiles knowingly and sympathetically when I explain the trauma we have been through. She has been there, of course, I've read it all before.

It is instinctive to protect your child from pain. This is a universal law. Most humans obey it. So do most animals, for that matter. So when it came time to take Eddie for his jabs, there was a little part of me still wedged in the front door, legs akimbo, arms folded, not wanting to budge. It said: 'You're going to what? Allow someone to plunge two needles into your baby's pristine thighs, and make him swallow a mouthful of polio? Oh, right on, sister. Great parenting.'

The rest of me said we had to go. Our government benefits and daycare aspirations depended on it. So boy and I made for the clinic.

There were about twenty people in the waiting room with infants of varying ages. I took a number and sat down, taking a sly glance at the rest of the little human pincushions. Yes, I had been right: my son was the most handsome, well-behaved and clever child in the world.

Well, actually, he couldn't be that clever because he didn't even look a little worried when kids kept disappearing behind a curtain and screaming 30 seconds later. After about half an hour of this, it was our turn. (Yippee!)

There were two nurses. One put a baby spoonful of anti-polio gunk in Eddie's mouth, which surprised him a little, but he swallowed it out of politeness. Then they prepared the needles, looked at each other and said 'one, two, three' as they stuck him with Hep B, Hib, tetanus, diphtheria and whooping cough.

Eddie went rigid and let out one indignant roar. And that was it. Tantrum over.

But my anxieties had just begun: I was watching for signs of a bad reaction. He was fine that day, but the next it seemed the light was leaving his eyes as his body used all its energy to fight off the invaders. For two days he was off-colour, dopey and miserable. This was to be expected. But it didn't make it any easier. All I could do was administer Baby Panadol and keep a close eye on him.

Which made me think of my grandmother and the story she used to tell about the night her baby sister Molly died of whooping cough; her exhausted mother's kerosene-lamp vigil as the child lay fighting for breath, pale and listless; how some well-meaning neighbours added to my great-grandmother's agony by telling her to stop giving Molly the medicine the doctor had left because it was bad.

Imagine wondering if the medicine you were giving your child was killing him instead of curing him. I could imagine it. I imagined it as I gave Eddie his Baby Panadol and kept my own vigil over his tiny body, pale and listless. I imagined my great-grandmother's terrible doubt and fear. I imagined all the scared mothers who once upon a time kept similar vigils.

I imagined what could happen to Eddie if he didn't get jabbed. The needles didn't seem so painful after all.

You see, Ed, your mum can put these things into perspective better than I can. I just wish she could stop the ache.

Love Dad

22 December 2005

On to more important things than the creation of new life. I know you'll be hanging out to know where my hair is at, as well as my head. Being heartily sick of the mousy colour, I went and got a dye job which is really close to my old hair colour but not quite so orange. It reminds me of the colour it was at my wedding. And those horrible curls are finally lengthening out a bit. It's still a shambles, but I don't feel like Kath from Kath and Kim *anymore.*

Before we made it back to Adelaide for Christmas, we had to shut the car boot. No easy feat. Packing the presents was like trying to solve a thousand-piece jigsaw puzzle. In the end I had to toss out the golf clubs and my fishing rods.

Kerrie was to blame. She had caught me completely unawares two days before leaving Cobram, grabbing the car keys and the credit card and mentioning something about ducking down the street for a last-minute item.

'There is one more thing I want to get for Eddie,' she said.

Building up to Christmas had helped Kerrie focus outside her swollen leg and mini-breakdown at the doctor's surgery. She simply loved buying gifts for others.

This last shop, however, was all about her son. She was gone for an hour and returned with half the town's toy store – stuffed figures from *The Lion King*, characters from *Madagascar*, *Toy Story* masks, a fireman's helmet, a wooden petrol station, Thomas the Tank Engine railway stations, Thomas the Tank Engine bridges, Thomas the Tank Engine holding sheds, Thomas the Tank Engine trains, balls you could bounce, balls you could squash and throw, a Bob the Builder briefcase and more and more and more.

I couldn't believe my eyes. Eddie was a great kid, but he wasn't going to know which way to look on Christmas morning. Our budget was blown. Kerrie had gone too far and I would have to tell her, break my vow of silence.

But she was too quick, reading my face and my mood.

'I know it's a lot,' she said. 'But I want to spoil Eddie this Christmas. It could be my last.'

25 December 2005

Dear Eddie,

Mum's buying spree pays off. She follows your trail of torn wrapping paper around Grandpa Des's carpet on her hands and knees, excitedly explaining each of her carefully chosen presents, while I stumble around in the background holding the video camera. Contrary to my fears, you revel in every gift.

'Another present! For me!'

'Yes, darling. You must have been a good boy for Father Christmas to bring all this,' Mum says.

'Look, Mum, it's Gloria the hippo. Gloria? Gloria?'

Mum takes up the game: 'Yes, darlin'?'

'You're nice and soft. I might take you to bed.'

'Thanks, darlin'.'

Next it's the wooden garage.

'I love it,' you announce dramatically, after tearing away the plastic.

'It's a petrol station,' Mum says.

'Yeah, and it's got a ramp.'

Present by present you tackle the pile, flicking shredded pieces of wrapping paper through the air like a mini-mulching machine. There's no denying, this is the best money your mum has ever spent.

When it seems there are no more parcels to tackle, Grandpa Des emerges from the passage with the *coup de grâce*, a mountain overpass for Thomas the Tank Engine and his friends.

'Wow, Grandpa. I love it.'

But when Kerrie opens the box, ignoring your insistence that she might need scissors, she can't put the pieces together. Not because she is in pain. Not because she feels weak. Because she is technically inept.

It's the one thing I can't understand about your mum. She's intelligent, understanding and a great exponent of common sense while holding discussions or making decisions, yet, when it comes to using her hands, she can't build a wooden train track. Which is probably just as well because it's one of the few things I'm good at. So while you and I race trains over the magnificent mountain pass, Gloria the stuffed hippo can lounge back and rest.

Happy Christmas, Ed.

Love Dad

25 December 2005

We spent Christmas lunch at Brendan's house and it was a heart-warming afternoon. While Kerrie nursed her niece, six-month-old Maggie, Eddie ran around with Ruby and Zac while Grandpa Des and I dipped into Brendan's cache of Crown Lagers.

For most of the afternoon, Kerrie was smiling and imparting her trademark wit, especially when her brother slipped around the corner and reappeared as Santa Claus. It was her turn to stumble around in the background with the video camera.

4 January 2006

Looking after Eddie while Kerrie was lost in fiction became my focus. I thought I was doing a good job. While she flipped through page after page of Alexander McCall Smith's *No. 1 Ladies' Detective Agency* novels or watched repeats of sitcoms on Foxtel, Eddie and I kept busy by rolling balls down the driveway, romping in the beach sand at Seacliff or feeding our faces with chocolate Paddle Pops.

We occasionally met up with Brendan, Jane and their kids, and once or twice I accompanied Grandpa Des on his daily two-hour visit to the pub. But, mostly, I remember struggling to stay locked on Eddie's four-year-old wavelength.

Kerrie saw things slightly differently: 'Dad hijacked Danny and poured beer and port down his throat and talked horses until he was hoarse, while I reclined in the air-conditioned lounge room watching *Will and Grace* marathons on Foxtel steadfastly ignoring my son while letting him eat crisps, biscuits and icy-poles on the carpet.'

10 January 2006

Linda looked after Eddie for a weekend while Dan and I sweated our little pores out in Moonta Bay. I loved it – we stayed at this new hotel on the beach with excellent restaurant and views – but Dan was disappointed with Yorke Peninsula scenery (except the sea, of course), the state of the roads (they ARE shocking), horrible drive from

Adelaide, and general tatty, down-at-heel feeling of YP towns. He was most upset about the lack of road guttering and verges, and the amount of shacks and caravans. Was also affronted by very over-rated Cornish pasties. Still, what can you do with a guy who worked at the Hyatt Regency in Coolum during his youth? The bar was set too high, too early.

Dear Eddie,

I'm driving back to Cobram. Mum's asleep in the front seat and you're asleep in the back. Strange silence considering Kerrie and I usually spend these trips chattering away, dissecting our time in Adelaide and the people we've visited.

Now I've only my thoughts, reflecting on our weekend in Moonta. I complained a lot, unimpressed with the tired and dishevelled towns with their beach shacks and dirt footpaths and unsightly TV aerials reaching for the sky. I'd wanted wild open seas, rugged coastline and a town with trimmings.

But as I think about it now it wasn't Moonta, it was my fear of death.

Kerrie's struggle is growing more difficult by the week. She couldn't make it to the end of Moonta pier when we went for a walk, having to stop a third of the way for a rest and wait for me to come back. It struck me how lonely that walk was, leaving her behind, continuing on at her insistence.

We later drove up the coast to Port Broughton and stopped for a break, further heightening the divide between our physical capabilities. I went for a walk on the jetty and she sat content in the car. I went to the pub for a bet and she sat snoozing in the car. I went for a walk to the fish and chip shop and she sat reading in the car.

On the Sunday, after checking out of our hotel, she hobbled down the beach and flopped down in the cool water, inviting the lapping at her dress and prickling of salt on her skin.

'This is beautiful.'

'It sure is, although maybe you should have put bathers on.'

'Why would you bother?'

She hobbled back to the car, having bathed in nature and feeling content. And now we are on our way home and she's asleep and I don't think she'll make it back to Adelaide again.

Love Dad

20 January 2006

Kerrie was conflicted. Part of her felt it was best to die sooner rather than later, relieving Eddie of the trauma before he was old enough to remember. I don't know how she could think with such foresight. I wanted to ignore the future.

'Danny, I want you to move on when I'm gone. Start again as soon as possible,' she said. 'Don't wait because you feel you have to.'

'Look, Kerrie, I probably will move on, but I don't want to think about it.'

'Eddie will need a mum. And a good one, so don't fuck it up, okay?'

'Sure, Kerrie, whatever you say.'

To hear your wife talk about death was tough, to hear her talk about life without joy was crushing. In the past week, her spirits had free fallen. She asked me to telephone the priest.

Father John was close on retirement age, but he acted young. I liked that. He sat down at our kitchen table and casually declined a cup of tea (there's only so many you can have in a day). While we waited for Kerrie, I explained our world of semi-denial, how I avoided words such as terminal or death. He nodded gently. I didn't have the chance to expand further when Kerrie plonked herself at the table.

'I'm dying,' she said bluntly. 'And the thing is, I'm not feeling any joy. I'm worried that I'll never feel joy again before I die.'

Okay, so we'd moved on from semi-denial.

'I'm not afraid of dying, Father, but at the same time I don't want to leave my husband and my son. I'm worried about how they will cope,' she continued.

Okay, so she's worried about death. I'd better hold back these tears.

'I don't want to rule from the grave, but the one thing I thought I would be good at is teaching Eddie about faith,' Kerrie said.

Okay, she doesn't trust me with Eddie. I'd better bite harder; these tears are building.

Father John interceded. He couldn't make promises to Kerrie, and I'm glad he didn't try. He told her to trust the values we had already put in place.

'You can't rule from beyond the grave because it's not that simple. When Eddie is a teenager and Danny feels he has to talk about religion, Eddie will probably slam the door in his face,' he said.

I sat there not saying a word. Kerrie's hole was an abyss. How could you face life without joy? Father John had better bloody well know.

'You two have a lot to talk about,' he said. 'You need to have a good cry together.'

And then he reminded Kerrie of my promise: 'To have and to hold, from this day forward, for better, for worse, for richer, for poorer, in sickness or in health, to love and to cherish till death do us part.'

He was right. The landscape had changed. While cancer was Kerrie's burden, we had joint custody of sorrow. For better or for worse. We had to embrace sadness, together. We needed to revisit our past, dredge up good memories and bad, remember the irate and the serene. If we could cry, we could feel joy.

Failing all that, Father John said, Kerrie's faith would allow her to find her heaven. She would feel joy when she passed into God's arms.

And maybe that's all she needed to hear. That she would, indeed, find God.

In the same way I'd missed the depth of Kerrie's mental anguish, I'd overlooked her physical state. But when my mother suggested Kerrie needed to see a doctor, I took it as an affront, an undermining of my abilities as a carer. I snapped back.

Not until I walked away did I know she was right. Kerrie was losing colour.

I found it hard to push my wife about her health. It was like pushing her a step closer to death. But I convinced her this was a way of feeling better, and Dr Chrissie agreed. Kerrie's blood count was incredibly low and Dr Chrissie was amazed she could walk without falling over.

'You must be exhausted,' Dr Chrissie said.

'You must be light-headed,' Dr Chrissie said.

'You must have a blood transfusion,' Dr Chrissie said.

26 January 2006

It didn't matter that anyone could drop a slippery bottle on a tiled floor; it didn't matter that my uncle and aunty could wait for a drink; it didn't matter that broken glass and spilled water wouldn't leave a stain, it mattered that Kerrie was on her hands and knees treating each shard of glass like a piece of her life.

'I can't believe I could be so stupid,' she kept muttering.

As I knelt beside her on the floor I knew there was nothing I could say to make her feel better.

During the middle of the night I heard Kerrie vomiting, violent retches from the bathroom broke my sleep. It was cruel and I shivered. Vomiting was the thing we feared most – a sign her bowel was blocked. A sign the tumour was running out of room.

Her body convulsed with every purge like she was being twisted from the inside out. She moaned with pain.

'Is there anything I can do, honey?' I asked, rubbing her back.

'No, I'll be all right.'

'You poor thing. I wish this didn't have to happen.'

'So do I.'

'Can I get you a drink?'

'Lemonade would be nice.'

Kerrie went back to sleep before I could. It wasn't a happy Australia Day.

* * *

27 January 2006

Kerrie checked in for a blood transfusion and didn't come home for a week. Her bowel was blocked and she was tired and exhausted.

During the inevitable and tiresome questions regarding Kerrie's medical history – I can't believe these things aren't on computers, accessible to all hospitals – the ward sister asked if we had registered with palliative care and whether the district nurses were visiting regularly. No and no.

She looked surprised. 'I'll get that sorted out,' she said.

I was surprised, too. Actually I was dumbfounded. If these services were available, where were they? How come they didn't know about Kerrie? How come they didn't know I was living with my parents, aged 35? Was the medical system so overstretched and understaffed that they simply forgot people?

I felt let down and wanted to wave an accusing finger in someone's general direction. But at whom? I couldn't wave it at myself. Could I? Was I incredibly naïve to think that help just presented itself at your doorstep?

And the answer was probably yes. That's the problem with cancer: there's a long queue.

By the evening Kerrie was suffering severe abdominal cramps. She was given morphine to settle the pain and by the time her aching tummy had been calmed night had fallen. I left her asleep in hospital, hooked up to a drip and a bag of blood, and walked under the streetlights to the pub where my family was having dinner with my uncle and aunty and waiting for my news.

2 February 2006

Don't mention the f-word.

Nurses were hounding Kerrie about bowel movements, appearing at the foot of her bed, poking their heads around corners and yelling out from the corridor. It's all they wanted to know. Have you farted yet? The f-word. Charming.

Kerrie didn't appreciate the interrogation.

'No. I'll tell you when I have, believe me,' she would reply tersely.

The question made her feel inadequate.

'It's like I'm letting everybody down. I would if I could. I want to, believe me.'

The problem was, Kerrie's immediate future relied on her passing wind, an ephemeral sign that her bowel was unravelling. And I was no better than the nurses, guilty of asking the same question, wanting to know whether the encouraging gurgles and rumbles picked up by the doctor's stethoscope had delivered on their promise.

'Have you farted yet?'

'Not you, too?'

'I'm sorry, honey. I just want to know, that's all.'

Of course, I wasn't always loitering around Kerrie's room. I had to get Eddie to kindergarten in his red shirt because the first day arrived quicker than a birthday.

Eddie wasn't nervous, I was. Looking out from the car at the gathering of mothers, knowing Kerrie would have joined the line, waiting for the kindergarten's door to open, sharing her expectations and doubts, making them laugh with her wisecracks. I couldn't take her place. All along, kindergarten, schooling and education were her concerns, things she worried about while I picked out horses. I couldn't join the line, not while she was in hospital, not without a parent to hide behind, or a leg to clutch on to.

It was Eddie who forged the way, barging through the front gate and up the path as if he had caught sight of The Beatles, introducing me into conversation along the way. He was a leg to hide behind.

But having an extroverted son didn't always prove to be a godsend because an hour after I dropped him off, I had to go back, for fruit duty. I was first on the roster. Figuring it was not something I would enjoy, but something Kerrie would have done, I'd volunteered first to get it out of the road.

'Hi, Dad. What are you doing here?' Eddie asked as I walked through the gate.

'I'm on duty,' I said. 'I'm here to make sure everyone gets their fruit.'

'Hey, Dad, this is my friend Cameron. Cameron, this is my dad.'

'Nice to meet you, Cameron.'

'Hey everyone this is my dad.'

Then Eddie embarrassed me further by coming over and hugging my leg, forcing me to half push him off while walking away, in case this wasn't appropriate parent–child behaviour in the kindergarten playground. Initial efforts failed because Eddie was dragging along the ground, clinging on to my left knee.

'Let go,' I hissed trying to shake him off.

Eddie thought it was fun.

'Eddie, let go,' I said with a deeper growl and a more forceful leg.

He refused to budge, so I reached down and prised him off, giving him a quick hug and telling him to go play. At least I wouldn't have to worry about such behaviour at secondary school. I'd probably be hanging on to his leg.

Later I sat by Kerrie at the hospital, telling her about my day.

'I cut up so much fruit it wasn't funny,' I said. 'They had five different tables of kids so I had to make up a plate for each. I cut up apples, pears, bananas, oranges and even kiwifruit. But kiwifruit is ridiculous. By the time you peel a kiwifruit and cut it in half there's hardly enough for one kid. And what kid likes kiwifruit? Anyway, I definitely overdid the fruit. They only had about three pieces each and the rest was thrown in the bin.'

'Did Eddie eat much?' she asked.

'He had a bit of apple and banana. But he couldn't sit still. He was turning one way and then the other, like he does at home. None of the other kids seemed to be as restless. He's definitely got ADD. I had to resist the urge to go and hold him still.'

'Oh dear,' she smiled.

'You should have seen them grabbing the fruit from the plate. They were meant to use a pair of tongs and put their fruit in a bowl. None did. They just grabbed with their hands. When they were told to use the tongs, they put the fruit back with their hands and used the tongs to grab another bit. Talk about hygienic.'

'What else did you do?'

'Not much. I raked the sandpit and washed the plates. I think Mrs Carmichael took it easy on me because I looked a bit lost. Then I decided to push Eddie and a couple of the other kids on the swing. Before you knew it they had all lined up. Even the Iraqi kids, who hardly speak any English. It just goes to show that playing is a universal language. Anyway, kids were pushing in, wanting two goes, wanting to go higher, wanting to go longer. It was a nightmare. I was lucky to get out of there alive,' I said.

'Oh Danny, you would have loved it,' she said, calling my bluff.

She was right. I did enjoy showing my son I could be king of the kids.

Brrrrrt. Fffffftt. Fffffft. Brrrrrt.

Was that what I thought it was?

Kerrie was able to give the nurses the answer they'd been looking for.

'Yes, I have,' she said.

With the good news came little rewards, such as icy-poles, and big treats, such as visits from friends.

'I feel great,' she said, pointing out new additions to the flowers surrounding her bed. 'I feel loved. It is wonderful to feel loved.'

If she felt loved, I felt on top of the world. The old Kerrie was back. Something we feared would never happen during our talk with Father John.

3 February 2006

Dear Eddie,

Kerrie arrives home happy with flushed cheeks and an appetite. Even her freckles look bolder.

She hugs you and showers you with kisses.

'Hello, darling. Mummy's home,' she says.

You respond, asking if she wants to play trains, or build a train track. You don't mind that she says no. You're happy to sit by her side and watch a DVD.

Love Dad

6 February 2006

Where would you like to die?

What a question. Most of us have a funeral song, or an offbeat idea for a wake, but not many I know have pinpointed a location for checking out.

Kerrie was given two options: at home, or in hospital.

It was hardly appealing. Not like picking a holiday with a stack of brochures strewn across the table, revealing exotic locations and their even more exotic people. No, it was home or hospital. Not so much as a coral reef.

Palliative care people, in order to provide quality of life and peace of mind for the dying, had to ask the shit questions. Like the proposal for terminally ill young mums: do you want to leave a memory box for your son?

I admired Kerrie for the way she composed herself in the face of these questions. I admired the palliative care nurse for asking them. I wanted to give my wife a hug, show how much I admired her courage. Instead, I had to grab a bucket because she started throwing up.

Two days later, Kerrie checked herself into what she called the 'dying room'. On face value it was the presidential suite of Cobram hospital with its ensuite, adjoining sitting room, fridge, kettle, microwave, TV and video player. It was basically a self-contained unit and had appeal if you could get past certain decorative aspects and Kerrie's unvarnished description. Even the nurses chuckled nervously.

She didn't say 'dying room' with loathing or trepidation; she was just good at cutting through the bullshit and describing the scene for what it was – a place where palliative care patients were afforded privacy and a splash of luxury.

Despite being sent home five days earlier, her bowel had not settled. Despite daily visits from district nurses, Kerrie had continued cramping and vomiting. So she was back in hospital, nil by mouth, frailer, hungrier and a little more desperate.

After Kerrie settled into her dying room, I stocked up on light reading – *Women's Weekly*, *Woman's Day*, *New Idea*, *Take 5* and *That's Life!*

When the magazines weren't distraction enough, Kerrie asked me to wheel her through the hospital gardens to see the flowers and smell their scents on the wind. At times she asked me to slow the pace, partly to offset the path's cracks and crevices jolting the rigid wheels, and partly to slow down the passing world.

'Be careful of the bumps, my tummy is pretty tender,' she said.

'Sure, honey. Is there anywhere else you'd like to go?'

'Let's go to the church.'

The church was empty save for a friend's dad doing spot repairs in the foyer. He stopped his hammering to chat, treating our meeting as if we were passing in the street, not placing any emphasis on Kerrie sitting in a wheelchair.

Next Kerrie had me wheel her to the altar, and then around the church.

'Let's see if we can guess all the Stations of the Cross,' she said.

'I think I'll leave that game to you, Kerrie. I'm not really up to speed with my Stations of the Cross.'

I don't know what Kerrie was thinking as we moved around the church, although I suspect it was a feeling of closeness. Not with me, but with her belief in God. It was her way of keeping in touch.

10 February 2006

Taking Eddie on a hospital visit proved a double-edged sword. He needed to spend time with Kerrie; he didn't need to be racing down the corridor with his extraordinarily loud voice almost shocking elderly patients out of dementia. Thankfully, the nurses never seemed to mind.

'Hi, Mum,' he would say, bursting into her room with me in his wake.

'Hello, darling,' she would say, never surprised to see him because his booming vocals had sounded a warning sign from half a hospital away.

And while she asked him about kindergarten and his new friends, Eddie would hunt around the room for a chocolate frog or an icy-pole. Sometimes his attention span lasted longer, particularly when we read him a book, but invariably he would become noisy and distracting, totally ignorant of our concerns for sick people in adjoining rooms. As a result I'd start feeling guilty and responsible and sometimes my edginess would rub off on Kerrie, who would also get annoyed, and I knew it was time to leave.

'It's time to go, Ed. Say goodbye to Mum.'

'Bye, Mum.'

'Bye, honey.'

I always misjudged the length of our visits, but by the time I'd dropped Eddie with Granny and Pa and returned to see Kerrie, she was fine. She never worried that letting off steam would ruin our family unit.

11 February 2006

Did I slag off the ambulance?

Call them bastards for grabbing my 2004 spring carnival punting money?

I take it back, now that we are bona fide members. They flew Kerrie to Melbourne and it didn't cost us a cent.

After a fortnight without a decent meal, worried nurses and Dr Chrissie agreed that Kerrie should return to Peter Mac where she could access a wider and a better-equipped support network.

For the first time, Kerrie talked about pushing the doctors for a colostomy bag.

'Anything that will help,' she said.

Dr Chrissie organised a shot of Valium, laughing when Kerrie revealed she was a nervous flyer. She also allowed Kerrie one more request.

'Can I have a biscuit, Chrissie?'

'Look, you know you shouldn't have one. But how can I say no?'

Rather than react adversely to his mum being whisked away by strange men in uniforms, Eddie treated the paramedics with reverence. After all, they had a kick-arse ambulance with flashing lights and blaring sirens. Far more impressive than our tired 1990 Ford sedan. Kerrie, too, was excited by the occasion. Apart from being booked into chillsville by her Valium jab, she was relieved that something was being done.

'How are you feeling? Are you nervous or anxious?' I asked.

'No, I'm not at all. I'm looking forward to flying,' she said.

Eddie trailed the paramedics to their ambulance as if he was trailing in the shadows of gods. Kerrie, who would be driven to Tocumwal to meet the plane, was chatting away dreamily. I wished they had room for me; it was one flight I did not want to miss.

'See you in Melbourne, honey. And don't go taking any detours, like setting a course for Ireland,' I said.

'Oh, wouldn't that be wonderful. I'll see you in Melbourne. I love you.'

'I love you, too.'

* * *

Hi Peter Mac, I'm back. Walking through your familiar foyer, past the same receptionists and the same café with its cancer victims and their hollow faces and their sad-eyed families. Back following the red line to the slow, clunky old Schindler's lifts. I never would have noticed the name if my observant wife hadn't pointed it out.

However, I did notice Kerrie's nasogastric tube. We were back on familiar ground, looking out the window at St Pat's Cathedral, and a plastic pipe dangling from her nose.

'I didn't have any choice,' she said.

'Is it okay?'

'So far. But it's harder to talk and swallow with the tube rubbing the back of my throat.'

'How was the flight?'

'It was fantastic; so smooth. One of the paramedics sat next to me the whole way, telling me where we were and how long until we landed. There was a little bit of turbulence flying in over Melbourne, but it was so much better than a jet. The way to fly, any day.'

'Did you fly over our old Pascoe Vale house?'

'I think so, I couldn't see because I was lying down.'

For the three years we lived in Pascoe Vale South, we knew the air ambulance by its distinct drone and lower trajectory into Essendon airport. I never thought it would be one day landing with Kerrie on board.

I made the 250 kilometres journey to Melbourne by road, hitching a ride along the Hume Freeway with Aunty Annette, talking about the ranges of emotions cancer evoked. Annette understood. She had lost her husband to the disease.

I told her that until recently cancer had largely shut me out, almost like the paramedics had kept me off the plane. It was Kerrie's journey, I said, and I only had a supporting role. I could only help when she asked. I couldn't make her do things, or eat things, or see people she didn't want to see. No one could. And many had tried. They couldn't comprehend that Kerrie knew what was on offer. That she knew what options were available. Kerrie had talked to experts, sought counselling, scoured the internet and each time arrived at the same conclusion: there was no cure.

I told Aunty Annette there was a black hole waiting for me when Kerrie died, but until then I took great comfort in her being alive. As long as I could be by her side, I said, I felt okay. I would worry about the hole when the lid was taken off.

12 February 2006

Kerrie's X-rays and scans sounded like a water board maintenance report: multiple loops with significant backlogs. Thankfully, Peter Mac's plumbers were confident of her pipes flowing again. A combination of the nasogastric tube, IV fluids, mild laxatives and enemas were expected to ease the constipation and faecal loading.

'We'll attack the problem from both ends,' I think was what the doctors said.

We felt more confident: specialised staff, a greater array of modern equipment and The Professor, Kerrie's surgeon. He'd helped us before, and she was hoping he could do it again.

Despite her suffering, I loved sitting by Kerrie's bedside. Few distractions, few interruptions. It's where I belonged.

Although I was occasionally dispatched on errands.

My first assignment: 'Bring me underpants and a nightgown.'

Simple. I'd catch Schindler's lifts to the ground floor, follow the red line to the front door, walk past Parliament Station to the Target store I had seen in Bourke Street and be back in no time.

'Just underpants and a nightgown? Was there anything else? No? Great, see you soon.'

Until then, of course, I wouldn't have been caught dead in the women's underwear section of Target. But you do these things for love.

The task proved more daunting than I anticipated – lurking in the shadows of underwear racks, wondering if female shoppers were looking my way. Paranoid thoughts started spreading like burning incense.

I'm being watched: *They are going to think I'm a pervert, aren't they? Why else would I be skulking around the ladies' briefs? I'd better make this quick.*

I couldn't remember Kerrie's size: *It won't matter if they're a bit big, will it?*

I didn't know what colour she liked: *I think she has some pink jocks, doesn't she?*

Or what style she liked: *Do they come in different styles?*

Then the tug-of-war started.

What about these ones here, they look all right.

Don't touch them, you fool, women are watching.

I wasn't doing anything. Oh shit …

Just grab them. Quickly.

But you said don't touch them.

How else are you going to get them off the rack? I meant don't fondle the bloody things.

Make up your mind …

Just grab the women's underpants.

Did you just say that out loud?

No, I didn't. I don't think I did. Fuck …

I snatched the undies from the rack, stuffed them under my arm, hoping they weren't the wrong size, wrong colour and wrong shape, and started looking for another two pairs so I could hightail it back to the hospital.

Then there was the girl at the cash register.

'Just these, thanks,' I said, smiling as I handed over my purchase. 'Just these three pairs of women's underpants.'

When I dropped the clothes on Kerrie's bed, I couldn't help myself: 'I hope you appreciate these after all I've been through.'

'Oh honey, you're so silly. They wouldn't have even noticed you were there.'

13 February 2006

Visitors were not always welcome. At times Kerrie wanted to shield people from her suffering, on other occasions she wanted to avoid their pity. There were also moments of throwing up or being pricked and prodded, none of which became miraculously easier when a well-meaning friend or relative appeared waving roses at the doorway.

I didn't mind playing guard dog because, within reason, I wanted Kerrie to myself.

During my travels throughout the corridors of Peter Mac, I noticed family members and friends sitting by bedsides in a myriad of poses – fidgety, staring into space, talking non-stop, holding hands, even eating leftover hospital food. Some visitors looked uncomfortable, some patients looked like they'd rather be left alone.

For me, being with Kerrie felt safe. The only time I looked at the clock was with reluctance at seeing the day running away.

'It's funny, but we talk better here than we do at home,' Kerrie said.

'We do. It's a bit like being in the car; there are no distractions. I don't feel obliged to go and play with Ed, or do the washing, or play golf.'

When the conversation ran dry, we would bury our heads in the newspapers and fill up the well, Kerrie often breaking the silence with a sense of outrage – 'Can you believe they are spending all this money on the Commonwealth Games?' – or me stopping to announce the races were on at Ballarat. We laughed about the absurdities or cleverness of letters to the editor, we discussed columnists and their rants, before turning to the crosswords and Kerrie would come up with solutions seconds after I had finished reading out the clues.

'How can I improve if I don't have time to think of an answer?' I complained.

'You're already good at crosswords,' she would counter.

Then there were more errands.

'You know what I need, some lip balm. I must have left the other stuff in Cobram.'

'I'll go down and get you some, shall I?'

'That would be great.'

'But I'm not getting any more undies.'

'No more undies.'

At 5.30 pm we would turn to the TV and watch *Deal or no Deal* with Andrew O'Keefe, Kerrie exasperated at the greed of contestants, while I took umbrage with those too prudent to take a risk.

'Take the money. Eighteen thousand dollars is a lot of money,' Kerrie would say. 'I can't believe how greedy some people are.'

'Yeah, but they could have two hundred thousand in their own suitcase. They could win two hundred thousand. They would be spewing if they took only eighteen thousand. And it's more exciting if they play on.'

Apart from the friendly banter there were many topics to discuss. After our heart-to-heart with Father John, I felt like I'd been opened. If something was playing on my mind, I could raise it with Kerrie.

Her father was different. Brendan had driven Des across from Adelaide and I think he aged each time he saw his daughter lying ill in bed. There was the perfunctory opener – How are you feeling, love? – followed by the weather or petrol prices.

They couldn't talk about dying.

'I'm fine, Dad,' was Kerrie's standard reply.

They couldn't change roles. She was his little girl and he was her soft and gentle father. They hadn't outgrown the picture on our wall: Des with Kerrie on her first day of school, his eyes sparkling with pride.

When Des walked through the door, Kerrie would will herself off the pillow, chirping like Julie Andrews auditioning for *The Sound of Music*, rather than a cancer patient in dire straits. But her weight was one change she could not disguise. And if Grandpa Des had tried to ignore her fading condition, her brother certainly could not.

Until then, Brendan hadn't said much. But we sat up all night talking about Kerrie, Brendan revealing he wanted to tell his sister that our kids would always maintain close links. He wanted our children to grow up knowing each other.

'Tell Kerrie,' I said. 'I think she'd love to hear it. Kerrie and I have already begun clearing the decks. We've said a lot of what needs to be said. We've spoken about funerals, we've spoken about how I will struggle to cope without her, we've spoken about how she struggles with the thought of missing Eddie growing up, and we've spoken about Eddie's future. Now it might be your turn, while she's well enough to appreciate your sentiments. I'll take Des for a coffee tomorrow morning so that you can have a chat.'

By then we could hardly keep our eyes open and there were no barriers left. Except one: Kerrie's time on earth.

'I just hope her suffering doesn't drag on too long,' Brendan said. 'I don't want her to suffer. It's too cruel.'

He was right, but I couldn't let go so easily. As long as she was alive, I didn't have to mourn. I was stressed by her illness, but I couldn't bear the thought of her gone.

Selfishly, I didn't want it over quickly.

Valentine's Day, 14 February 2006

Dear Eddie,
I arrive at hospital to receive this letter from your mum. I think it's my most prized possession.

My darling Dan,
It is just after dawn here in Peter Mac and I woke to loving thoughts of you. It is quiet and a good time to write down the things I was thinking before the breakfast/doctors' rounds chaos begins.

Actually, this is your Valentine's card, immobile cheapskate that I am. I know some couples today will lavish gaudy jewellery or a hot-air balloon flight on each other. As always, words are all I have – but I think somehow you prefer it that way (well, you'd better!)

And what was I thinking this morning about you? How I can't believe it has been 10 years since that infamous night at Someplace Else. That's nearly a third of our lives now. How I can't believe how much we've grown, individually and together, in that time. How I can't believe we're the same people we were in 1996. We've been so heedless and carefree and had so much pointless fun.

And now our stories are very different. And I'm so proud of how we – especially you – have dealt with all the sadness and trauma that has seemed to rain down on us since our marriage.

We have raised an incredible life-force of a boy through all of this and our union has just got deeper and stronger. C.S. Lewis said something like we are plain slabs of marble under the sculptor's chisel. It is his blows which hurt us so much that ultimately make us perfect.

You are perfect to me, Dan. You are a man in the truest sense of the word. You have walked with me through my darkest days, never flinching, helping steady and comfort me. Putting up with so much, so graciously.

Embracing my family with more grace than I do. Your generosity and good will still astonish me.

I look at you and feel proud, but also a little bit humbled when so often my own reserves of cheer are low. I look at the boy I met and see the man he has become and am so damn grateful that somehow God saved you for me. Do you see now why I trust and love Him so much?

Yours, forever
Kerrie

15 February 2006

I began each day the same, meeting Brian at The Galleon in St Kilda, sitting among the baggy-eyed patrons and their coffees, wondering what sort of day they had ahead, whether they too might be preparing to visit a hospital or a sick friend. I liked meeting Brian at The Galleon. It seemed an appropriate start to the morning. Kerrie and I had history at the place. We went there ten years ago on our first official date, sharing a bottle of red among its organised clutter, perched on our stools looking out on to Carlisle Street and feeling out each other's personalities. She let me do most of the talking all those years ago, and I remember being secretly chuffed at how interested she was in my goals and dreams. Without saying much, she made me feel taller, broader and smarter.

But that was then. On these mornings, mostly, I let Brian do the talking, allowing my mind to be filled with anything other than Kerrie's health – his work at Luna Park, horses, or dysfunctional stories about our dysfunctional friends.

Coffees finished, we would go our separate ways, Brian returning to work while I caught the 96 tram to the city, sneaking glances at fellow travellers, trying to read their faces behind iPods and commuter masks, wondering what traumas they had in their lives.

Those mornings helped me feel alive, watching the hustle and bustle of St Kilda's diverse human traffic, moving among their collective pulse. It was the reason I could arrive at Peter Mac with a smile

But on this day the smile was wiped from my face. Kerrie was told she could live for another two years.

On face value, these tidings couldn't have been better and I should have been doing backflips. But while Kerrie couldn't contain her joy, I felt awkwardly ambivalent. Even hollow.

Here was my dilemma: I'd begun bracing for Kerrie's death, not her bouncing back to good health and carrying on for another two years.

Did that make me a shit?

The positive prognosis had come via her oncologist.

'He said because my tumour had remained localised and not spread to other organs or parts of the body it could be better managed. And he said with proper management there was no reason why I couldn't live for another couple of years. Isn't that great?'

'Yes,' I said.

The oncologist had sat with Kerrie on a good day. He told her his research team had made a breakthrough, and she said he'd almost levitated with excitement. The sense of achievement spread to Kerrie. She, too, almost floated out of bed.

I felt like a traitor because I didn't believe it was true.

I didn't want to feel bad. I didn't want to feel stupid for having triggered the panic button, subtly preparing myself, family and friends for the end. Despite Kerrie's new-found verve, it was a hard feeling to shake.

'Does this mean you will see visitors now?' I asked.

'Maybe one or two,' she smiled.

I shared my conflicting emotions with two people that night: Brian and Brendan.

'Kerrie's physical state doesn't allow me to believe she can live for another two years,' I said. 'Am I wrong to think this way? I mean, it seems a ridiculous thing to tell her if it's not true. How can she be okay for another two years when they haven't got on top of this current problem?'

Brian suggested that I should focus on Kerrie's reaction to the news. And in some ways he was right.

Brendan, however, was less circumspect. His eyes, too, told him other than two years.

'But let's hope he's right and we're wrong,' he said.

'Let's hope so.'

16 February 2006

Kerrie's first visitor was a newspaper colleague and good friend, Steve. They were chatting when I arrived at the hospital, Kerrie holding a McDonald's Coke in her hand. She was explaining matter-of-factly that her bowel obstruction was merely a hiccup, she was fighting fit and had a good couple of years left in her yet. She seemed to discount that not eating a decent meal or sitting on the dunny for three weeks amounted to slightly more than a hiccup. But that was Kerrie's way. She sifted for gold.

'You can't beat a McDonald's Coke,' she said, sipping away.

When she had been flown to Melbourne from Cobram, I queried whether she would return. The answer had become yes. She was on a light diet, felt bright and the doctors agreed she could go back to Cobram in two days.

Later I told Kerrie of a guy I had overheard on the tram. He was a lean man, aged in his twenties, talking through a goatee, wearing a white T-shirt, faded jeans and standing in a door-well explaining to a stranger that he was fresh out of jail and looking for a job. While this ex-con had jolted speech and crude grammar, I was captivated by how candidly he spoke about his new-found liberty, rolling through the city streets without a curfew, not having to answer to screws, and free of a claustrophobic cell. He didn't look like a bad person, more a lost soul, probably caught in the wrong place at the wrong time.

'Perhaps everyone is getting a second chance this week,' I said to Kerrie.

18 February 2006

The night before she was to be released, Kerrie bled internally and suffered a fever, shaking uncontrollably in the middle of the night. Doctors told her the tumour might be breaching her bowel, which in turn was releasing 'nasty bugs' into her system. Her haemoglobin had plunged to 76 grams per litre – the normal range is between 120 and 150 for a woman – and with it the door to freedom slammed in her face. She was treated with IV antibiotics and given a blood transfusion. More needles, more tubes, more time. Rather than being disappointed, Kerrie said she was glad to have caught the problem before we went home. She said it with a sense of resignation.

20 February 2006

Dear Eddie,

I know we haven't seen you for a more than a week, but Mum is still having trouble with her tummy. We think about you every second and I hope you enjoy the toys and DVD in this parcel. Granny and Pa say you have been entertaining all their friends, and loving kindergarten.

I don't know when we'll be home. I'm staying at Brian and Chel's flat and visiting Mum every day. Believe it or not, the thing she talks about most, apart from you, is food. I sneak into Chinatown for lunch and she makes me recall the meals in depth, devouring every morsel of detail. It sounds perverse, but she practically eats the answers. She even made Brian and Chel describe their Valentine's Day dinner.

'I shouldn't really be talking about what we ate,' Brian said, slightly embarrassed.

'Oh, don't be silly,' Kerrie prompted. 'I want to know. It all sounds so delicious.'

The back of her eyelids must resemble a cookbook, covered with images of different cuisines, allowing her mind's chef to recreate the meals. She's odd, your mum.

Speaking of odd, a pregnant Indian woman fainted at the foot of Kerrie's bed today. She's a doctor, part of a palliative care team reviewing your mother, and she complained of feeling light-headed and needing to sit down. Before I could make room, she collapsed, thankfully into the arms of a female colleague.

Kerrie almost jumped out of bed.

'Oh, are you all right, darling? Oh, you poor thing. Here have some of this water. Danny, get her a seat so she can sit down.'

The Indian doctor regained consciousness quickly. She must have been surprised to see us gathered around peering down.

'I'm okay,' she said, slightly embarrassed.

'Are you sure?' Kerrie persisted. 'Here, have some water.'

She poured a cup from her bedside pitcher and asked me to pass it across to the pregnant doctor who was now seated on a chair, regaining her composure. Apart from the initial scare, it became a beautiful moment: your mum, the dying patient, wanting to comfort and care for the doctor.

Hope to see you soon.

Love Dad

21 February 2006

The pregnant-Indian-doctor-fainting episode inadvertently resulted in Kerrie having a fall. She looked sheepish when I greeted her mid-morning.

'Hi, Kerrie. How are you feeling?'

'Okay, but the most embarrassing thing happened to me during the night,' she said, glad to be getting it off her chest.

'What?'

'I thought I heard Joyce calling out for help from the bathroom in the middle of the night. I got up and said, "Are you all right, Joyce?" and in my rush to get across the room stumbled and fell over.'

'Did you hurt yourself?'

'No, I'm fine. But I must have imagined it because Joyce was still in bed and said she didn't say anything. I feel so stupid.'

'Don't feel stupid, you thought you were doing the right thing.'

There were two fall-outs from Kerrie's mid-night accident: she was embarrassed and her file was marked 'prone to falls'.

Prone to falls? This was outrageous, I thought, grossly unfair. Kerrie said she tripped over. I would have an indignant word to these nurses and tell them to change the file back. My wife wasn't an invalid.

Was she?

And then I studied the evidence: Kerrie was rarely getting out of bed. Apart from the odd trip accompanying me to the canteen, she didn't leave the room. She was too tired to use her legs.

If only I could think like a woman. I mean, that had to be the reason I didn't buy Kerrie moisturiser or massage her legs. Chel beat me to the punch, waltzing in one afternoon carrying creams and lotions from The Body Shop, making Kerrie feel indulged and glad to avoid hospital-issue shampoo and soap.

I was slightly jealous of Chel's foresight and annoyed at myself for ignorantly overlooking my wife's need for pampering. To make matters worse, a nurse started rubbing these creams into Kerrie's swollen and irritated legs, filling the room with the most delicious aroma, stopping noses in the corridor, and eliciting groans of pleasure from my wife.

'I could have done that,' I said. 'I could have been doing that for the past three weeks. Why didn't I think to massage your legs? Why didn't I think to buy you creams and lotions? Why didn't you ask?'

'You can't think of everything.'

The big difference between Kerrie and her two roommates was their age. They were grey-haired, retired and grandmothers. Kerrie was thirty-six. That didn't stop her from making friends. She also liked the nurses, adroitly manipulating the conversation so they felt comfortable talking about themselves. Undoubtedly, though, her favourite was Jimmy, the food trolley man. Jimmy didn't have medical qualifications, he couldn't administer painkillers, and yet I think his sunny disposition was Kerrie's best medicine.

Jimmy was Asian, and could always read her mood. If she was tired and miserable, he flitted in and out, hardly making a sound. If she was feeling okay, he would stop for a chat and his smile would make her laugh. I never felt jealous of Jimmy. How could I when he gave me so many biscuits?

Occasionally I needed a friend, too. Apart from my nightly chats with Brian and Chel I organised to meet my brothers Pete and Chris. After filling the ward with laughter and obscenities, we bade Kerrie goodnight and adjourned to a nearby restaurant. It always struck me as incongruous to be enjoying a meal while Kerrie was wasting away. Nevertheless, by the time we had finished and Pete had dropped me off at St Kilda, I felt like there was a collective arm of support resting around my shoulders.

22 February 2006

I didn't understand medicine.

Kerrie's pain-relief tablets could cause constipation. So her palliative care team suggested she used slow-release patches instead. They would relieve her discomfort and wouldn't clog her pipes.

There had to be a catch. There had to be. Otherwise my sarcasm was justified.

'Kerrie, a month after your bowel is blocked, some bright spark decides that patches will help. They'll help alleviate your pain and ease your constipation. That's pretty quick thinking, isn't it?'

'As long as they work, I don't care,' Kerrie said.

How could she not care about going a month without a decent feed? Four weeks without a bowl of pasta? Thirty days without a steak? How could she not care that some bloody bright spark hadn't produced these patches a bit fucking earlier?

No, what she did care about was an upcoming meeting with The Professor, desperate to know if he'd discovered a rabbit up his sleeve.

'We've got to try anything we can,' she said.

We were seated in the patients' lounge watching TV when The Professor arrived, bringing in his serious face. The smiles didn't follow.

If, as he suspected, Kerrie's tumour was eroding the wall of her bowel and releasing nasty bugs into her system, a colostomy bag couldn't help. Nor would deblocking the tumour. In other words, there was no rabbit.

He told Kerrie he would operate if that were her wish, but the risks were great. She was incredibly weak.

'I don't want to have surgery if nothing can be done,' she said.

Kerrie was deflated, but far from falling apart.

'Don't look so glum,' she told him.

But how else could he look? He was telling her precisely what she didn't want to hear. This was the end.

'You should go home and be with your family,' he said.

28 February 2006

For the past month I could walk out the front door whenever I felt like a break – there were trains and trams to catch, people to study, shops to stroll past, CD stores to browse through, coffees to drink, even traffic lights.

Kerrie had missed four weeks of the world.

'You must be looking forward to getting out,' I said.

'I am, but you get used to being institutionalised. Sometimes it's hard to imagine doing anything different.'

When we checked out, doctors told Kerrie to keep in constant contact and book in to Cobram hospital for blood transfusions whenever she needed them.

'Oh, I don't know about that. Other people might need the blood more than me,' she said.

With cancer, unlike mainstream life, the highs and lows flow in closer sequence. Kerrie spent half of her first night back in Cobram with her head in an ice-cream container. The excitement of coming home, the three-hour drive and the KFC had taken their toll. I emptied the container in the toilet and washed it out with disinfectant in the laundry sink. Kerrie said sorry each time I returned to bed. The answer was always the same: 'Don't worry, honey, it's not your fault.'

But by morning she was no longer vomiting and was, in a vague sort of way, content. She had her pain-relief patches, breakthrough drugs and pay TV. She re-ignited her love affair with *Little House on the Prairie* and its star, Michael Landon. But as the day wore on, I became more alarmed. Kerrie was stoned. She was falling in and out of sleep, sometimes nodding off halfway through an article, the newspaper still in her hands. I called her name and she opened her eyes, returning to the paper and reading again as if she hadn't dozed off at all.

I asked her a question and she slurred a response. My razor-sharp soul mate was fading to grey.

Kerrie woke me during the night to go to the toilet. I helped her out of bed and into the bathroom and there's probably no other way to put it other than things just happened. For six weeks she had barely passed more than a pebble or a nugget but this night it flowed. There was nothing to do but laugh, at the noise, at the breakthrough and at the new sense of hope. If her system was working, she could eat properly again. And if she could eat, she could regain weight. I started to believe in the two years. Kerrie, however, was as bewildered as she was relieved.

'It's a little bit strange, don't you think?' she said as I helped her back to the bedroom.

'What do you mean?'

'Well, that they kept me this way for so long and then all of a sudden I can go to the toilet. It's too good to be true, don't you think?'

'I don't get what you mean. I think it's great you can go to the toilet, but who are "they"?'

'Never mind.'

2 March 2006

'They' turned out to be a conspiracy theory. And so was I, according to a more lucid Kerrie, who had slept off her drug-induced haze. For the past 24 hours Kerrie had believed that doctors, nurses and myself were purposely keeping her weak and frail.

'I thought there were two Dannys,' she said, shaking her head.

'What?'

'I thought that the real Danny had been taken away and that you were a second Danny put in place to keep me in this state. I didn't think you were a bad person, just not the real Danny,' she continued.

'Are you serious?'

'Yes. That's what I believed last night. And that's why I thought it was so odd that suddenly I was able to go to the toilet.'

'But you think I'm the real Danny today, don't you?'

'Of course I do, honey,' she laughed.

'Because I am the real Danny. And I'm not trying to keep you sick. I'm so glad you went to the toilet.'

As far as I know, the second Danny was wiped from existence when the palliative care nurse arrived at our front door the following afternoon and immediately noticed Kerrie's drug-taking was out of whack. She said Kerrie was having too many breakthrough painkillers on top of the slow-release patches.

I was right, she was stoned out of her brain.

From now on, I was told, I should take custody of the medicine box. This meant changing Kerrie's patches every three days, dealing out breakthrough painkillers when necessary, making a note of all the pills that were swallowed and, as a result, further eroding my wife's independence.

What a boxful of pills they were – Coloxyl, Coloxyl with senna, dexamethasone, paracetamol, pantroprazole, cyclizine, metronidazole, oxycodone and the fentanyl patches. Some were swallowed half a pill a day, some were taken three times a day and all of them had different purposes, from pain relief to alleviating constipation.

Typically, Kerrie wouldn't swallow them all.

'I'm starting to rattle I'm taking that many pills,' she said. 'And half of them don't make any difference.'

The patches, however, had been a revelation.

3 March 2006

I forgot our wedding anniversary. I didn't give it a thought.

Kerrie remembered and she was the one on drugs. I walked into the lounge room and noticed a bottle of Moët on the table.

Kerrie had pasted her favourite wedding photos on a hand-made card:

March 3, 2001
D
On this date
my life gained
meaning & purpose
thank you for five
years of overwhelming
love & tenderness

x x x x x
K

Amid the pain and suffering, Kerrie never stopped making me feel special.

I popped the cork and poured two glasses. Kerrie managed little more than a sip.

6 March 2006

I couldn't pick up a baseball bat or a brick lest I smashed every mirror in the house. Kerrie didn't need to see herself all skin and bone, looking like she had stepped out of Changi Prison and the Second World War. No person should see herself or himself that way.

I helped Kerrie undress and into the shower cubicle, but not before she turned and lamented her reflection, malnourished and underfed, her ribs jutting out like they'd been living in Ethiopia for six months. I had to disguise my shock.

'Look at me,' she said, peering at herself in the mirror, which I felt like ripping from the wall. 'I'm just skin and bone. I look awful. Oh Danny, this is not me! This is not me!'

I tried my best not to cry.

'Kerrie, I know who you are.'

'I wish I could put on weight.'

'If you keep having chocolate thick-shakes and continue to keep food down, you'll put weight back on. And no matter what, Kerrie, you are still beautiful. I'll always think that.'

I helped her sit on a special chair under the shower and as she washed her hair, I stripped to my boxer shorts and washed her legs, exfoliating the flaking skin. As water ran down my arms and legs onto the bathroom floor, I was gripped by the change in our lives – not until Kerrie became an invalid had I ever done anything truly special for her.

When she finished showering and I ensured every soap sud had been rinsed from her hair, I placed my arms under her shoulders and gently lifted Kerrie to her feet. When she was at full height, apart from the cancerous stoop, she kissed me gently on the neck. I didn't want to let go.

7 March 2006

Apart from helping Kerrie in and out of her lounge chair, I became her eyes and ears, explaining how Eddie bounced into kindergarten each morning, saying hello to the mums and announcing that he was wearing a red shirt. Just in case they hadn't noticed.

'Red's my favourite colour, you know?'

I told Kerrie how I would invariably have to stop Eddie racing for the toys because he had forgotten to hang his backpack and pull out his lunch. She smiled at the image of our son turning in bewilderment and the obvious question written across his face – if it's so important to hang a bag and grab a lunchbox, why don't you do it, Dad?

On this day, however, I spent all morning at kindergarten. My second fruit-duty shift. During a break, I sat and listened to Mrs von Appen read a book about families to the class. The book made mention of identical twins.

'We have twins in our class, don't we?' she said, looking up at the circle of nodding faces. 'Can anyone tell me who they are?'

I told Kerrie I felt proud when Eddie piped up with their names, Peter and Josh, two boys who happened to be absent that day. And I told her how I stifled a laugh when another boy quickly added: 'We know they're twins because they're both the same colour.'

The book then moved to the father of the story, which prompted a whispered response from a little girl.

'What did you say?' the boy beside her asked.

'My daddy's in jail,' she said, louder this time.

'What did he do?' the boy asked, his eyes widening and the whole class tuning in.

'He was naughty.'

I told Kerrie I pulled Eddie aside and sternly instructed him not to associate with the jailbird's daughter.

'Oh, you did not,' she smiled. 'Kids are just so innocent, aren't they?'

'They sure are. We'd better be careful what we let Eddie overhear in future.'

'That's right, otherwise the whole town will know our business.'

'Oh, it's too late for that. This is a small town, remember.'

The next kindergarten adventure was an excursion to the library. Kerrie had wanted me to push her in the wheelchair, but by the morning of the excursion couldn't muster enough energy. Eddie didn't mind. He was thrilled to have one parent along and made me hold hands as we started off in an orderly fashion, two by two, for the library. As I said, the walk started orderly, but it wasn't long before it resembled a drunken conga line with bodies spewing from side to side, kids breaking rank to run their hand along a wooden fence and the group having to stop at least twice because someone's shoe had fallen off.

Kerrie brightened at the recounting of these stories, wanting to know what books the librarian read to the group, which friends Eddie sat with and whether the line was more orderly on the return journey. It wasn't, of course.

While she missed these adventures, she made up for it with attention at home. The one thing she could always do for Eddie was offer warmth and love. Always a hug and a kiss before kindergarten and a hug and a kiss when he got home.

11 March 2006

Dear Eddie,

If your mum needs to feel loved, she has had it in spades this weekend.

Mardi is first to arrive. She has practically flown straight from Mexico, cutting short their year abroad, to see Kerrie. Then again, Kerrie is her daughter's godmother. Mardi's husband, Alex, has amassed some heavy artillery, including a made-in-Mexico Rosary bracelet, courtesy of his sister's hands, and a container of holy oil that he continually rubs on Kerrie's forehead. I hope it doesn't bring out any pimples.

Next to arrive is Uncle Brendan, who pre-warned us by saying he would 'pop over' for a visit while on his work rounds. 'Pop over' being a seven-hour drive from Renmark – I don't know if he'll trust internet maps again. As usual, a roast dinner and a couple of bourbon and Cokes cure his driving fatigue.

Kerrie is gravitating to her brother like I've never seen before, wanting to talk constantly about the fond memories of their childhood.

Everything starts with a question. 'Remember when …? Remember the time …? Remember how we …?'

I don't recall the exact nature of every story, apart from the ones I've jotted down, so that's something you'll have to take up with your uncle later on in life when you're looking to hear a cheery tale. He's good at telling yarns.

Well, at least Kerrie looks satisfied.

Love Dad

* * *

13 March 2006

Our visitors had gone, but Kerrie was not alone. She was sharing her body with a shivering attack. She felt it coming on, complaining of a sore jaw, chattering teeth and aching joints. I grabbed her painkillers, placed a hot water bottle across her chest and buried her body under a mountain of blankets. She shook like a pensioner locked in a deep freeze, her body fighting to maintain control over those 'nasty bugs' being leached into her system. We'd learned to minimise the length of these episodes by keeping her warm. Otherwise there was nothing we could do.

The attack lasted about 30 minutes before the shivering stopped.

Unfortunately, her mouth ulcers were still causing her misery.

14 March 2006

Defying cancer and its shivering attacks, Kerrie said she felt like a holiday, telling me to fill the car with petrol because she had booked two nights in a Beechworth cabin.

'Your parents said they would look after Eddie,' she said.

Kerrie was bossing me around, pointing out a suitcase, handpicking her clothes to be neatly folded inside, and chastising me for grabbing the wrong toiletries bag. Instructions kept coming thick and fast, causing me to prickle – 'In case you haven't noticed, I've been trying pretty hard lately' – but Kerrie laughed at the notion I was feeling sorry for myself.

'This is going to be great. I'm so excited about going away for a couple of days,' she said.

I could not believe this was the same Kerrie. The woman who'd spent the best part of February in hospital, the woman distraught at the reflection of her naked body, and the woman who not long ago thought I'd been replaced by a look-alike Danny.

'You're not Kerrie No. 2 by any chance?' I asked.

'Don't be silly. Now, make Eddie's bed before we leave.'

Yes, boss.

'And ring the district nurses to say we'll be away.'

Yes, boss.

'And pack me a pillow for the car.'

Up yours, boss.

'What's that?'

Nothing, boss.

Did someone mention time warp?

On the south side of Wangaratta, about an hour into our drive, we lost our way. Déjà vu Paris and Amsterdam. We hadn't changed at all. I still had a misguided confidence in my sense of direction and Kerrie had an equally misguided confidence in her ability to read a map. I stopped the car and grabbed the paperwork.

'Hey!'

'Bloody hell, Kerrie. Give me a look at that thing. You've no idea where we're going.'

'And I suppose you do?'

We found our way to Beechworth in a roundabout, sightseeing kind of way, checking in at reception and waiting for an ebullient Kerrie to crab up a set of steps. She then settled on a cabin with the steepest path, the most steps and the prettiest views.

'Isn't it gorgeous?' she said with a cheerful shrug of the shoulders that I also recognised from the past.

'It's lovely, honey. Are you sure we can afford this?'

'Of course we can.'

I immediately felt stained. We were battling financially, it was true, but what was the sense in saving pennies?

Whereas we had walked around the Louvre or stumbled into Amsterdam coffee shops, today we were tourists with a wheelchair.

As I pushed her around Beechworth's historic cordial factory, Kerrie treated her lap like a supermarket basket.

'Oh, I think your dad would like this shortbread,' she said, 'and these Bum Hummers pickled onions. Look, here's some plum sauce for a stir-fry. I reckon your mum would like this.'

We even bought some red cordial without thinking of the consequences, namely our already active son imbibing one sip and turning into the Tasmanian Devil.

It didn't matter that rain started falling, Kerrie had me push her from veranda to veranda, shop to shop, wheeling slowly past pictures, sketches, prints, ornate plates, vases, pottery, figurines, soaps, oil burners, oils, incense sticks, incense cones, creams, books and clothes. Did I mention the flowers and woodcarvings? I set a personal best for standing around shops as Kerrie continued to chat to owners, sales assistants and innocent bystanders, all the time amassing possessions.

Conscious of my contribution, she parked her wheelchair on the footpath, and sat with a lapful of candles, incense, creams and assorted knick-knacks while I ducked into a PubTab for a bet.

'Are you sure we can afford it?' she laughed.

'Not if it loses.'

'It won't win. Your horses never win.'

She was right. Chetwynd South lost. Again.

By nightfall Kerrie no longer wanted to dine out or sit in a spa surrounded by her new candles. She was content to sit propped up on the couch watching TV.

16 March 2006

Yesterday we took our step forward and this morning it was time for two steps back.

Kerrie was so exhausted, having suffered another shivering attack, she couldn't get out of bed. I paid for a late checkout, telling the owner my wife wasn't feeling well. No sympathy there. Maybe it was a common excuse.

The two hours ticked by and I managed to dress Kerrie and seat her by the door.

'Okay, Kerrie, we'd better get going. I'll walk you to the car,' I said.

No sooner had she taken two steps than she fainted, folding into my arms. I lay her on the floor and placed a pillow under her head, relieved she quickly regained consciousness but anxious about what to do next. I didn't want to call an ambulance because we were two hours from home in a town without family or friends, but I didn't know what else to suggest. Kerrie said no.

'Just give me a few minutes to rest and I'll be all right,' she said.

The phone rang. It was the owner. He wanted to know when we'd be leaving.

I explained my wife was feeling faint and we'd be out of the room as soon as possible. Still no sympathy. In fact, he was rude. He said the cleaner was on her way around.

'Sure,' I said, exasperated.

I struggled to remain diplomatic. I wanted to scream down that phone line and tell the obnoxious prick to give us a fucking break. But how could that help Kerrie?

The cleaner was surprised to see my wife lying on the floor and I realised it was the one time I should have taken a stand. I should have told the impertinent owner Kerrie was dying and if they were so desperate for the room, I would gladly pay for another night. But the chance had gone. I picked Kerrie up and carried her to the car, ignoring protests that she could walk.

'I'm taking you to the hospital, Kerrie,' I said.

'No, I'll be fine. I'm feeling better, I'm just a bit weak that's all.'

'No, I'm the one who's weak.'

1 April 2006

It was my thirty-sixth birthday and Kerrie presented me with a watch. Rather trusting of her really, considering I had lost so many in the past.

After slipping on the gift and admiring her choice, I casually asked the price.

'It doesn't matter,' she said. 'You know I wouldn't buy you a cheap watch. What do you want to know for? I can't believe you're asking.'

'I just want to know that's all,' I teased.

'I'm not telling.'

'Let me guess then.'

'No way. You don't do that with gifts.'

'A hundred bucks?'

'Danny, I'm not saying. I can't believe you're asking me this.'

Kerrie was annoyed. I'd either caught her by surprise or she'd forgotten me because it was the same question I'd always asked. And it was the same question she'd never bothered to answer. I tried to atone by saying I loved the watch for how it looked and for what it represented, but Kerrie only half-smiled. After being pushed around a jewellery shop in a wheelchair, I guess she deserved more than that.

Kerrie went to the movies for my birthday, with her friend Nicole. I was left at home with Eddie and Nicole's son Sam. So we had a party: mini sausage rolls, party pies, cocktail frankfurts, chips, Cheezels, lollies and soft drink. We sang happy birthday to me, blew out candles on a chocolate mud cake and then clawed it apart. It was wonderful to feel ten again.

At the culmination of our face-stuffing, we packed a bag of lollies and went fishing. For the most part of our angling expedition we threw rocks in the water or ate more lollies, but finally we landed a tiny Murray cod. Sam was shocked when I gave the tiddler a Rex Hunt-style kiss and tossed him back in the river.

'What did you do that for?' he asked, his eyes wide in disbelief.

'What?'

'Throw him back in.'

'Because he's too small.'

Sam wasn't convinced. He didn't argue but I could tell he was wrestling with my logic. Why go fishing just to throw them back? At least Eddie didn't care. He didn't care if we caught one fish or ten. He didn't care if we stuffed them into our fishing bag or threw them all back. He didn't care how much my watch was worth or how it looked. He just kept eating lollies.

* * *

5 April 2006

Dear Eddie,

Have I told you how much I love your mum?

We're on the road again, having abandoned the house for the day. She needs to keep moving, anything but sitting around waiting to die. She's unstoppable.

We park the car at Echuca's historic wharf area, help Kerrie into the wheelchair and push off, you bouncing around like a sheepdog, accosting people as they walk past.

'Look how excited he is,' Kerrie says. 'We should take him on adventures more often, Danny. He is just so happy to go somewhere different.'

Your mum is amazing, behaving like she has the time and energy for a thousand more such trips.

As we walk through the historic precinct, I keep Kerrie's wheelchair on the smoothest part of the dirt road trying not to disturb her delicate stomach. You take turns of helping me push and walking by her side. Our immediate goal is to find a suitable café for lunch.

When we do, Kerrie pores over the menu.

'Oh that sounds lovely,' she says. 'It all sounds so lovely. I feel like ordering it all.'

'Why don't you order a couple of dishes and whatever you don't finish, I'll eat?'

'Oh no, I'm just being greedy. I think I'll have the vegetable soup.'

I know she wants lasagne as well so that's what I order. But Kerrie is right. She struggles to finish half her bowl.

Next we step aboard a paddle steamer.

A paddle steamer, can you believe it?

Some people jump out of aeroplanes for kicks.

It takes some effort to crab down the steep riverbank with Kerrie, but once on board the excitement is palpable. You run to the stern, turn around and gallop back to the bow, walk upstairs, climb along the seats and then return to the deck. Then we stop to say hello to Mum, who is parked at the front of the boat looking out at the brown water and the haunting river gums.

'I can't believe how beautiful the river is,' she says. 'It's gorgeous. I've never appreciated it in this way. You see it from such a different perspective on the water. The gum trees, the birds, they all look so different.'

'You'll have to come out in the tinny with Dad and me when we go fishing at home one day,' I say.

'I'd love to. I never realised how beautiful it is. Isn't it gorgeous, Eddie?'

But you don't answer because we're off again. Upstairs, downstairs, clambering around seats at port and then crawling across to starboard. I can safely say we cover every square centimetre of the boat, save for flopping around on the paddle wheel and putting our heads in the engine's wood-fired furnace.

Eventually you need a break and we sit beside Kerrie as the engine chugs and the paddles churn. Mum is wan and gaunt and yet as beautiful as Kate Winslet sailing on the bow of the *Titanic*.

By the time we dock, Kerrie's tummy is beginning to ache so she pops a couple of painkillers and closes her eyes for most of the 80-minute drive home. I think she is dreaming about the steady ripples of the river.

Love Dad

6 April 2006

'What else can go wrong?' Kerrie pleaded more and more about her ailing health.

She wasn't alone.

I was asking myself the same question, but not because I had mouth ulcers or was leaking blood. I raged over housework.

Becoming the housewife had brought with it a feeling of helplessness that manifested itself in even the simplest of daily chores: such as finding a disintegrated tissue in the washing. They spread like little nuclear explosions, tainting every item of clothing in the machine. One tissue infected an entire load, spotting shirts and pants and socks and jocks and anything else that had been whizzing around my tub during the spin-dry cycle.

'I can't fucking believe this,' I ranted. 'I checked every pocket and still a bloody tissue gets through. How do they make so much mess? They're only fucking tiny, for God's sake.'

I shook these clothes with fury, turning our backyard into a gigantic snow-dome. Then I started fighting with the bed sheets. I couldn't keep them off the ground. I would peg one end to the line and the other would drag in the dirt. I would hold both ends and the middle would sag to the ground. I would hold the middle and … well, fuck it, I'd had enough. They could stay dirty.

Dropped plates, burnt sausages, I was cursed.

I didn't choose to become a housewife. I didn't choose for Kerrie to become sick. I didn't want to move back in with my parents. It was cancer.

Either unaware of my petulant outbursts or choosing to ignore them, Kerrie hobbled out of the bedroom and said we were going shopping. Improved from a blood transfusion and on antibiotics for her ulcers, she had me push her around the kids' clothing section of Target while Eddie fled to the toy shelves.

Before long Kerrie became frustrated at being pushed too fast or too slow and stood up and started walking. But it wasn't a walk, it was a pitiful shuffle. Her clothes hung from her body like hessian bags.

I was embarrassed for my wife. It would have been clear to anyone in the store she was dying, and while I didn't think she deserved that sort of scrutiny by strangers, I didn't get the chance to share my concerns.

I couldn't say anything because Kerrie didn't give a stuff. She was focused on skivvies, jumpers, jackets, cord pants, tracksuit pants and pyjamas. Item by item, as she determinedly shuffled along, she piled Eddie's new wardrobe on the trailing wheelchair.

'Oh, I like this,' she would say, lifting a jacket from the rack and twirling it around in front of her face. 'What do you think?'

'Yeah, it looks great,' I would reply, and onto the wheelchair it would go.

I blocked out my pity for Kerrie. As much as I detested shopping, anything was better than wrestling bed sheets.

15 April 2006, Easter Saturday

I lost Eddie at the races. Not my money, my son. And it wasn't to the bookmakers. I turned my back for a second and he disappeared among a sea of legs, discarded betting tickets and crushed VB beer cans.

And the worst of it was, none of those VB cans or tickets were mine.

I'd been sitting with my friends' wives for most of the afternoon and was beginning to understand why it was that wives and mothers didn't actually like going to the races. Not being a woman, this was new territory to me. I usually hovered around the bookies, the bars and the parade ring, blissfully free of paternal responsibilities. Not this day at Tocumwal. The first thing I'd done was lay out a ground blanket, checked if Eddie wanted something to eat and then half-listened to the girls chat about family life and the fluffy dressing gowns in Target.

I was drinking light beer because I had to drive and talking fluff because no one else on the ground rug was interested in talking horses. We could have done this at home.

It wasn't all sitting around, though. I decided Eddie needed to burn off some sugar on the bouncy castle and on the return route I would amble past the bookies, just to see what it was I was missing.

I instructed Eddie to stay 'here in this spot and don't move', while I took five steps into the bookies' ring to have a bet. It's not a good look to be walking around with a four-year-old in the ring so I left him 'right here, right beside this pole'.

While I was fumbling for change, I noticed the odds were better down the row, so I took ten more steps and discovered even better odds another ten steps away. I began calculating a wager and the likely winnings when a voice called out: 'Dad ... Dad ... Dad ... where are you?'

A hundred fatherly faces look around, but I knew the voice, the kid was mine.

'Dad ... Daaaaad ... Daaaaad?'

Shit! He was getting louder. That's all right, I'd have a bet and get straight back. And then I spotted my fellow fathers at the bar, laughing and joking and having a wow of a time talking to some girls from some office. While I was gawking at them, and wishing I could join in, Eddie went quiet.

Shit! I backtracked to the waiting spot – except it was just a spot because Eddie was no longer waiting. I'd lost him at the races.

I didn't want to panic, but I was in no position to consider logic so I pushed wildly through the crowd. He wasn't in the toilets so I tried the bouncy castle. No luck. I was becoming alarmed. What would Kerrie say?

'I don't mind you losing money at the track, but our son?'

I returned to the ground blanket to ask the others what to do; mums were good in these situations. They had experience. They knew how children thought. Us fathers knew how to mow the lawns and put the bins out.

I was just about to spill my fear when I noticed Eddie sitting on the rug, playing with his mates. The panicked thoughts stopped bouncing around my head and treating it like a jumping castle.

'Did you know he was back here?' one of the mums asked.

'Ah, well, um, no. He ran off,' I said.

She gave me a reassuring smile, as if this was what commonly happened when you took kids to the betting ring. I was grateful for that smile, but Eddie wasn't getting off so lightly.

'Eddie, come here,' I said, trying to sound stern but not so loud that a thousand racegoers would hear. 'Don't ever walk off on me again.'

'Sorry, Dad,' he said, stealing a glance back at the kids and the toys.

'I'm very disappointed. And I was worried. I didn't know where you'd gone.'

'Sorry, Dad.'

'Don't do it again. I don't want to lose you. Mum would never forgive me.'

'Sorry, Dad.'

I dropped the subject when I saw Kerrie shuffling through the crowd on her walking frame. What was she doing here?

'Hi, Kerrie. I didn't think you were coming,' I said.

'Well, you sounded like you wanted me to come this morning and Chel wanted to go for a drive,' she said, sounding remotely annoyed.

Hmm, wanted her to come to the races? I had asked her, that was true, but I was only being courteous. I was only trying to make her feel welcome and included. I hadn't expected her to actually turn up, struggling with every step. I didn't think she would enjoy herself. Hell, I wasn't enjoying myself.

'Well, I didn't want you to come if you weren't comfortable,' I said. 'But I'm glad you're here. Do you want to have a bet?'

'No, thanks.'

She smiled, but she didn't appreciate the joke. I played it straight instead.

'Do you want a drink?'

'I'd love a Coke, thanks.'

Kerrie sat down on the rug and settled into conversation, telling the group how she had been at my mother's art show. As she retold the splashes of colour I realised she was so much better at rug talk; she could discuss anything from theology to Target dressing gowns.

Unfortunately, she lost her nerve when it came time to pack up and leave. Kerrie was passed by hundreds of people as she crept towards the exit, step by painful step, stopping to hitch her tracksuit pants over her hips. Each time she paused with her arms on that walking frame I had to resist the urge to pick her up and carry her to the car. Maybe I should have because within touching distance of the gate she cracked. She fought back tears and started apologising to people for slowing them down.

One woman tried to set her straight, 'Don't you be sorry, honey. You have nothing to be sorry about.'

She was right, of course, this stranger. Everyone believed her, except Kerrie.

Don't ask me how to put those days into perspective. Don't ask me how we could have done things better. I don't know. As soon as Eddie was tucked into bed, and Kerrie was comfortable, I went to the pub and got drunk.

16 April 2006, Easter Sunday

My head pounded, my throat rattled, and I couldn't move. It was up to Kerrie. She willed herself out of bed, recovered from the exhausting and humiliating end to yesterday's races, and joined the egg hunt.

For weeks she had looked forward to Easter Sunday, stockpiling eggs like they were food for winter. She had scattered them around the house and now she walked, stooped and sore, beside her wound-up son.

Lifting my leaden head off the pillow I heard his excited cries.

'Look, Mum, there's another one.'

'Yes, darling, and look under the rose bush as well.'

'More Easter eggs, Mum!'

I pray Eddie remembers that day.

19 April 2006

Tensions mounted in the house. Instead of helping Kerrie, we inadvertently patronised her, patting her on the head like a child, asking her every second minute if she wanted a drink or a thick-shake or a sandwich when all she wanted was to be left alone.

Kerrie became irritated.

She chastised me, I passed it on to my mother and Mum took it out on Dad. We all took it out on Ed.

Frustrated, Kerrie raised her voice at Eddie for not paying attention, the rest of us censured Eddie for getting in the road.

'Not too loud, Eddie. Don't run around the kitchen, Eddie. Don't jump on the couch, Eddie. Careful of Mummy's tummy, Eddie.'

Kerrie was right. This wasn't her. This wasn't us.

In a bid to stop going mad, Kerrie started knitting. No plans or patterns, just the rhythmic calm of clicking and clacking and knitted wool flowing to the floor like paper out of a typewriter. All that mattered, the only prerequisite to buying more stock, was wool that was soft on her hands.

My outlet was golf. I became obsessed. Whenever Kerrie slept and my parents were home, I would throw the clubs in the car and head for the driving range. Sometimes I took Eddie after kindergarten, bribing him with a lollipop to keep out of the way, telling him to play in a nearby bunker or chase the ducks.

The reason I could turn my mind to a sport when Kerrie was in bed with cancer was control. By continually practising I could make something better, even if it was only my swing.

My fixation with golf didn't seem to bother Kerrie, but she began to guard our time. She took umbrage when my father asked me to go fishing. She waited until he left the room and then broke into tears.

'I just want to spend time with my husband, doesn't anyone understand?' she said. 'They all try and take you away. Don't they realise the reason we came up here was to spend time together?'

But that was exactly the problem: no one could understand how Kerrie felt. She'd always been selfless. She'd never demanded much of anyone. On the contrary, in the past she had always encouraged Dad and me to spend time together, complaining when we sat in the same room reading different newspapers and not engaging in conversation.

After her outburst, she started apologising.

'I'm sorry for doing this to you, Danny,' she said.

'Kerrie, I'm doing this because I love you and because I want to.'

'But I'm ruining your life.'

'You are my life. Look, Kerrie, taking care of you not only gives me a purpose, it allows me to do other things that I love. I don't have the stress of work, I am spending more time with you and Eddie, I can play golf, read books, watch DVDs. You shouldn't feel bad. I'm grateful that I can help.'

20 April 2006

It was 8.30 am, bloody freezing because no one else was up to turn the heating on and I had fifteen minutes to get Eddie to kindergarten.

There were two problems. No one remembered to turn the dishwasher on last night and I forgot to grab one of his red shirts off the line. They're stiff as a stuffed cat because of the morning frost and we don't own a clothes-dryer. I tried to break the news to my son as gently as possible, tapping into my feminine side.

Me: 'Here, put this blue skivvy on.'

Son: 'But I want to wear a red one.'

Me: 'They're dirty. Put the blue one on and hurry up. We're running late.'

He looked at me in disbelief, before his eyes filled with tears and his lip broke into a tremble. This was where his mum usually took over, but she was in bed with cancer.

The reason I was in this predicament, the reason I flicked off the office computer and walked out of multi-storeyed office life to become her carer was to do something more for the person I loved than jumping up and down on an overstuffed garbage bin every Sunday night just so we could fit in the last bag of rubbish.

As Father John said, this was upholding our wedding vows: through sickness and in health, till death do us part. We'd been married only five years; how did those words come to pass so quickly?

I started to tell Eddie that we couldn't always wear what we wanted, that I didn't have any good clothes when I was a little boy. He was still sobbing.

I told him I had to wear hand-me-downs from my older brother and sister. More sobbing.

Last-ditch effort. I told him little children in Africa didn't have any good clothes, and *they were starving*. He ran off to the bedroom and slammed the door.

What's with red? No one wore a red shirt ... except Murray the Red Wiggle. And if he'd walked into the room right then, I would have grabbed his damn electric guitar and wrapped it around his head, shouting something along the lines of, 'Why couldn't you pick a bloody blue shirt like Anthony the Blue Wiggle? We've got stacks of clean blue shirts.'

But that wasn't helping get my son to kindergarten. I knocked on his bedroom door.

'Are you okay in there?'

'I'm not going to kinder. I want you to write a letter and tell them I'm never going again.'

'All right, I'll write a letter.'

'Write a letter to Matthew, Cameron, Sam and Lewis and tell them I'm never ever going again.'

'Okay. But you'll have to come with me to drop it off. And you can't go in your pyjamas, so you'll have to put the blue skivvy on.'

After a short time he reluctantly agreed, but only on the condition that he stayed in the car while I delivered the missive.

So he came out and put on his blue skivvy, while I wrote a formal note to his kindergarten teachers and his friends Matthew, Cameron, Sam and Lewis, explaining that Eddie was never coming again, all because Murray the Wiggle picked a red shirt instead of blue.

But there was one more problem: someone forgot to turn the dishwasher on last night. There was nothing clean on which to make his lunch, and no clean lunchbox to hold his sandwiches. We were already ten minutes late, and there'd be no cool trucks left to play with when he got there ... that's if I could convince him to go inside. Matthew, Cameron, Sam and Lewis would be playing with them all.

I grabbed a plate and wiped it with my shirt. We were in a hurry. Then I grabbed a knife and wiped it with my shirt. We're saving time. His lunchbox didn't look too dirty so I saved my shirt for later.

We pulled up outside the kindergarten and I grabbed the letter before pretending to see Matthew, Cameron, Sam and Lewis having the time of their lives.

There was a short pause and then a breakthrough.

'Dad, I think I'll probably go inside now.'

'That's great, son.'

'You'd better screw up the letter.'

'I will, son.'

So I left him at kindy and drove down the street to buy five more red skivvies, wondering if I should blame God.

I didn't want my wife to die. I wanted to travel the world together when I retired and tell her she was still beautiful when she turned eighty. So if I was going to be deprived of this joy, why did everything else have to go wrong?

Kerrie said she had cancer for a reason; that her suffering was part of His plan.

But why did He have to let tissues sneak their way into my wash?

I thought marriage ended happily ever after, and that being a housewife was easy.

It brought all kinds of tears to my eyes: sadness, helplessness, frustration and even the feel-sorry-for-myself crying of a four-year-old. Maybe I should write Him a letter.

22 April 2006

Dear Eddie,

I won the monthly medal at Cobram Barooga Golf Club.

I tell you this partly to brag, but mainly because your mum reacts as if I've won the British Open.

'That's great, honey. I am so proud of you. I can't believe you've won on your first day of competition,' she says.

She shouldn't be surprised, I've been practising practically every day for more than a month.

I offer to place the medal around your neck, but you're not interested.

Maybe in a couple of years.

Love Dad

24 April 2006

While I was well enough read to know where Mongolia was on the globe, I didn't know how they cooked their sheep.

Which was a pity because that was the task I found myself confronted with.

Kerrie had set the menu for the coming week, poring over the many recipe pages she'd torn from women's magazines during her extended stays in hospital.

Now that she needed help to walk, she saw setting the menu as her way of contributing to the household, one of the few ways of preventing cancer rotting her self-esteem.

And one of the dishes she settled on was Mongolian lamb.

If there's one thing I learned from my wife, it's that you couldn't 'live' on meat and three veg alone. You could survive, but you couldn't 'live'.

The country had diversified and so, too, had the menu. Where we used to have sausages and three veg we could now have fancy curries; where we used to have T-bone steak and three veg we could now have penne with tuna and tomato sauce; where we used to have rump steak and three veg we could now have Mongolian lamb.

So I was off to the supermarket with my pre-school son to round up the 'special' ingredients. It wasn't long into the shopping when I asked myself: where have I had my head buried not to notice the revolution? The choice was ridiculous – sixteen brands of soy sauce. So where was the hoisin sauce?

While this fruitless search took place, my son tugged at my shirt wanting to move to brighter aisles.

'Dad, can we go and look at the yoghurts?' he said, as I tried to brush him aside.

'In a minute, son. I have to find the hoisin sauce.'

'What's a hoisin?' he asked.

'Good bloody question.'

'Ah, Dad you swore. Now can we go and look at the yoghurts?'

'Not now. Can't you just wait a minute?'

There's no mention of this in the recipe under preparation time: search for two tablespoons of hoisin sauce for about 25 minutes with a persistent four-year-old boy hanging off your leg.

Beaten by the badgering, I submitted to his demands by taking a detour past the yoghurt fridge – which had even more variety than the soy sauce section and looked like it had been sponsored by Disneyland.

But I wasn't falling for my son's charm, ignoring his appeals for the *Cars* packaging, which was dominated by the movie's star, Lightning McQueen.

'You don't even like yoghurt,' I argued.

'I'll like the Lightning McQueen yoghurt,' he countered.

He'd made the same forecast about Alex the Lion, of *Madagascar* fame, and the cute little clownfish with the gammy fin in *Finding Nemo*, and I'd ended up eating all the yoghurt.

So he whinged and I grew even more infuriated and before I knew it we'd bought the *Cars* yoghurt and I was back in the kitchen about to destroy the misconception that no man could stretch his thought process beyond one thing at a time.

Jamie Oliver might be able to open a new restaurant, he might be capable of saving the unemployed, but could he cook Mongolian lamb while running a bath and unpacking the dishwasher at the same time? I shouldn't think so.

I started with the onion and it wasn't long before tears were streaming down my cheeks.

'Why are you crying, Dad? Are you sad?' Eddie asked.

'It's the onions, son.'

'Why, what did they do?'

'They just make me cry.'

'Why, what did they do?'

'Just go and play with Lightning McQueen.'

With the slicing, dicing and crying done, I loaded the wok. The recipe said to add water and red capsicum and then stir in cornflour paste. But I'd already added the cornflour paste. Damn those instructions, why didn't they spell it out more clearly? That's the problem with recipe books, they're like trying to watch a French film without the subtitles – it looks delicious, but how do you make sense of it all?

And I needed the wooden spoon. Where's the wooden spoon? Ah yes, it's in the dishwasher, which I'd forgotten to unpack, which reminded me ... the bath.

'Ah, Dad you swore,' Eddie said as I jumped over his play mat and dashed for the bathroom before it started to emulate Lake Eyre after a deluge.

Floor saved, back to the kitchen and I'd unpack the dishwasher later.

The Mongolian lamb was bubbling along nicely and it was time to dish out the rice and ... shit, I'd forgotten the rice. Did my wife really have this much trouble?

'Ah, Dad you swore,' my radar-eared son piped up again.

'All right, all right Mr Swear Man, here's a dollar for your jar, now go back to playing with your cars.'

Another twenty minutes later the rice was cooked, the Mongolian lamb was cold and I was all set to serve.

Eddie ran to the table and upon seeing what was before him screwed up his nose.

'I don't like it,' he said.

'How do you know, you haven't tasted it?'

'I just don't like it.'

'But it came in Lightning McQueen packaging.'

He didn't buy it, and I resorted to the only thing left to convince my son to eat his dinner: I cooked sausages and three veg.

30 April 2006

Dear God,

My wife fell over on the way to the bathroom during the night and bumped her head on the tile floor. I heard her fall and heard her whimper. She sounded meek, like a lost child.

'Oh dear. Oh no,' she said.

I jumped out of bed and picked her bony frame off the tiles and cradled her head in my arms. I couldn't believe I had let her make the trip alone. I couldn't believe I'd wanted to sleep.

'I think I'll be all right,' she had said before leaving the bed.

I think I'll be all right!

And I let her go.

There was nothing to do but gently rub her head. She didn't utter a word. She was defeated.

Why, God? Why does Kerrie have to suffer this way?

I took her to hospital and watched as a drip was placed in her arm. I watched nurses swab her mouth ulcers, sores that are so painful she winces with every sip of water. I watched them draw blood from her arm in an attempt to pinpoint her temperature.

And, do you know, God, Kerrie's faith never wavers. She doesn't blame you, and I don't understand.

Right now she wants to be in hospital. She wants to remove the burden from those she loves.

How can I make sense of this to my son when I can't make sense of it myself?

She says we have to trust in you. And I tell her I will try. But what I really need is an answer.

Danny

2 May 2006

Kerrie had a new worry.

Not about herself, but the miners trapped underground in Beaconsfield, Tasmania. She prayed for their rescue and she prayed for their families.

She prayed that Larry Knight's soul would rest in peace.

I, on the other hand, was numb to it all. To me it seemed a world away, like a bus crash in China.

5 May 2006

Kerrie rallied. Strong antibiotics healed her mouth ulcers, she'd been given more blood, she'd been pampered by the Cobram nurses, her patches had been increased to lessen the pain and her father had arrived from Adelaide.

We brought her home.

Each morning Kerrie and her father scanned the newspapers or watched TV for news of the trapped miners. I wondered if Kerrie felt the same, trapped in a crumbling body with each solution and every rescue mission failing to set her free.

The frenzied media pack was desperate to get inside the heads of Todd Russell and Brant Webb to understand how it felt in their claustrophobic, underground cell. Maybe Kerrie knew.

Regardless, she didn't tell her father. Together they read out the newspaper quiz, did the crosswords and watched TV. She joked and laughed and talked about what we were having for dinner. But she never mentioned cancer.

'How are you today, darling?' Des would say, reaching over and kissing her forehead.

'I'm okay, Dad,' she would reply.

'Would you like a cup of tea?' he would ask.

'No thanks, Dad.'

Out of the blue, Kerrie expressed an urge to chance her luck.

'I want to go to the Sporties tonight,' she said. 'I feel lucky.'

'That's great, love,' Des said.

'That's brilliant, Kerrie,' I said.

'We'll all go together,' my parents said.

But as the hours ticked away our excitement wilted. Kerrie's energy levels buckled. While the patches were helping mask the pain, the swelling in her right leg had shifted to her hips, making her tired and uncomfortable. She lost the drive to leave the house.

But no matter, she said, Des could take her money and buy $20 worth of raffle tickets and she could still chance her luck.

The Friday night raffle was like a mini game show, in which twelve numbers were drawn throughout the course of the night and the lucky contestants played off against a host for 'the money or the egg'. One of 40 eggs hid $1000, while the other 39 covered prizes of varying worth. Contestants had to decide between the cash on offer or a yet-to-be-revealed prize.

Kerrie decided her minimum was $200. If her number was called out, she told her father, he should take the prize unless he was offered more than $200 in cash. He hugged her for luck.

And then I chipped in: 'If the thousand dollars has gone off, take a hundred bucks. They won't offer you very much money if the thousand bucks has already gone off.'

It was an innocuous comment, me having a say for the sake of joining the conversation. It wasn't designed to sting Kerrie.

'Why doesn't anyone listen to me?' she cried after Des and my parents had left the house for their night out. 'Nothing I say counts. I have lost all authority. I'm just useless.'

'Kerrie, of course what you say matters,' I replied, knocked at her outburst.

'Well, then why did you go and tell Dad to do something different from what I had told him?'

'I don't know.'

'Nothing I say counts.'

Des came home a winner. He won $200. I was asleep on the couch, as had become the nightly custom until Kerrie was ready for bed, when the other three burst through the doorway whooping and hollering about his good fortune. I was narky at having been woken up, while Kerrie reacted like she had won the money herself.

'Good on you, Dad, that's fantastic,' she said. 'You always have luck at the Sporties.'

6 May 2006

Nine days before Kerrie died, she played the poker machines. After Des's good fortune from the night before there was no way she would miss out again.

We couldn't agree more.

Way to go, girl! You get out there and rake in the big bucks!

We scrambled over the top of each other to help her into the car. Dad grabbed the wheelchair, I grabbed Kerrie and Des grabbed the door.

We would help her win. Our positive thoughts would rub off.

My enthusiasm, however, flagged when we walked into the club. Our friends at reception, two burly, good-natured men, could barely hide their shock. It took them time to recover their composure, fumbling through their embarrassment. I knew what they saw and I felt faint. In four months my wife had become a 90-year-old woman.

I wheeled Kerrie to her favourite Hearts machine. She fed in cash, but didn't have any luck. We tried a Pyramids machine and then one with a rock'n'roll theme. None of them paid a cent. But Kerrie didn't mind. What bothered her was the three of us hovering, threatening to smother her with good intentions. It was exactly what she didn't want, being tapped on the shoulder every 30 seconds and offered a drink. We offered her cash; we offered her luck. Eventually, she told us to leave.

'I can play by myself,' she said. 'Go and enjoy yourselves. You don't need to keep checking to see if I'm all right. I'll be fine.'

Des and my father walked off, but I stayed. She needed help to move the wheelchair from machine to machine, I reasoned. But I still wished for luck, begging those damn machines to show some compassion.

'Pay out, damn you,' I willed those computerised screens.

Kerrie read my mind.

'You don't have to pretend to be excited, honey,' she said.

'Oh, actually I wasn't pretending.'

'It doesn't matter if I don't win. I'm just enjoying being out.'

I'd forgotten luck didn't discriminate. It was like cancer, you either got it or you didn't.

Kerrie looked like a dying person. She looked like a woman who had flirted with hope, diced with luck, and the odds hadn't fallen her way.

After she lost $50 and proved that she could get out of the house, she asked Des, Dad and me to take her home.

'The pain is getting too much,' she said.

Monday, 8 May 2006

Dear Eddie,

It's time to go.

Your mum has been in so much pain during the night that we increase her fentanyl patches and give her extra painkillers.

I sit her in the lounge room for her morning TV and she becomes alarmed at her inability to hold a breath.

'I need to go to hospital,' she says.

'Do you want me to drive?'

'No, call an ambulance.'

While we are waiting, a district nurse visits and I explain an ambulance is on its way. As she speaks, Kerrie vomits.

'I just don't know what to do anymore,' Kerrie complains. 'I just want to go to hospital and get knocked out. I just want to be made comfortable.'

When I walk into the 'dying room', Kerrie's face is sadly defeated.

'I don't think I'll be coming home this time,' she says, 'it's too soon since I was last here. I'm not scared of dying, I just thought I had more time.'

I can't believe it, Eddie.

We are still having meaningful conversations about politics, and mine rescues, and what we have done in life, and what we want for you. The oncologist said two more years. We are still in love. How could she not be coming home?

I nod, trying to mask my torment.

'Don't worry, honey,' Kerrie says.

She then asks me to go home and collect a diary she is compiling for you. She wants you to know her favourite foods, her favourite movies and her favourite music.

I hold up the diary, bringing a smile to her melancholy face.

'You know me too well,' she says.

'I brought it just in case.'

We start the list: *Shadowlands*, *Remains of the Day*, *African Queen*, *Eternal Sunshine of the Spotless Mind* … salt'n'vinegar chips, chocolate Paddle Pops, Coca-Cola, beef and black bean sauce, tuna pasta … and by the time we reach music, and I pen Jeff Buckley, the morphine closes her eyes.

Love Dad

Monday, 8 May 2006

Kerrie slept most of the afternoon, but by evening she became distressed. She was anxious and scared of the pain.

'What do you want, honey?' I asked.

'I just want to be bombed out.'

'That means we won't be able to talk anymore.'

'I know, honey, but I am in agony. You don't mind, do you?'

'Of course not. You can't be in pain.'

'Thanks, sweetheart.'

'I love you,' I said.

'I love you, too.'

Tuesday, 9 May 2006

The beginning of hell.

Despite the morphine driver, Kerrie had not settled and it was decided to sedate her with Midazolam and later Serenace.

A blessing for her, a nightmare for me. Her eyes were open and she said hello, but she was mentally lost. I didn't know who she was.

The thought of her dying had always been assuaged by her strength of mind and comforting words. All of a sudden, her counsel was gone.

I waited to see Dr Chrissie on her afternoon rounds.

'Do you think Kerrie will be coming home?' I asked.

'I think that's something we need to talk about,' she said.

'Because I want to know if it's time to start making phone calls. Should I be calling Kerrie's family and friends so that they can say goodbye?' I asked, praying she would say no.

'I think it would be a good time for that.'

But when Dr Chrissie tried to discuss it further with Kerrie, she was still in a daze.

'Kerrie, you don't really understand what we are talking about, do you?' Dr Chrissie asked.

'No, not really,' she said in a dreamy, remote voice.

'Perhaps we should talk about it in the morning?'

'Okay,' Kerrie said.

Dr Chrissie explained to me that the sedatives helped Kerrie forget that she was in pain. They also helped smother anxieties and fears. She was no longer vomiting and no longer breathless. I nodded my head to indicate I understood, but what I really wanted to know was whether my wife was coming back.

Wednesday, 10 May 2006

I couldn't find the brake.

I wanted to stop this mess, but I couldn't find the right button.

Dr Chrissie had brought Kerrie out of her daze and I listened to them speak. Their chat was brief.

'Kerrie, do you want me to give you anymore blood transfusions?' Dr Chrissie asked.

'No,' she said.

'And if your heart stops, do you want us to administer CPR?' Dr Chrissie asked.

'No. Let me go,' she said.

And that was that. I was looking at Kerrie and her serene face when she asked to be let go. I couldn't have been more than a metre from her bed and yet it felt like I was a kilometre away.

I was not ready. I needed more time. What had I been doing fucking around playing golf?

When Dr Chrissie left I didn't feel like I had much else to say to Kerrie other than, 'So this is it?'

'Yep, this is it,' she said.

'Well, at least I can talk to you. It's so nice being able to talk to you. Yesterday you were really spaced out. I missed you.'

'I know, honey, but you said you wouldn't mind if I was bombed out.'

'I know. I did. It just came as a bit of a shock. I'm glad to be able to talk to you now.'

'Me too.'

'Oh, by the way, the miners were rescued this morning.'

'That's wonderful news.'

'I'll turn the TV on to get an update.'

'Okay, honey.'

When Kerrie had fallen back to sleep, I drove home. It was time to tell Des his daughter was dying. He knew, of course, he always knew, but it had to be acknowledged.

I walked into the house and burst into tears. Des took me in his arms.

'She's not coming home,' I sobbed.

'Oh my dear boy,' he said. 'I'm so sorry.'

All along, deep down, I didn't think we'd run out of time. I knew Kerrie was terminal and that she would die young, but I didn't want to admit that the days were gone. I rang Kerrie's friend Jude in Melbourne to pass on the news.

'If people want to say goodbye to Kerrie, now is the time,' I told Jude. 'She's in hospital and she hasn't got long to go.'

At Des's request I telephoned Father John and asked him about last rites. I asked whether he had discussed the issue with Kerrie.

'We didn't talk about it,' he said. 'We just talked about politics. But I'll come across to the hospital tonight.'

Trust Kerrie, I thought. When she should have been discussing her own spiritual needs, she turned the topic to all the shits she thought were stuffing up the world.

Next she would be turning us into angels. And that's exactly what she did.

As Father John called us to the foot of her bed to share in the last rites and we hovered, not really sure what to say, where to stand and what to do, Kerrie whispered: 'Look at my angels, I can see my angels.'

Des, being a religious man, took her literally.

'Can you, love?' he said, sounding as if he was in the midst of a miracle. 'You really can see angels, can you, love?'

I started to laugh. If only life were so perfect.

'I think she means us, Des,' I said.

'Oh,' he muttered.

'God bless you, Dad,' Kerrie smiled.

Then we all laughed. By the time we stopped none of us felt awkward or that we were imposing on Kerrie's faith. It felt right to hold hands around the bed and it felt right as Father John led us – Des, Brian, Chel and myself – in prayer. We didn't feel sad.

Well, Des was a little sad, but more so because of his own gullibility.

'What a silly old bugger I am,' he grumbled. 'I thought she could see angels.'

Thursday, 11 May 2006

It wasn't the last day Kerrie and I spent together, but it was one of the best. Less sedated and her pain bearable, we rediscovered the fullness of joy.

I mentioned a phone call from her Aunty Win and Uncle Doug, passing on their best wishes from Adelaide. Just the mention of Uncle Doug made me smirk. Not because he was silly or strange. No, Uncle Doug was handsome, engaging and intelligent. It was just that his name was rhyming slang for 'a tug'. A … well, you know.

I fell into a schoolboy guffaw, while Kerrie grabbed her chest as her beaming smile threatened to stretch beyond her face.

'Oh, you're so silly,' she said, 'get out of here and get me those lollies.'

I almost burst with happiness as I drove to the supermarket. She wanted 'Fruit Tingles', 'Paddle Pops', 'jubes', 'pineapple lollies' and anything remotely 'tasty and chewy' as long as it wasn't a supermarket home brand.

As Kerrie sat munching on sweets, her mood brightened further with a visit from her father and brother. She waited until Brendan was in the midst of explaining how he was taking up surf lifesaving again before cutting him off mid-sentence.

'I can't believe you passed your bronze certificate. You're so fat,' she said with a barely disguised grin.

'Thanks a lot, Kare,' he said. 'I'm glad you have so much faith in me.'

Then it was Des's turn.

'Dad, don't pick your nose. You do it all the time at Kath and Pete's house. It's uncouth. And that jumper is appalling. You've had it on all week and it should be thrown out. Haven't you got another one?' she said.

'I didn't even know I was picking my nose,' Des said.

'You do it all the time. It's like a nervous reaction.'

'All right, love, I'll try and stop it.'

I said to Brian later that day, 'If you didn't know she was dying, you'd almost think she was getting better.'

* * *

Friday, 12 May 2006

I tried to meet every visitor at the door, warn them about the state of their friend. But no one could be properly prepared. And I would be lying if I said I wanted them there. I wanted every last minute to myself. Even when I left the hospital for a break, I wouldn't last ten minutes before I was anxious to return.

I did get time alone with Kerrie by the afternoon and I asked her if she had any requests. I asked her whether she needed anything said or done.

'No,' she replied, 'I feel cherished. That's enough.'

I then asked her if she would like me to read out a tribute I had spent hours compiling on the computer. She declined. She said it would make her feel too sad. She said she wasn't scared of dying, just the leaving. The one pain morphine couldn't mask.

Instead, her gift to me was to cope with pain. The nurses said she kept saying, 'I want to stay awake for my husband.'

This was the first night I slept at the hospital, and Kerrie was as excited as a ten-year-old girl preparing for a slumber party.

I kicked myself for not having done it earlier. I'd wanted to provide stability for Eddie at home and, to be honest, I was slightly embarrassed about nurses seeing me in my boxer shorts. I mean, it doesn't happen at home, nurses marching through the bedroom door, opening the blinds and asking if you're ready for breakfast.

'What will I wear to bed, Kerrie? I don't want to get caught going to the toilet during the middle of the night in my undies,' I said.

'They won't care what you wear. The hospital is full of people in their pyjamas.'

'I know, I know. But what if they come in and complain of boy's smell?'

'You are being silly. It will be great. It will be just like a sleepover, I'm so excited. We can sit up and watch TV together.'

The nurses set up a bed in Kerrie's room and I turned on the TV. Kerrie fell asleep. I wished she hadn't. I wanted her to laugh with me during the *Chaser's War on Everything*. I wanted it to be like the old times when we sat up with a bottle of red and giggled in disbelief at the irreverence of *Father Ted*, or snickered at *Time Gentlemen Please*, or shook our heads at the vulgar brilliance of *Little Britain*.

Saturday, 13 May 2006

No one mentioned my boxer shorts. The night-shift nurses were too busy attending Kerrie. Sometimes I climbed out of my bed to help her roll over or move, but I couldn't administer the morphine. It was a restless night.

'That was fun, honey, I think I'll stay again tonight if you don't mind,' I said in the morning, managing to shower and change while nurses were out of the room.

'I didn't think you would stay again after they moved me all night,' she said.

'Actually, I slept well. I was able to doze off without any problems.'

'That's good. I'd love if you could stay again.'

'Actually, I might go nude now that I'm comfortable.'

'I dare you.'

Despite the interrupted sleep, Kerrie was feeling well enough by mid-morning to have Weet-Bix and a plate of ham and salad for lunch.

Her last supper.

When Des, Brendan and my brother Chris called in, we sat around her bed and did the *Herald Sun* quiz.

Her last quiz.

As usual, she and Brendan aced three-quarters of the questions while Christ and I battled to make up the rest. Kerrie's memory was astounding. I reminded her it was not too late for a shot at *Who Wants to be a Millionaire?*.

'Oh, I'd be no good,' she said. 'I'd be too nervous in front of the cameras.'

'But you're so smart,' I complained.

'I'm not smart. It's all useless information. What's any of it good for?'

'Winning *Sale of the Century*.'

'You're kind, Danny, but really I wouldn't be any good.'

Against my better judgement, I left Kerrie for the afternoon because she had fallen asleep, but when I returned nurses were buzzing around her bed because she was in severe pain. Her system had rejected the Weet-Bix and ham.

'I just want to be bombed out again,' she told the on-call doctor.

He agreed to increase her dosages.

'This means I won't be able to talk to you,' I said.

'You said you wouldn't mind.'

'I did. I don't mind, honey,' I lied.

I don't know exactly what prompted Kerrie to say it, whether I was moving her in bed, or giving her a sip of water to ease her dry lips, or refilling a hot water bottle to place under her aching back, but I'll be forever grateful.

'My darling husband, what would I have done without you?'

Sunday, 14 May 2006

Time was running out, but cruelly it slowed down. Every hour in that 'dying room' stretched out like a day because Kerrie wasn't there. She was awake, able to acknowledge when Des, Brendan or I gave her a kiss, but she wasn't there.

The drugs made her forget she was in pain, but they took her back in time. They took her back to my parents' lounge room, looking out at the river. She didn't notice that Eddie had left a Mother's Day card beside the bed.

Instead, she kept telling me, 'It's time for my breakthrough painkillers' or 'I want to go to bed now'.

'You are in bed, Kerrie. You're at Cobram hospital,' I said.

'Oh,' she would say, looking around slightly confused.

Later, I changed my answers.

When she asked to be taken to bed, I would put my arms under her back and pretend to pick her up – 'One, two, three,' she whispered as a signal for me to lift. And then I would pretend to put her down.

'There you are, Kerrie. You're in bed now,' I said.

'Thanks.'

I pretended to give her painkillers, and handed her a glass of water to wash them down.

Then she asked me to take her for a drive.

A drive!

How I would have loved to take her for a drive. Take her away from all that suffering. But all I could do was pretend.

'We've just arrived in Echuca,' I said, and Kerrie nodded. 'We'll park here at the old wharf, go for a walk and look for a restaurant. Eddie is so excited. He's blabbering on and running up and down on the spot. We'll stop here at this little café for lunch. It looks nice. Look at the menu, Kerrie. There's vegetable soup and lasagne …'

I kept talking because Kerrie seemed to be listening.

'… After dinner we go for a ride on a paddle steamer. For a moment there I thought we were going to lose control of your wheelchair while creeping down the bank and have you end up in the water. The river is beautiful. There are egrets wading for yabbies and kookaburras in the gum trees. The place is alive …'

Kerrie had stopped listening.

Instead she whispered, 'My mind is still strong, but my body just keeps letting me down.'

All night Kerrie moved her hands in front of her face, occasionally picking at her sheets, her eyes staring straight ahead. She was knitting.

'Kerrie?' I would say.

'Yeah?' she would whisper.

'Go to sleep, darling.'

'Okay.'

But she wouldn't. A couple of times I placed her hands gently on her chest, but as soon as I let go she started again. She knitted an invisible blanket.

Monday, 15 May 2006

Brendan was right. The suffering was too much. I asked Dr Chrissie if there was anything we could do so that we didn't have to see her in this confused, pitiful state. But there was nothing; we had to wait for Kerrie's body to let go.

The only comfort came with the arrival of Kerrie's best friends, Linda and Margie. They cried, of course, but then they regaled us with stories of Kerrie's youth, talking about their teenage pal who had a crush on INXS singer Michael Hutchence. They told us that Kerrie once turned up outside an Adelaide hotel because INXS members were staying inside, only to have to duck and hide when they came out because she'd forgotten to shave her legs.

Linda and Margie also told me to change the music.

'Haven't you got any Enya?' Margie asked.

Shit! Of course, we had Enya.

What was I thinking?

Why didn't I think of Enya?

How could I do this to Kerrie?

No one should die listening to *Hooked on Classics*.

Tuesday, 16 May 2006

It can't be easy telling a child you're leaving. Kerrie did it with style.

She explained that, 'Mummy is getting very old.'

She explained that, 'Mummy can no longer play on the floor, or drive you to kindergarten, but she still loves you very much.'

It was beautiful, and Eddie had a beautiful way of accepting her explanation.

He didn't seem to mind that Dad was not getting old at the same accelerated rate; that Dad wasn't wasting away to the ravages of cancer as an old person succumbs to a century of years.

In the months leading up to Kerrie's death, my four-year-old son was happy to have his Thomas the Tank Engine trains, and his afternoon treats, and his books before bedtime. He was just happy to have his mum and dad around.

But then it came my turn to explain. It was unavoidable that my wife's time was growing short, and the question had hovered above me like a troubled angel: what was I going to tell our son?

Our palliative care nurse suggested that we prepare him for the end.

'It might be a good idea to tell him that she's dying and then take him into the room when she's gone so that he has a reference point, and doesn't think that she's on holidays and might be returning. It could be very confusing for him otherwise,' she said.

I believed she was right. One day he would comprehend what had happened and at such time it was important, even if he did not remember, that he knew he was a priority right to the end. So I found myself in hospital, outside her room explaining to Eddie that, 'Mum is going to heaven soon to be with Grandma.'

'Why is she going to heaven?' he asked.

It was a good question. Throughout my life I had been a fence-sitter when it came to contemplating the after-life, not brave enough to make a jump in either direction, but at this stage it was the best explanation I had and one in which my wife had invested total faith.

My son understood that people became sick, but he did not understand the varying degrees of suffering, and he certainly was not ready to understand cancer.

I reiterated that she was getting old and that God had decided he needed her by His side. It was also what I desperately wanted to believe.

At that time, as I looked at his chubby face, and into his earnest blue eyes, I felt myself starting to choke with tears.

'And He will make her all better, because you can have parties whenever you want in heaven, and eat as many lollies as you want and you don't get sick.'

My son said these words, but they belonged to my wife. It had been typical of her, paving a smoother passage for me by explaining what a hoot the good souls from this earth had when they died.

I laughed. He had cured the tears because he was too young to understand. He thought his mother was going to one giant party in the sky and one day we would all join her. And what child wouldn't want to go to a place where there was no cap on the amount of sugared goodies you could stuff in your mouth?

With our son temporarily prepared, we walked into her room and I held him across the bed to give her a kiss and tell her he loved her. She was far away, and not capable of mustering a tender response. It annoyed me that we weren't going to get a Hollywood ending, that my wife could not impart wisdom and contentment before a final peaceful sigh. All those movie endings had been a lie.

'I'm going to miss Mummy,' Eddie said as we left, and I agreed. He held in his hand one of the Freddo Frogs that we had stocked in her bedside drawers to ensure each visit had made the room a happy place.

That was two days ago and now Kerrie has gone. I've shed my tears and now it's Eddie's turn to enter the room and say his last goodbye. Far from being upset, he treats the parting as if he's kissing her goodnight and going to bed.

'Goodbye, Mummy, I love you,' he says, before taking one final peek in the drawer for a Freddo Frog.

We walk into the courtyard to join a small gathering of family and friends. At the same time a Qantas jet passes overhead, its white kangaroo rushing through the sky.

'Grandma's jet,' I say. 'It's come to get Mum.'

And this is when Eddie turns wide-eyed to Father John, proud of his mum and the fashion in which she has departed this world.

'Mummy has gone to heaven,' he says. 'She bursted out the window and got on a jet plane with Grandma and flew all the way up to heaven.'

1 February 2007

Dear Kerrie,

It's eight months since you've gone and almost every morning since I've woken up to a click of the door, a 'hi Dad' and a little body crawling under the Doona.

'What time is it, Dad?' he asks.

'It's only seven o'clock, it's way too early (for me), so just lie there and don't kick, and go back to sleep for a little while, okay?'

'Okay, Dad.'

The 'okay, Dad' usually lasts about ten minutes before he can no longer contain the wiggles and squirms and the kicks to the midriff.

'Eddie, it's still too early, go back to sleep.'

'I'm not tired, Dad, I want to get up.'

'All right, you get up but I need more sleep.'

At which time he usually goes and knocks on Granny and Pa's door, knowing they are not slaves to sleep and more vulnerable to pleas for a playmate.

This morning starts out much the same. He crawls in about 7 am and says he has to 'wipe the sleep out of my eyes because every time I go to bed I get sleep in my eyes'. But this time he returns to an unshakeable slumber. On the first day of school. Do not disturb. Not even by 8 am. No longer 'way too early' for me to arise.

I am disappointed. Grandpa Des has flown across from Adelaide and Eddie doesn't want to face his momentous day.

'C'mon, Ed, it's time to get out of bed. You need to get dressed,' I say.

'I'm not going. I'm too tired,' he mumbles from under the covers.

I grab the Doona, hover above the bed and contemplate whether to yank it away. But we still have 45 minutes, and with extra time in bed he won't be wandering around school like a sleep-deprived zombie, inviting his teacher to think of me as an incapable layabout who doesn't properly care for his son. So I gently let go of the Doona and head to the kitchen to prepare lunch.

My parents are at the breakfast table and Grandpa Des is stirring. Lunch made, bag packed, I try again: 'C'mon, Ed, it's getting late. You've got to get up and get ready so YOU CAN GO TO SCHOOL!'

This time I sell the concept like an overzealous telemarketer. We only have 30 minutes left.

'I'm not going. You go by yourself,' he mumbles.

'But if I go by myself I'll have no son to hug and kiss goodbye. And besides, I spent thirteen years at school and I've done my penance and there's no way I'm going back.'

'I don't care. I want to go to kindergarten.'

'Mate, no one will be at kindergarten. All of your friends will be at school.'

'What about Peter and Mitchell?'

'No, they will be at a different school. But Jordan and Ryan and Lily and Evie and Lewis will all be at your school.'

Forgive my churlishness, Kerrie, but this isn't the way things are supposed to happen. This is meant to be a 'great day'. How can I remain calm? He is going to be late? What will the other parents think on seeing that I can't get my son to school on time, or in a school uniform, or with combed hair, or in a good mood?

I leave Eddie in bed and prepare the cameras. We still have twenty minutes, and at least he has an ally in Granny Kath.

'He might be like me, I refused to go to school for the first six months,' she says.

'Six months?'

'Well, it was a long time. I did not want to go.'

Great, we are in for six months of this shit.

The next time I check Eddie he is sitting up, rubbing his tired eyes. A good sign, despite there being just quarter of an hour to get dressed, fed, photographed and into the classroom.

Finally, he walks into the kitchen and is momentarily overwhelmed by the attention – the four of us gushing about it being such a 'special day'. And then Pa points out the window at a school bus driving past.

'What's wrong?' I ask.

'The bus,' Eddie says, wiping tears from his eyes.

'Don't worry, you're not catching the bus.'

'Who's the bus for?'

'The kids who live on farms and whose parents are too busy to drive them to school.'

'Well, what school do they go to?'

'The high school, and the primary school and St Joseph's,' I say, hoping for a reaction because we have less than ten minutes to make it on time, and I haven't taken a photo. Not that it matters if we are on time, right? Because it doesn't matter what the other parents think.

Inexplicably and without warning, Eddie springs into action, telling us to watch his special method of getting dressed, which isn't that special really, but if it's quick, I don't care. At the same time the camera sharks move in, clicking like crazy as our son turns publicity-starved B-grade actor hamming it up on Granny's brown carpet.

'I still love you all,' he declares as he slips on his shirt, his socks and his shoes. 'Thank you for the happy new year, Grandpa,' he says as he collects his bag.

'Watch how fast I can run,' he says, thundering along the passage before turning around and tearing back.

And next thing you know he is running for the car. And when we pull up at St Joseph's he is running from the car, leaving Grandpa Des and me trailing behind.

'Are you a teacher at St Joseph's?' he has time to ask a lady who is walking past.

'No,' she replies.

'Oh, well I'm a St Joseph's kid now.'

When Des and I catch up, me hoarse from yelling at him to slow down, he is waiting at the front gate. He's so excited, he starts walking backwards. Our son, the first child to arrive at St Joseph's Primary School the wrong way around.

All of this is so much fun, Kerrie. Grandpa Des and I can't help looking at each other with pride. This kid is ready for Grade 6!

The classroom is full of clucky parents milling around their children, and Miss Kelly welcomes us into the classroom, pinning a name badge on Eddie's shirt.

'You're the lucky last,' she says.

'I didn't want to get out of bed,' he declares.

'Good, well you won't be tired for today.'

Miss Kelly then has to latch on to Eddie and show him where his bag belongs. He doesn't even think to take off his hat because he's saying hello to his old kindergarten friends and following Miss Kelly around the room to show her a model aeroplane he's found in the corner.

Grandpa Des and I kiss him goodbye and quietly slip out of the room, past the doting parents finding it harder to close the door.

And that is when the tears come. Not because our little boy is growing up; not because he doesn't need me to stay, but because you aren't here.

Miss you,
love Danny

6 February 2007

Dear Kerrie,

Did you know you can buy a Yummy Drummy for 60c, a chicken burger for $2.30 and a Hawaiian pizza for $1.90? Or is that a Hawaiian burger for $1.90 and a chicken pizza for $2.30? And what the hell is a Yummy Drummy?

Welcome to morning canteen duty.

The mother showing me the ropes says not many men turn up for canteen duty and I know why: we are bloody hopeless. I am chaotic. I have bags from Prep T mixed in with bags from Grade 3/4, plastic spoons where the straws should go and I start putting mayonnaise sachets into lunch bags instead of tomato sauce.

Kids are going to starve, and it's *all my* fault.

The instructions are simple enough: write down the lunch orders, lay out the brown paper bags in preparation for the lunches, sort the money and ring the bakery.

So why am I walking around in circles?

'They're in the freezer,' the helpful and slightly bemused-looking mother says.

'What are in the freezer?' I reply.

'The double choc-chip muffins.'

'Oh. Okay. Yep. Here they are, the double choc-chip muffins with the triple twist. And what did you say about Prep kids and lollies?'

'You can put lollies in the Prep bags, but grades one to six have to buy their lollies from the canteen window.'

'Oh. Okay. Preps lollies, big kids no lollies. And what is a Yummy Drummy?'

'They're like chicken nuggets.'

'Right. And where do I find the triple-twist muffins with the double chiccy-choc?'

'The chocolate-chip muffins are in the freezer. You were just looking at them.'

As soon as the lunch bags are laid across the bench in room order, the money is counted and the bakery is phoned, I bolt. I don't want to be around when the noon shift volunteers move in to sort out my mess.

I can't believe I've volunteered for canteen duty. I mean, I wasn't even a visible presence for Eddie. His classroom was half a school away and when I asked him, he didn't know what the canteen was.

At least he's still heading into his school days at a run. From the moment we pull up each morning, about 1 km from the school gate on account of us being among the later arrivals, he is out the car door and bolting to the front gate, occasionally stopping to ask other kids questions or to make bold statements such as 'Grandpa gave me Sarge from the *Cars* movie.'

The excitement doesn't translate to his artwork, largely because he appears to have inherited my shaky genes when it comes to being creative with paintbrush or pencil. He brought home a peculiar drawing today; a child's face with a bizarre make-over. He coloured the nose yellow, the ears green, the eyes and eyebrows red, and the rest of the face a dark brown.

Grandpa Des and I are intrigued. We ask for an explanation.

'Because some people are black,' Eddie says, barely looking up from his Bush biscuit.

'That's right. Do you know any black people?' I ask.

'Well, Peter. He's black.'

'And what about his brother Josh?' I ask.

'Yeah, he's black, too.'

So the artwork is a semi-tribute to his kindergarten buddy Peter and his twin brother Josh. I'm just not sure who he's modelled the yellow nose and green ears on.

Soon after putting Eddie to bed, Grandpa Des and I sit out the front, watching the Murray River flow by, sipping on straight whiskey and doing the *Herald Sun* quiz.

We're often stumped by questions – such as 'What does boanthropy mean?' – and I always say, 'I wish Kerrie was here, she would know the answer to that.'

And Grandpa Des says, 'Yeah, she was a real trick, that girl. She knew the answers to a lot of questions, dear girl.'

Maybe we need to ease back on the whiskey to help our cause. But he's a hard man to resist, your father. If I say no to a whiskey, he usually gets me a port, or a beer, or a glass of wine. But I rarely say no. What else can we do? Play Scrabble?

Miss you,
love Danny

7 February 2007

Dear Kerrie,
Your father and I go to mid-week Mass, the second time I have set foot in the church since your funeral. I see your coffin at the altar. But this time when I look up at the microphone from where I delivered your eulogy, I realise I no longer have the same courage. That person, dressed in black, with your wedding rings hanging from a chain around his neck, extolling your traits and nuances, is a different me, another untouchable person from my past.

I was late to your funeral. I couldn't face people while waiting for the pews to fill. I left Eddie with Nanna Vogel, a family friend, and Dad drove me to the church, meeting Brian at the door, feeling nervous and removed, like I was about to take centre stage in a tragic play. I walked to my seat, unable to look at anybody and sat beside Des. It had been a tiring three days, reminiscing about you, picking a coffin, signing papers, wading through readings, penning 'Prayers for the Faithful' with Father John, taking phone calls, accepting flowers, feeling grateful to people for their soups and cakes. I needed a rest. I looked for the undertaker and gave him a nod. It was time to say goodbye.

Your brother spoke first, followed by Mardi. They were kind and humorous and nervous. Then came my turn, my chance to tell everyone about my wife: the Kerrie I knew, the Kerrie I loved and the Kerrie I lost.

Three times I practised the eulogy at home and three times I broke down, unable to reach the finish. For this reason I asked Brian to follow me to the microphone in case it happened again. But by then I was okay. I felt strong.

No, I didn't cry at the rostrum, I waited until 'Calling all Angels' floated from the speakers. The tears continued as I followed the pallbearers with your coffin and we parted forever, a silver hearse taking your body away as the church bells tolled and my heart wept.

And before I had a chance to search for meaning I was mobbed. Mourners popped up like shark's teeth. As soon as one was gone another was standing in their place. I didn't know which way to face or what to say. By then I was out of tears.

I had to sit down at the wake because the day had taken its toll. People came to speak but I could barely understand. My ears felt like they were full of bathwater. I was dizzy and tired and felt like I was going to faint. People spoke and I nodded dumbly in return. I went outside for fresh air and stayed there for the rest of the evening, scared to move in case my ears filled with water again. We later went to the pub and sent you off in style, Pete, Chris and I not making it home until 4 am.

After Mass, Father John meets Grandpa Des and me outside, dressed in shorts, thongs and puffing on a fag. Once again he light-heartedly admonishes Des for handing over a bottle of South Australian wine.

'Des, you shouldn't have,' he says.

'No, no, you deserve it, Father. You've been very good to us,' Des insists.

'Oh, I haven't done anything, Des. You should keep the bottle of wine for yourself. Or give it to Danny.'

Yes, I think, give it to Danny.

'No, Father, you were very good to our girl. I want you to have it,' Des says.

Okay, don't give it to Danny.

I'm not sure but I think that makes bottle No. 12. And before Des oversteps his devotion and promises to bring another dozen reds, I tell Father John that your brother Brendan had asked me to be Maggie's godfather.

'They obviously don't know my past history very well,' I say. 'That's why I dropped in today, to polish up.'

Father John laughs.

'Actually Brendan rang two nights ago to ask, but it came with one condition: that I turn up on time. When he had his other two kids christened, Kerrie had to run up the aisle because she was running that late.'

'I'm sure you'll make it on time,' Father John says. 'I think it's a lovely gesture.'

We bade him farewell, standing by the church door, puffing on another fag.

Miss you,

love Danny

9 February 2007

Dear Kerrie,

School is great for Eddie, keeping his fertile mind growing and providing him with friends. It's home I worry about. I don't have a natural instinct for parenting. So many times I brush him away when he tries to come between the computer and me. Then guilt creeps in and a depressing sense that I'm letting you down. I always think about that silly 'Cat's in the Cradle' song in which a father dismisses his son because he's too busy. I feel compelled to apologise, which I do today, and Eddie accepts, giving me a hug.

'We love ourselves don't we, Dad?' he says.

Then he corrects himself: 'We love each other don't we, Dad? I love everybody, but I don't love myself.'

'Well that's no good, because there's a lot to love about you,' I counter.

'Nah, I don't love myself.' I think he is fishing for compliments.

'Well, they say to love others you should first learn to love yourself,' I say. See what I mean about my missing instincts? As if a five-year-old is going to understand this nonsense.

'I do love myself, but I don't listen to my brain,' he says.

'Go on.'

'I don't listen to it, I don't think about it, I don't love it. I think it's silly.'

'Oh?'

'Who's your favourite Ninja Turtle, Dad?'

'What?'

'Who's your favourite Ninja Turtle?'

'Leonardo.'

'I knew you were going to say that. I love Raphael because he's a rebel and he wears red.'

'I'm sure he would love you, too. And your brain. You're both a couple of rebels. Now off you go and let me do some work.'

'Okay, Dad.'

Miss you,

love Danny

10 February 2007

Dear Kerrie,

You'll be glad to know, or sad, however you care to interpret it, that I still possess the ability to go walkabout. A few beers after tennis turned into a massive session and I found myself staggering home from the Gemmill's pub in my thongs, tennis bag slung over my shoulder, at 3 am. As usual, the last remnants of the night have become a sea of faces and lost words and I'm paranoid once again that I've said the right things to the wrong people. Or is that the wrong things to the right people?

Whatever, my parents aren't impressed. They suggest that I am too old with too many responsibilities to be falling through the front door during the early hours of the morning – as if it were ever acceptable. I think Grandpa Des is also surprised. At least it doesn't upset Eddie. He still crawls into bed, demanding that I get up and get him breakfast.

Miss you,

love Danny

Dear Kerrie,

Grandpa Des is a celebrity at the Ouyen café. You know Ouyen, that dying town in the middle of the Mallee? A woman behind the counter recognises Des when we stop for lunch on our ten-hour road trip back to Adelaide. Des, as you can imagine, is chuffed, especially after we've driven hundreds of kilometres through arid paddocks, rendered lifeless by this dreaded drought. Little more to see than motionless tractors and road kill.

'I always order your lovely home-made soup,' Des announces.

'I know, I recognise your face,' the woman replies.

Obviously not many people are driving through the Mallee and stopping at Ouyen these days because the last time we ordered soup was October. The comment puffs Des's chest. He is the soup man.

'Kerrie put me onto this place,' he tells me proudly. 'She told us how good it was on one of your stopovers so Elsa and I called in and ordered the home-made soup. I've had it ever since.'

The vegetable soup is thick as a sponge and comes with a fat slice of bread. Des struggles to finish, while Eddie refuses to eat because he wants to save his stomach for McDonald's, despite it being a five-hour wait (Adelaide is the next McStop).

He's had a disappointing trip. We couldn't get a Happy Meal 'and boy's toy' an hour and a half into our journey because the Echuca McDonald's was still serving breakfast. He couldn't get a Happy Meal three and a half hours into our day because the Swan Hill store was also on breakfast time. But Eddie decides the Happy Meal toy, some form of plastic alien, is still worth the stomach-rumbling wait and he doesn't want to ruin his appetite.

I'm not hungry, either. I'm still a bit shaky from the car trip. I let Des drive. For the hour leading into Ouyen I almost shit my pants. I certainly couldn't sleep. Each time the car hit a bump or rounded a long, sweeping bend, I opened my eyes for fear that we were flying into the Mallee scrub. Still, he didn't make a mistake until he arrived in Ouyen and drove up the wrong side of the main street.

'Oh I'm a silly old fart,' he chided himself.

'Don't worry, Des, I can take it from here.'

Our next stop is Pinnaroo. I need an ice-cream. My tongue is welding itself to my palate in sympathy with the dusty paddocks. Des ducks into a pub to use their toilets and soon makes friends with the publican. He momentarily leaves his pot of beer and excitedly beckons Eddie and me inside as if we are about to meet the Queen. Except the Queen isn't inside, it's a man behind the bar. And he's been to our home town, Cobram.

Des thinks it's a miracle, but I'm not surprised – everyone knows someone from Cobram. Reluctant to leave his beer-serving, well-travelled friend, Des eventually agrees that we have to hit the road and finishes his drink, grabbing four stubbies for the journey.

'Two for me and two for you. But I'm sorry, Dan, you'll have to wait until we get home until you can have yours,' he says with a grin.

Three hours and no beers later I'm exhausted, my eyes sore and strained from the passing road. Eddie, however, is full of beans. We are in Adelaide, he's finally having his Happy Meal and playing with his Happy Meal toy.

Miss you,
love Danny

13 February 2007

Dear Kerrie,

Job No. 1 when we get home from the city: clean Grandpa's car. There's budgie feed scattered across the back seat.

'Louie's cage tipped over when I picked him up from Wally's place and I haven't got around to cleaning it up yet,' Grandpa Des explains.

So we drive my car into Adelaide's CBD, arriving 30 minutes late for Des's appointment because we've mixed up the times. We needn't have bothered. The specialist tells Des the damage caused to his bladder by radiation is irreversible.

'The specialist said I'm stuck with the problem,' Des relays, dolefully.

'What can they do to manage it better?' I ask.

'Nothing. I just have to learn to live with it.'

'So there's nothing they can do?'

'Not that I know of.'

'What a pain in the arse.'

'Yeah. Well a pain in the front region, anyway.'

With the sobering news that his bladder is prone to blistering and bleeding, and his urethra in danger of being blocked at any time, we stop at his local pub for a couple of beers. And as Eddie entertains and annoys Grandpa's friends sitting around the 'table of knowledge', we forget all about the budgie's mess on his back seat.

Miss you,
love Danny

17 February 2007

Dear Kerrie,

Eddie won't eat his breakfast. He's hardly touched a meal since we've been in Adelaide. I'm beginning to worry about his loss of appetite until uncovering insider trading: your father has been sneaking him Bush biscuits and Kit Kats. The kid's full. Until now I thought Des was running each offering past me, keeping in good with the kid's father. And now I discover this collusion, with cunning Eddie waiting until I am outside or reading in my room to catch Grandpa at a vulnerable moment. No wonder you were a chubby kid.

I also think Eddie's considering becoming a vegetarian. We went to the movies yesterday and *Charlotte's Web* had more impact than I first thought. This morning he asks me if people really do eat pigs.

In between scoffing popcorn, slurping Coke and running up and down the aisle, he must have been listening. I was. I almost cried.

Almost. I was sad because Charlotte reminded me of you. Not the eight legs, the fact she was prepared for death.

I remember you talking about this film, Kerrie. It obviously left an indelible mark because you suggested Debbie Reynolds's version of 'Mother Earth and Father Time' from the soundtrack as a possible song at your funeral. Honestly, Kerrie, who remembers a song from their childhood as an appropriate signing-off tune?

Apart from worrying about our son's diet, I've been sifting through the family videos and discover a tape of your twenty-first birthday.

I should have left it on the shelf. Seeing footage of you alive and well, mixing with family and friends, drinking, eating and laughing around the bricks and mortar of 2 Waite Avenue leaves me unexpectedly melancholy.

I switch off the tape and walk outside. Nothing remains but the backdrop – the rainwater tank next to which the speeches were made, the Hills Hoist under which people stood during the celebrations, the open carport in which the meals were served and the little section of lawn (now a dead brown because of this damn drought) where Brendan played barman. Was this the emptiness you felt returning home after Elsa died?

I don't know how Des copes. He says he stays in this house for the memories, but is it any wonder he gets sad at the thought of Eddie leaving and the house falling silent again?

Miss you,
love Danny

18 February 2007

Dear Kerrie,

I hardly dare turn my back on Eddie. Each time I'm away for as little as a night I swear he grows a centimetre, adds another three or four words to his vocabulary and becomes a step more independent. And so it is this morning. He has stayed at Linda's overnight and I meet them at Glenelg's new amusement park to pick him up for Maggie's christening.

Eddie doesn't need any help to make it to the top of the waterslides nestled somewhere among this building's rafters. He clicks his pass through the turnstile, disappears up the ramp and then comes hurtling down the chute, arriving at the bottom on a wave of water.

'Did you see me, Dad?' he shouts.

'I sure did.'

'How did you see me?'

'Because they have a video camera at the top of the slides and you can watch kids coming down.'

Only yesterday I would have had to carry him up that ramp.

Linda, too, is amazed at the rate in which he's growing and how quickly time is passing since your death. We take turns being sad.

She thought of you on Friday night during a wedding reception in a city library.

'When I stopped and looked at all the books, it hit me how much I really miss Kerrie,' she says. 'Because she would have been fascinated. She would have asked me a hundred questions about the library and the three storeys of books and the wedding, and she would have made me take her there to have a look. It's the sort of place she would have loved.'

Linda and I never let the sadness take over. We never shed a tear. Invariably we break into a laugh or change the subject. And I don't know why. That's the whole bloody point of missing someone you love, isn't it?

Love Danny

18 February 2007

Dear Kerrie,

There are two hurdles to our getting to Maggie's christening on time: my suit had not been dry-cleaned in the three months since the Melbourne Cup and Eddie's good pants have a dirty spot.

I've got to clean the bloody things with a damp cloth. I curse my lack of preparation. I'll have to stand at the altar facing backwards.

Thankfully, the clothes scrub up to an acceptable level and Uncle Mike swings by to get us to the church early. This is my promise to your brother, don't forget.

I remember you standing at this altar as a godmother for Maggie's sister and brother three years ago, but I don't feel sad. Maybe it's because of dear little Maggie. She reminds me of your mother – curly blonde hair, cheeky and bossy.

Hang on a minute, there's a woman running up the aisle to join her family.

It makes Brendan laugh.

'At least someone is keeping up the tradition,' he says.

The christening is the first time I've come back to Adelaide since your death that I don't feel like I'm chasing your memory. I'm here because I've been asked, albeit in your honour, and it feels like I belong. It helps later in the day when Des takes me in his arms and says he loves me like a son.

Miss you,
love Danny

19 February 2007

Dear Kerrie,

I take Eddie to Seacliff beach to splash in the shallows and play sharks and crocodiles before saying goodbye to Des and his friends at the pub. It seems more appropriate than leaving him at the top of his driveway.

Of course, Eddie puts on a show before we depart, asking what football team everyone barracks for.

'My favourite team is the Sydney Swans because they wear red and red is my favourite colour. My second favourite team is the Cobram Tigers because I live in Cobram; my third team is the Adelaide Crows because Grandpa lives in Adelaide, and my fourth team is the Carlton Blues because my dad barracks for them,' he announces.

Throughout the performance, Des keeps turning to his mates and saying, 'It's going to be quiet at my house this afternoon.' They all agree.

But it's only quiet for an afternoon, because by the following day your dad is in hospital.

It's hard not to think about you on this drive back to Cobram.

We spent so many hours together crossing the Mallee.

Those memories are pinging around my head. I can almost taste the Eskimo pies, hear your Wiggles renditions and breathe the same summer air. I remember the words you wrote about our first crossing.

Eddie is a redhead. And a Scorpio. We all know about the gingernut reputation for volcanic tempers. But it's a little-known fact that Scorpio is Latin for 'child with incredibly loud cry and colossal distaste for car capsules'.

It was with this twin terror in mind that we set off for Adelaide to give my mum and dad the only decent Christmas present I have ever given them: unfettered access to a grandchild.

I had been dreading the motoring marathon (ancient Greek for 'uncomfortably long, hot, boring journey'). And now here it was, inevitable and unenviable.

The Falcon (old German for 'sensible family car') loomed in the driveway like a prison guard waiting to take a condemned man to the gallows. And I trudged towards it muttering a vain prayer that Eddie's temperament would pay no heed to his hair colour or his star sign, that it would be over quickly and I wouldn't feel a thing.

God must have been listening, because the child was an angel for the first half of the journey as we ticked off the towns flashing by, each bringing us a step closer to a nice cup of tea and clucking grandparents who would take our precious bundle off our hands long enough for us to go out for dinner together.

Then we met our Waterloo. It was a hot, gusty, fly-blown, post-apocalyptic stretch of Mallee highway tantalisingly close to Ouyen. Napoleon – sorry, Danny – had made this our objective, to be reached by 1700 hours. Except drummer boy Eddie started a chorus for his supper. And I was only too happy to dance to his tune. Not Napoleon. 'C'mon Ed, cheer up soldier. Only 10 minutes to Ouyen. Then we can decamp and you can get your milk rations.'

I tried to explain to Danny that nine-week-old babies don't know what 10 minutes is, and don't care, even if it means Daddy doesn't get to make it in time to the PubTab to put a bet on a hot tip. When that didn't work, I told Danny to !#@*ing pull over before our son passed out from the exertion of his tantrum.

And what a tantrum. The boy burst a blood vessel in his eye. Result: two harassed, guilt-ridden parents who spent the rest of the trip on tenterhooks, waiting for little whimpers to turn into full-blown wails.

Eddie had one more major fit of pique just before we reached the wide brown suburbs of Adelaide that resulted in Mummy sitting in the back desperately trying to console and entertain a very unimpressed bundle of boyhood.

And when we rolled into the driveway of 2 Waite Avenue, Grandma was waiting on the porch to commiserate with Eddie on his lousy parents putting him through such torture.

The homecoming cup of tea was bliss. As I sipped gratefully, I could feel my jangled nerves start to repair themselves. Until I realised that in one week we had to make the return journey. And this time there would be no clucking grandparents waiting on the porch to help.

You'll be glad to know, Kerrie, that Eddie's no longer a redhead – his hair is a browny blond – and I no longer set a stringent schedule. There's no departure time and we stop often: for toilet breaks, for a stretch, for an ice-cream and always for Maccas. But despite Eddie's amusing dialogue or role-playing requests, there's still too much time to think. And it's at these moments I wonder whether God could spare me five minutes of your time.

I'd like to tell you how much I miss you. Just so you know.

Love Danny

21 February 2007

Dear Kerrie,

Des is still in hospital with his bladder problem, but says he's improving.

As for me, I'm still doing your jobs. It's Eddie's day off, but we meet with his teacher, Miss Kelly, so she can run him through a few literacy and numeracy tests.

They soon become frustrating. I'm finding it hard not to butt in when he stumbles on shapes, or counts from 1–29 and forgets 30, or when he writes his name as Ebbie because he's having difficulty with d's.

I stop myself spitting out: 'Your name is Eddie, son, not Ebbie. You know that a d is a d and not a b. You know what a rectangle looks like, and that 30 comes after 29. Come on, son, you're making me look bad here.'

I sit there and keep my sweaty palms on the desk, smiling each time Eddie looks up.

Why doesn't she test him on money? He knows all about money, and banks.

This morning he refused to hand over his coins.

Look, I'm no fan of the greedy, money-grabbing bastards either, but I couldn't convince him the money would be safe in the bank and still his to spend.

'I want to keep my money here,' he told me.

'Eddie, you put the money in the bank so you can start saving some more,' I reasoned.

'I'm not going to.'

'You can still get the money out of the bank. It's still your money, and by emptying the moneybox you'll be able to fill it with more coins. I'm offering you the opportunity of a lifetime, kid!'

'But I want to keep it at home.'

'We'll talk about this later. Put your shoes on, we've got to get to school to meet Miss Kelly.'

'I'm not your friend anymore.'

'That's fine. Sometimes sons aren't friends with their dads.'

'Well, I won't talk to you anymore either.'

'That's no good, because when we become friends again you won't be able to ask me to take you to the playground or the toy shop.'

'Well, I'll use sign language. How do you do "toy shop"?'

And this, I suspect, is the reason for his aversion to banks. He'd rather spend the money on toys. It's a dilemma because I've been talking long-term saving, eighteenth birthdays and cars.

Which raises the question: when does the money become his to spend? If I don't want to hand over control of the loot for another thirteen years, why did we open the account in his name?

No, I'll bank the coins for his own good. He'll thank me later. I'll wait until he's not looking. When the coins are gone, he'll have no choice but to start saving again. I'll make a capitalist of him yet.

He finishes his session with Miss Kelly and on the way to the car I remind him of 30 and rectangles and the letter d. But when we arrive home I discover our son's smarter than I give him credit for – the piggy bank is nowhere to be seen.

Miss you,
love Danny

3 March 2007

Dear Kerrie,
Happy wedding anniversary.
I remembered.

Six years since we were married.
Six years since we took the vows.
I think I'll get drunk.
Miss you,
love Danny

5 March 2007

Dear Kerrie,

Our son is being terrorised by the Fishy Monster. It's no joke. He doesn't want to leave the classroom at lunchtime. Ed's teacher discovered the trouble last week after finding him hiding behind the door, sobbing. He complained of being slapped across the face.

Thankfully she is taking steps towards solving the problem, banning the Fishy Monster – a Grade 1 boy – from playing with Prep students and encouraging Eddie to seek out a yard duty teacher if he feels threatened.

I don't know what to do or say. It's all a bit surreal and scary. I thought he was making the transition from kindergarten seamlessly and now a month into the school year he's being bullied. He's still got twelve years and three terms of school to go!

I'm shocked because I thought Eddie would be all right. I didn't think he was vulnerable. And yet here I am meeting his concerned teacher, being encouraged to reassure Eddie he will be safe in the playground. I agree. The classroom is no place for a happy, boisterous five-year-old during a lunchbreak. But what can I do to make him feel safe?

I wait until after school and ask Eddie about the Fishy Monster. He confirms being slapped and feeling scared, but says the teachers will protect him. This makes me feel more confident. At least he's open.

Eddie has played an unwitting part in this drama. The Fishy Monster evolved from the Kissy Monster game, Eddie's habit of chasing around classmates and threatening to plant a smooch on their cheek. Suddenly the game is no longer fun.

Maybe I should march into the schoolyard and grab this Grade 1 kid by the neck and threaten him with tough justice if he scares my son or hijacks his playtime again. But it's not what I want to do. I just want him to leave Eddie alone.

Miss you,
love Danny

6 March 2007

Dear Kerrie,

Day 1 post-Fishy Monster and Eddie emerges from the classroom with his bag over his stomach and laughing with a friend. He seems okay.

'Hi, Dad,' he says.

'Hi, Ed. Any problems with the Fishy Monster today?'

'Nah, he's not allowed to play with the Preps.'

'So you went outside during playtime?'

'Yeah.'

'So what did you do?'

'Ah, I don't really want to talk about it now.'

'Sure, mate.'

And I feel relieved because I can relate to the lethargy. I've been there most of my life. He's not retreating; he's not too scared to talk. Like most kids, he simply couldn't be bothered discussing his school day.

I take Eddie to my football training at Katamatite and it soon becomes apparent his confidence is not lost. He is five going on twenty.

'Come on men, catch up,' he shouts, darting between the players' legs.

I tell him to go away, but he ignores me and strives to remain at the front of the group, claiming victory when we complete the lap.

'I win,' he shouts.

Then as the coach, Gypsy, calls the team together to lay down some important ground rules for the season ahead, Eddie again interrupts.

'Gypsy, I want to tell you something,' he says, calling the coach down so he can whisper in his ear. 'When you have finished talking to the men, I want to make a command.'

Gypsy straightens up, trying to keep a straight face, and announces we'll have a guest speaker.

'Guys, when we raced before, I won, didn't I?' Eddie says.

'You sure did, Ed. Now go over to the sidelines,' I say, as the players break away from the group shaking their heads.

Miss you,
love Danny

15 March 2007

Dear Kerrie,

Life, death, Jesus and Ned Kelly. How do I explain these things to a five-year-old?

The significance of Easter has been discussed at school and Eddie feels sorry for Jesus, particularly because he was put on a cross and left to die. He's not the only one. A girl from his class went home and told her mother, 'Bad men killed Jesus. Last year!'

Of course, now I've got to make sense of Jesus and heaven.

'How come you know everything, Dad?' Eddie asks.

Thankfully, he is distracted by rain on the roof.

'Mum must be sad,' he says of the falling drops. 'She misses me. She's crying. And all the people with children who have died and the old people who have gone to heaven are crying. See, I do know something. But you know everything, Dad.'

He's wrong. I don't know much about Ned Kelly.

How did we start talking about Ned Kelly? Good question.

When Eddie suggests we could have called him Ned instead of Ed, I tell him that people who are christened Edward can be called Ned, such as Ned Kelly. Then I explain that Ned Kelly is a famous bushranger. Bushrangers, I tell him, steal horses and rob banks. I leave out shooting policemen.

'But Ned Kelly lived a long time ago and he's dead now,' I say.

'So he's in heaven?' Eddie asks.

'I guess so.'

'So he's a good person now. And is he looking down on his children?'

'He didn't have any children but I'm sure he's looking down on his family.'

'Yeah, his family. How did he die?'

'Ahh, would you like an Easter egg?'

'Sure, Dad.'

Miss you,

love Danny

22 March 2007

Dear Kerrie,

The Fishy Monster crisis has been solved. Eddie says he is friends with the Grade 1 kid and wants to invite him to his birthday, despite it being in October. Apparently it was an errant slap, and not intended to cause harm. Eddie no longer feels victimised. Which is a good thing because we've just arrived at the dentist.

Eddie is blissfully unaware, having read in well-meaning kids' books how innocuous it is to lose a tooth. Maybe the authors are ignorant, too.

We are called into a room and Eddie gladly climbs onto the chair, opening his mouth for inspection.

'Now, Eddie, there is a hole in your tooth and it is going to need a filling,' Steve the Dentist says gently.

'I know that. Dad told me,' Eddie replies.

'Oh right, okay. Do you brush your teeth?'

'Yes, every night.'

'Do you count to five on every tooth?'

'What?'

'You need to count to five while brushing every tooth. You count to five for me.'

Eddie rattles off five in record time so Steve the Dentist suggests wedging one thousand between each digit to slow him down. He has his fingers in Eddie's mouth.

'One, one thousand, five thousand, ten thousand,' Eddie slurps.

Steve the Dentist tells Eddie he needs practice and then says he needs to take an X-ray of the tooth because an abscess suggests decay may have reached the root system. Eddie happily marches off to an adjoining room, plonking in another chair but instead of sitting back and keeping still starts peering into the lens of the X-ray machine, saying, 'Nice camera.'

Steve the Dentist asks him to sit back, keep still and bite on a mouthpiece while he snaps some photos.

'Watch out, I have a licky tongue,' Eddie says.

'I can see that. Now I need you to keep your tongue still, clamp down tightly on this with your teeth and not move.'

Each time the mouth clamp touches the back of Eddie's throat, his eyes water and he starts to gag.

Mouth X-ray, Take 13. Success. But the evidence is damning and we return to the original chair with Eddie still charmingly unaware that his tooth has to be ripped out. By this stage I'm starting to sweat.

Steve the Dentist smears anaesthetic gel across his gum in preparation for a needle, but Eddie reacts to the flavour and starts spitting it on to his bib. Still, we think enough has been smeared to deaden the gum. Steve the Dentist asks my son to look at the roof and count to thirty, while he stealthily raises the needle for a jab. Eddie stops counting at twelve and starts crying in both fright and pain.

I'm sweating more and starting to feel like Judas.

Blood trickles from Eddie's mouth and he is sobbing inconsolably, forcing Steve the Dentist from the room and leaving a nurse to comfort my son. There's no way this tooth is coming out. Mercifully, we are set free and told to take a course of antibiotics to tame the abscess. But before we leave we are instructed to make an appointment … to come back.

I leave the surgery feeling terrible. Guilty. Guilty as charged. Steve the Dentist, I've given our son too many sweets, failed to micro manage his brushing and should have brought him in for a check-up six months ago like my mother suggested. But I knew better. 'They are only his baby teeth,' I had said. 'He gets a second chance.'

But Mum was right. And maybe she is right about all the other things I choose to ignore – he's going to bed too late, his hair is too long, his table manners are non-existent, he needs to have friends over, he has an unhealthy obsession with his tattered red Power Ranger suit, he watches too many violent cartoons, and ... you get the picture.

I feel alone. I know I couldn't cope without my parents' support. And I know I'm often impudent instead of grateful for their advice, but I feel like everything I do is wrong. I miss you telling me that I'm doing okay; that I'm a good father.

Miss you,
love Danny

25 March 2007

Dear Kerrie,
Eddie has worms. The poor boy is falling apart.

I have returned home from a two-day football training camp worn out and hung-over only to be told by Mum she has discovered worms.

Great, we'll be ostracised by the school community.

'The poor little kid without a mother has worms,' they will say. 'And he needs a haircut. And he talks with his mouth full. And his dad spent all weekend drinking down the river.'

Thankfully, Eddie doesn't know anything about stigmas or lepers. He just wants to be rid of the irritation. He doesn't want an itchy bum.

'I have to have medicine to get rid of the worms in my bottom,' he tells me.

'That's good, Ed,' I say, 'but let's keep that to ourselves, okay?'

My mother has changed the bed linen, washed the towels, washed Eddie's clothes and vacuumed the floors. In some ways I'm glad I was training down the river.

By nightfall Eddie's mind is ticking over.

'Dad, how come I'm getting so many sores?'

'Why? Where are you getting sores?'

'Well, first I got a sore tooth and then I got a sore bum. Then I got a scratch on my face.'

Oh, did I mention the scratch on his face?

Someone hit him with a stick in the playground. Eddie says it was an accident. Apparently, someone pushed someone who fell into someone who was holding a stick that scratched Eddie's face.

'I don't know, Ed, these things just happen to people when they grow up,' I say. 'But we can make them better.'

'Yeah, I know. But I don't want to have sores.'

'Me neither.'

Miss you,

love Danny

28 March 2007

Dear Kerrie,

We are getting on top of the worms and Eddie is booked in for a haircut. As much as I like the Huckleberry Finn look, I can't take the risk – Mum keeps reminding me there's been cases of head lice reported at his school (what are these kids' parents doing, drinking down the river?).

Eddie points to a picture of a David Beckham-style mohawk and tells Jess the Hairdresser that's what he wants. But I put my foot down.

'You can ruin your hair when you're a teenager,' I say.

It sets him thinking because he asks why I don't have any hair.

'It fell out,' I reply.

'Why?'

'Because I ran too fast.'

'How old were you?'

'I was a man. Don't worry, your hair is not going to fall out. Just don't run too fast.'

'I won't.'

The questions are becoming more complicated, Kerrie. Next poser comes from the bath.

'Dad what are these round things near my doodle?' he asks.

'They're testicles, Eddie.'

'What are they for?'

Fuck. What am I going to say about this one? Surely five-year-old boys aren't ready for the reproduction minefield? He stares at me expectantly.

Possible answer No. 1: *You need them to make babies.*

No way, there's another thousand questions right there.

Possible answer No. 2: *They are to stop your legs rubbing together.*

Doesn't have the ring of truth about it.

Possible answer No. 3: *They're to keep your doodle weighed down.*

Aahhh … probably not.

Possible answer No. 4, and I'm running out of time: *They're there to help you do wee.*

Yep, that'll do, he'll buy that one.

'They help you do wee, Ed,' I say, almost convincing myself.

'Oh, because when I grab them they hurt.'

'Well, don't grab them. It's bad to grab them.'

'Yeah, because I'll break them and I won't be able to do wee.'

'That's right. Now go and put your pyjamas on and go to bed.'

'Okay, Dad.'

Miss you,

love Danny

29 March 2007

Dear Kerrie,

Thankfully, there's an upside to parenting – compliments.

Praise has added balance to the run of disasters and my flagging confidence. Eddie is all right! A mother told me so at school this afternoon.

'Do you have a boy in Prep?' she asked as we crossed the road and headed into the playground to collect our kids.

'Yes, Eddie. He's in Prep K.'

'Eddie! Oh he's such a delightful boy. My Amy loves Eddie. She talks about him all the time. He's so talkative and well mannered. He's such a beautiful little boy.'

'Is he?'

'He's gorgeous.'

Then on arriving at the classroom a fill-in teacher meets me at the door, insisting Eddie is a constant source of entertainment and a delight to teach.

'You've only had him for two days,' I counter.

I don't know why I jest in the face of these compliments, especially when they are in regard to our son. Why do I shift uncomfortably, deflecting praise by suggesting he's no angel at home, or that he never stops talking or never sits still?

Why can't I say, 'thank you' and 'he makes me feel proud'?

Miss you,

love Danny

3 April 2007

Dear Kerrie,

Socks and hankies for my birthday!

Two days after I turn 37 and there's Eddie waiting with Granny Kath at the Cobram bus station, hiding gifts behind his back and beaming.

'Happy birthday, Dad,' he says, hands folding out to reveal a present.

You would have thought he was carrying the complete boxed set of *Little Britain* or a new iPod, the way he expectantly waits for me to melt with appreciation once the wrapping is torn to reveal my … packet of socks.

'Thanks, Ed. They're great.'

'Granny and I bought them.'

'Well, you bought wisely. These are the best presents I've ever had.'

Socks and hankies?

Do I need any more proof that you're no longer here, Kerrie? At least you never stooped any lower than boxer shorts.

But I shouldn't pick on our son. My best mate is no better. Brian bought me a CD by Nick Cave's band Grinderman, decided he wanted a listen and hasn't removed it from his CD player. I don't ever expect to see that one, despite him continually extolling its artistic merits.

I had a good birthday, celebrating with Brian and Chel and a couple of friends at Lola's, a Spanish restaurant in St Kilda. We sat up chatting well into the night.

It's escaping to Melbourne once a month, having a break from Eddie and my parents, that keeps me sane. And now I am comforted in the knowledge that the next time I set sail for the Big Smoke, I'll have fresh hankies and clean socks to go with me.

Miss you,

love Danny

8 April 2007

Dear Kerrie,

For the second year running I can't make it out of bed for the Easter egg hunt.

At least Granny is here to chaperone Eddie around the house, filling his basket with an inordinate amount of chocolate goodies.

These things invariably happen when my brother Chris comes to stay. We never know when to call it a night. He probably blames me. It's not as if I've been completely neglectful, however. During our boozy session we managed to scatter the eggs. I even threw a couple across the road towards the river.

Eddie is surprised by the amount. I hear him through my bedroom window.

'I must have been a good boy,' he keeps saying to Granny.
Miss you,
love Danny

10 April 2007

Dear Kerrie,

Nothing like camping to strengthen the father–son bond. We've set up the tent at Jamieson caravan park – about 50 metres from where you and I stayed in a cabin three years ago – and Eddie is treating our temporary abode like a cubby house, running in and out and diving on the swag. Mountain backdrops, bubbling rivers and pristine air mean nothing to a five-year-old, especially when he's distracted by a bed of canvas and half a dozen fold-up plastic poles. I pull out the video camera.

'What should I say, Dad?'

'Whatever you like,' I tell him from behind the lens.

'Ninja Turtles.'

'What's that got to do with camping?'

'I just wanted to say it. Ninja Turtles.'

And so begins the next obsession: Goodbye Thomas the Tank Engine, farewell Lightning McQueen and your petrol-munching pals from Radiator Springs, move aside Power Rangers, the Teenage Mutant Ninja Turtles are No. 1.

Of course, Eddie's favourite is Raphael. He wears a red bandana and 'red is my favourite colour'. A small Raphael figurine shares Eddie's bed, sits beside him at the barbecue and plays with him on the slide.

Eddie is fast becoming a Turtle expert, watching their videos, copying their martial art moves and imitating their voices. Despite their propensity for violence, including karate kicks on unsuspecting trees, I can't bring myself to rein in this new focus on 'hurting the baddies'. It doesn't seem long ago I was enamoured with superheroes, wanting to brandish a stick like martial arts dynamo Monkey.

Anyway, distractions are a good thing when you're failing to catch a fish. We've only hooked sticks. Lots and lots of sticks. But as Eddie points out, 'We are still learning.'

Which won't get us fed so we drive to Mansfield for supplies and the Turtle obsession turns sour. As a reward for being an enthusiastic camper, I tell Eddie to look out for a toy store. Unfortunately, the shop is light on Turtles and rather than Eddie picking a gift he doesn't want, I tell him to wait until we return to Cobram and we'll buy the head-kicking Raphael doll he'd been coveting last week. Soon as we agree on this, he develops an aversion to camping.

'When are we going back to Cobram, Dad? I want to go home,' he says.

'Not today. We're not going back for two more days so I don't want you nagging about Raphael all the time or else we won't get him. You're going to enjoy our holiday.'

He tries a different tack. Instead of talking about Raphael, he muses about how much he misses Granny and Pa, saying it will be lovely to see them again … soon.

I call his bluff, and we have a standoff.

I can't win, Kerrie.

I've given him an inch and he's taken me on a marathon.

Miss you,

love Danny

11 April 2007

Dear Kerrie,

We're sitting around the campsite after breakfast when a pair of European wasps land on our leftovers, forcing Eddie out of his seat and into the car. He locks the door, and won't be coaxed out.

'They won't bite you, Ed. If you don't hurt them, they won't hurt you,' I assure him.

'Get them away, Dad.'

The wasps won't be dissuaded, lifting away from my waving arms before darting sideways and approaching our table from a different angle. Eddie, too, is stubborn, refusing to open the car door even when I move our wasp-attracting garbage a good 20 metres from the tent. Temporarily defeated, I make the decision to clear out, jumping in the car with Ed and driving off to find a fishing hole.

Assured the river is wasp free, Eddie climbs out of the car and decides he's not interested in fishing because he's discovered a box of Saladas on the back seat and takes up residency beside a tree.

'What are you doing, Ed?' I ask, while wrestling with a nasty green lure.

'Eating Saladas.'

'I can see that. Don't you want to go fishing?'

The lure hooks into my finger. Fuck.

'It's too boring,' Eddie says. 'Fishing isn't that boring, I just think it's boring for me. It's not boring for you.'

I wish I was sitting beside him dipping into the biscuit box rather than wrestling with my rod … and reel … and lure. I haven't made the water yet. Fishing takes patience, I remind myself, and after minutes of pulling, threading, weaving and swearing I'm knot free. It's time to catch a fish.

'Dad?' Eddie asks.

'Yes, Ed?'

'When are we going home?'

'Tomorrow, why?'

'Oh, it's just that I want that Raphael toy.'

Miss you,

love Danny

16 April 2007

Dear Kerrie,

Round two at the dentist and Eddie's no longer ignorant.

He's semi-traumatised, sitting in the chair, crying and refusing to have numbing gel wiped on his gum. He remembers the taste. As much as I try to placate his anxieties and convince him the process is for the best, his mouth stays clamped. He knows a needle is next.

I hate this place, too. I didn't want to bring my son to the dentist. I wanted to stay at home and wish the problem away. I didn't want to feel sick in the stomach knowing Eddie was scared and about to suffer pain.

But what can you do?

'If you don't get the tooth out, you'll get sick and have to go to hospital,' I say.

Eddie's mouth is still shut.

'If you do what the dentist says, we'll go to the toy store and buy a toy,' I say.

That doesn't work.

'C'mon, Ed, just lie back for me. The gel will make the gum go numb and it won't hurt. Lie back, that's a boy.'

No luck. Just sobbing.

It's apparent there's no tooth coming out today and I'm sad and frustrated. Mum has been on my back: get the tooth out for Eddie's sake, she keeps saying. She suggests I might have to hold him down, but I can't. I don't have the strength.

As we step out the door Eddie miraculously reverts to normal and asks about the toy shop.

'What?'

'What about the toy shop, Dad?' he asks.

'No way. The only reason we were going to the toy shop was if the tooth came out,' I snap.

His face drops, and his eyes moisten.

'I don't want a toy anyway,' he says, starting to sob again.

All of a sudden I'm struggling to feel sympathy for our son. This bloody tooth saga doesn't seem to have a happy ending in sight and I've got to go home and tell my mother we've failed again.

Miss you,
love Danny

Dear Kerrie,

Each day Eddie is taking a step farther away. I drop him at school this morning and before I can ask if he's happy enough to go off alone, he's running.

'Hey wait a minute, what about a kiss goodbye?' I yell.

He skids to a halt. 'Oh yeah, I forgot.'

He runs back, gives me a kiss and off he runs again, his backpack swinging from side to side and his little legs working overtime. I wish time could stand still, or play in slow motion. He's running too fast.

Days are flying past. Not long after I drop him off, I'm back parked among the line of cars, among the mums and dads, waiting for Eddie to finish school. I see him appear and decide to let him cross the road alone. When the lollipop lady walks out and blows her whistle, Eddie marches across like he is walking the red carpet.

'Hey, I can cross without my parents,' he keeps announcing to anyone who will listen. 'Hey, Dad, I can cross without my parents, can't I?'

'You sure can, Eddie. You're a big boy now.'

Further proof comes at night when we're lying side by side with his school reader. After discussing the pictures, as teachers have suggested, I read the story and then hand over to our son. He sits up, holds the book out front, almost flaunting it like a conductor's baton, and repeats the words by rote.

'I can jump,' he announces with verve.

He is becoming increasingly interested in letters and their place in words. Of course, the book is so dull it traverses boredom by countries, but none of this matters to Eddie because it's his turn to read and he's stepping farther away.

Miss you,

love Danny

Dear Kerrie,

Round three at the dentist, this time in Shepparton, and Eddie is spitting, crying, screaming and almost hyperventilating. I'm backing into a corner. Someone get the tranquilliser darts. We've got ourselves a polecat.

Adding to my confusion, this new dentist claims his eyetooth can be maintained with a filling and won't need removing.

'But the other dentist took an X-ray,' I say. 'Wouldn't that be fairly conclusive?'

'No, it only needs a filling. Here, have a look.'

Have a look? Do I look like I've been to dental school? And besides, I'm not putting my fingers near that rabid beast.

I stand back and give her the nod. If she says it needs filling, it needs filling. Who am I to question her authority? She's obviously important; in this place they're called dental therapists.

None of which matters to Eddie. He's so scared he's worked himself into a frenzy. Someone has closed the door because they can hear his screaming in the waiting room. We're both petrified.

The dentist moves her mirror close to Eddie's mouth and then reprimands him for spluttering. 'Open up,' she barks. Her domineering tone annoys me so I sit beside Eddie and hold his arm. She fills half the tooth before Eddie's breathing becomes so rapid I fear he's going to pass out. I'm about to say something, when she stops, puts away her equipment and tells us to return next week.

I'm surprised she'll let us near the place.

'Oh, I've had worse than this who are a lot better the next time around,' she says.

Worse than this? Does she also work on feral cats?

When we leave the room, Eddie is eerily quiet. He walks up to a plastic cow, about the size of a Labrador, in the waiting room, and starts stroking its head and talking to me in broken English.

'Daddy pat cow?' he keeps saying.

'I will in a minute, Ed, I've just got to make another appointment.'

'Daddy pat cow?'

'You can talk properly,' I say, hoping this side effect isn't permanent.

'Dad, do you want to pat the cow?'

Phew. He's back. But what's this fixation with plastic cows?

'Yeah, sure. Hi, cow. You look lovely today.'

Eddie gives me a funny look as if I'm a lunatic talking to a plastic cow, which I am. His recovery from then on is swift. Unfortunately, mine is not.

While he is sitting in the back seat playing Ninja Turtles, I'm struggling to focus.

'Daddy drive car,' I keep telling myself. 'Daddy drive car.'

In the end I manage to turn the key, start the car and drive off, all the time thinking we've got to go through this again.

Miss you,

love Danny

26 April 2007

Dear Kerrie,

Eddie had a nightmare last night. He woke up crying about 12.30 am, saying we abandoned him – Granny, Pa and myself driving off in a car, leaving him at traffic lights (the little green man had turned red so he couldn't cross). He could see my face looking back from the rear window.

Complicating things further, he wet the bed.

'Dad, you're not going to get killed, are you?' he asks.

'Of course not,' I say.

'We're not going to go to heaven now, are we, Dad?'

'No, not for a long time.'

'Not until we get really old.'

'That's right.'

He often asks why you had cancer, and I never know what to say. I mean, why did you get cancer? Was it something you swallowed as a child? In the end I have no answer other than to say it was God's choice.

I'm glad Eddie is constantly thinking of you. He took our photo to school for 'family week' and he's so proud that Miss Kelly 'wanted to put it on the wall'. He tells the class you are in heaven.

'Why did God want Mummy in heaven?' he asks me after school.

'Because she had done so many good things on earth that it was time for her to be rewarded,' I say.

'But why?'

'Because you can do anything in heaven. You can eat as many lollies as you like, you can have parties all the time and Mum doesn't feel sick anymore.'

'How can God make people feel better?'

I almost say he is magic.

'Because God can do anything and everything.'

'What does God look like, Dad?'

Okay, here we go. What does God look like? The Sistine Chapel painting? A woman?

'God looks like whatever you want Him to look like,' I say, pretty happy with myself.

'Well, I want Him to look like a Turtle.'

'That's great, Eddie. If you want Him to look like a Turtle, that's fine,' I say, unsure if there's substance behind my sentiments.

'Well, I mean a good Turtle, not a bad Turtle, Dad.'

'I'm sure you do.'

At this rate, I'm going to start wetting the bed.

Miss you,

love Danny

8 May 2007

Dear Kerrie,

Round four at the dentist goes marginally better than the third, with Eddie confessing he 'eats lots of treats' before trying to bite the

Therapist's drill. There is less kicking and screaming, just, but in a fit of pique the Therapist tells me Eddie needs to grow up. To which I almost reply, 'That's exactly what he doesn't need.'

I feel like telling her to fuck off and that the kid has lost his mother and to give him a break. But I don't, because we've got to come back.

That was a week ago and here we are, again, back for the final round. Two old foes to fight it out.

Ladies and Gentlemen, in the blue corner, waving a whiny drill and with a perfect knockout record, is champion of the surgery, the Therapist.

And in the white corner is poor little Eddie Russell.

Except Eddie is up for the challenge, walking through the door and slapping his hand on his forehead with Homer Simpson-like irreverence before pulling his hood down to hide his face.

'Most kids feel that way, but none of them express it like you,' the Therapist says.

What's going on? She's smiling and warm. She has feelings. She's no longer a sadistic monster. I smile, too.

Eddie procrastinates for a short time, lifting his hood to look at how-to-brush-teeth posters, before sitting in the chair. He doesn't squirm, and while he asks me to sit by his side, I don't need to restrain his arms. He flinches a little during the drilling, but doesn't cry or scream. No one closes the waiting room door, and soon the job is done. We don't have to come back for twelve months.

Hooray. Yes. We're done. No more torment. No more Mr Evil Dad dragging his son to the torture chamber. It's over.

Eddie sits up and says brightly, 'Can we go to McDonald's, Dad?'

Ah, um ... well, it's ... um, you know ... how do I get out of this?

'It's a bit too early for McDonald's, isn't it?' the Therapist interjects.

I enthusiastically agree, but Eddie sees my sly wink.

Miss you,

love Danny

Dear Kerrie,

All roads lead to 'why?' and it's driving me crazy.

'Why, Dad? Dad? I'm talking to you, Dad.'

'What's that?'

'Why, Dad?'

'Ed, I just need you to leave me alone for a second.'

'I just want to talk, that's all. I just want to ask some things.' And then he asks why the Sydney Swans play the St Kilda Saints.

And then he asks why the Adelaide Crows beat the Sydney Swans.

'Because they kicked more goals. They had better players on the day.'

'Why?'

'Shit, I don't know. Ask Paul Roos or Neil Craig. They're the coaches.'

You were so much better at the whys. I'm only good at the why nots.

I love that he is inquisitive and I love that he wants to learn, but I'm not very good at filling that rapidly expanding sponge in his head, especially when I'm taking my own thoughts for a walk.

'Dad?'

'Yes, Ed?'

'Why do elephants have trunks?'

Sometimes, at least, I have tolerance for our son. I can recognise that he's putting his mind to the right things at school, bringing home a certificate this afternoon for 'using my best manners'. He is so proud and we make room on the fridge door. I kiss him on the head and rub his back. Well done, son.

Most of the horrors of the past two months are behind us – no bullying, dry beds, worms eradicated and teeth filled. The only anxiety to overcome now is his fear of death. He's worried about things that can kill him. Scary things like crabs in mangrove swamps and seemingly innocuous things like rain (although floods have been in the news lately). I guess it's understandable, having lost his mum at a young age, and I try to placate his fears. But what do you say? I mean, things can kill us. Things such as cars, fires, floods, murderers, stingrays and, you know, cancer.

Actually, here he is now.

'Hi, Ed.'

'Hi, Dad. Dad, why do people eat crabs?'

Shit! Gotta go, Kerrie. Will talk soon.

Miss you,

love Danny

13 May 2007

Dear Kerrie,

It's Mother's Day and I'm stirring early in preparation for a drive to Melbourne airport to pick up Grandpa Des when I hear Eddie talking in his room.

'Dear God, can you please look after Mummy because I love her very much. In the name of the Father, the Son, Holy Spirit, amen.'

It breaks my heart and I walk in to tell him how thrilled you will be to hear his prayer.

'But we can't hear her, Dad, can we?' he says.

'No. But she would be very proud of you.'

His shoulders broaden and we scoff down breakfast before hitting the road.

Eddie falls asleep for the first part of our journey and I'm lost in thoughts when he suddenly wakes and says, 'The bees would be awake now, wouldn't they, Dad?'

'Oh, yeah, definitely. But there's no bees around here.'

'Why?'

'Because there are no flowers.'

'Why?'

'I don't know.'

'Dad, imagine if a car was driving along and a bee stung it on the tyre.'

'Couldn't get through. Tyres are too thick. People have thin skin.'

'Yeah, but remember when Lightning McQueen burst a tyre?'

'During the race?'

'Yeah, his tyres wore out, didn't they?'

Ignoring Eddie's fixation with animated heroes and all creatures with a propensity for biting, nipping and stinging, I turn in to the airport, park the car and we rush across the footbridge to find Grandpa Des sitting in a waiting lounge, waving at us in his customary manner, as if he's flicking away bugs. He is sunk back in the seat, looking smaller, frailer and older.

Eddie yells out 'Grandpa' and runs along the passageway to give him a big hug. These moments are worth driving across the country for, let alone a state.

'It's good to see you, Grandpa,' he says.

'It's twice as good to see you.'

Then he learns Grandpa has brought a surprise from one of his pub buddies.

He doubles the reverence: 'It's *really* good to see you, Grandpa.'

Miss you,

love Danny

16 May 2007

Dear Kerrie,

The anniversary of your death starts with your dad and me dropping Eddie at school and ends with five of us in darkness at Cobram cemetery, your dad talking about a man who had his finger cut off in a hire-car door.

Mum and I have set up a picnic table beside the plaque that contains your ashes, well most of your ashes, and Dad is seated beside Des listening to the unfortunate fate of his fingerless friend.

Despite the oddness of our night-time homage, it feels right. Of all people, Kerrie, you will understand. You will comprehend both my melancholy and joy. Sad without you, and yet smiling because we are gathered in a graveyard, under the vast dark sky with its pinpricks of starlight, drinking champagne, eating tuna mornay and talking shit. Three of your favourite things.

Eddie is running around with a torch, stopping by our table for a chip or a drink of apple juice before running off. He isn't scared, sad or confused. He is happy to be having 'a picnic with Mum at the cemetery'.

Eddie and I have come a long way without you, Kerrie. It is hard to believe.

He can write his name, wash his hair, put his face under water, bear the thought of spending a day without wearing red, entertain an entire classroom, charm the elderly and amuse people from all walks of life. I get the feeling he is something special.

I'm sorry you can't be here for these wonderful achievements, Kerrie. I wish you were. But I am learning to live with God's decision.

At least we are going to be all right. Despite the hole in our lives, and despite the obstacles and questions that Eddie will encounter, we are going to be all right. And I think that is what mattered to you most.

Miss you,
love Danny

Dear Eddie,

I want you to know, my love, before you hit your teens and go through all the wonderful, awful weirdness of adolescence, that you are never alone. My heart will always be connected to yours and I'm sure I'll be walking each step of your life with you.
Mum

Acknowledgements

Like my son, my father lost his mother when he was a young boy. Dad still misses her desperately and clasps tightly to the handful of memories that remain. For this reason, I started writing to Eddie about his mum.

I would particularly like ot thank Ian Fuge for the phone calls and the laughter, and the daring suggestion that I should introduce these experiences to the *Sydney Morning Herald*. He later provided me invaluable advice and much-needed confidence. I am indebted to Fiona McGill for running these columns and to Hazel Flynn for bringing my story to Murdoch Books. Thanks too, to Steve Acott for giving me the courage to write with honesty about his good friend, Kerrie.

Last, but never least, I want to thank Eddie. He is imaginative, talkative, fun-loving, stubborn and undoubtedly his mother's son. I truly know no other like him.

First published in 2008 by Pier 9, an imprint of Murdoch Books Pty Limited

Murdoch Books Australia
Pier 8/9, 23 Hickson Road
Millers Point NSW 2000
Phone: +61 (0) 2 8220 2000
Fax: +61 (0) 2 8220 2558
www.murdochbooks.com.au

Murdoch Books UK Limited
Erico House, 6th Floor
93–99 Upper Richmond Road
Putney, London SW15 2TG
Phone: +44 (0) 20 8785 5995
Fax: +44 (0) 20 8785 5985
www.murdochbooks.co.uk

Chief Executive: Juliet Rogers
Publishing Director: Kay Scarlett

Commissioning Editor: Hazel Flynn
Editorial Manager: Colette Vella
Editor: Karen Ward
Concept and Design: Gayna Murphy
Production: Monique Layt
Painting of Kerrie and Eddie by Kathy Russell

National Library of Australia Cataloguing-in-Publication Data:
Author: Russell, Danny.
Title: Dear Eddie / Danny Russell.
Publisher: Sydney, N.S.W. : Murdoch Books, 2008.
ISBN: 9781741962086 (pbk.)
Subjects: Russell, Danny—Correspondence. Cancer—Patients—Family relationships.
Children of cancer patients.
Dewey Number: 362.196994

Printed and bound in China in 2008 by Imago.